CHRONIC VENOUS INSUFFICIENCY

First edition. February 27, 2024.

Copyright © 2024 Ram Malkani.

ISBN: 979-8224210411

Written by Ram Malkani.

Table of Contents

Chronic Venous Insufficiency International Research ABSTRACTs
Dr Ram Malkani

1

FOREWORD

Chronic Venous Insufficiency(CVI) of the legs or Varicose Veins in the legs is a common symptom affecting almost one third of the population. Most are asymptomatic. Amongst the symptomatic, all do not come forward for investigation or treatment, except those aesthetically conscious, those developing pigmentation, stasis eczema, intractable itching and development of ulcers.

The final reason for symptoms is Venous hypertension or Stasis, which is pooling of blood in the veins near the ankle and a little above. The valves inside the vein when fail to prevent reflux, because of space between them when they close (incompetence) the stasis occurs, below the level of the incompetence of the valves in the superficial or deep venous system. The valves in the superficial veins or in the deep vein can be affected by infection, trauma, congenital causes, overweight, hypercoagulability leading to clotting or sluggish flow of blood, or because of long periods of not being ambulant.

Surprisingly in almost 40 percent of the CVI patients could develop a DVT which resolves spontaneously (subclinical DVT) leaving behind consequences of incompetent perforators leading to reflux.

All patients should undergo an ultrasound, colour Doppler which is the Gold standard for diagnosing CVI or DVT or reflux or incompetent perforators.

Amongst blood tests CRP, D Dimer, Lipid profile, Liver function test, Homocysteine Levels are mandatory.

This book, a collection of Abstracts of references is expected to be useful to the medical fraternity to understand a common ailment which is ill understood.

Dr RAM MALKANI MD DVD DDV FRCP
ram@drmalkani.com Cell No. 9820027456

INTRODUCTION

Venous Insufficiency

Robert Weiss, MD; Chief Editor: William D James, MD

Background

In venous insufficiency states, venous blood escapes from its normal antegrade path of flow and refluxes backward down the veins into an already congested leg. Venous insufficiency syndromes are most commonly caused by valvular incompetence in the low-pressure superficial venous system but may result from valvular incompetence in the high-pressure deep venous system or rarely both. Untreated venous insufficiency in the deep or superficial system causes a progressive syndrome involving pain, swelling, skin changes, and eventual tissue breakdown.

Deep venous insufficiency occurs when the valves of the deep veins are damaged as a result of deep venous thrombosis (DVT). With no valves to prevent deep system reflux, the hydrostatic venous pressure in the lower extremity increases dramatically. This condition is often referred to as a postphlebitic syndrome.

Superficial venous incompetence is the most common form of venous disease. In superficial venous insufficiency, the deep veins are normal, but venous blood escapes from a normal deep system and flows backwards through dilated superficial veins in which the valves have failed.

The valves in superficial veins can fail for a variety of reasons. Most commonly, congenitally weak vein walls may dilate under normal pressures to cause secondary valve failure. Direct injury or superficial phlebitis may cause primary valve failure. Congenitally abnormal valves can also be incompetent at normal superficial venous pressures. Normal veins and normal valves may become excessively distensible under the influence of hormones (as in pregnancy).

Most cases of superficial vein valve failure occur after primary points of high-pressure leakage develop between the deep system and the superficial system. High pressure causes secondary valve failure when otherwise normal superficial veins become so widely dilated that the thin flaps of the venous valves can no longer make contact in the lumen of the vessel. Over time, these incompetent superficial veins become visibly dilated and tortuous, at which point they are recognized as varicose veins.

High pressure can enter the superficial veins as a result of the failure of key valves at any point of communication between the deep system and the superficial system. The 2 major sources of high- pressure leakage from the deep veins to the superficial system are junctional valve failure and perforator valve failure.

Junctional high-pressure disease most often results from failure of the primary valve at the junction between the greater saphenous vein and the common femoral vein at the groin (saphenofemoral junction). Vein incompetence then proceeds distally from the groin, and patients perceive that a large vein is growing down their leg. A less common form of junctional reflux results from failure of the primary valve at the junction between the short saphenous vein and the popliteal vein at the knee (saphenopopliteal junction).

Perforator high-pressure disease results from failure of the valves of any perforating vein. The most common sites of primary perforator valve failure are in the midproximal thigh (Hunterian perforator) and in the proximal calf (Boyd perforators). When the primary high-pressure entry point is distal, large clusters of veins are first noticed in the lower leg, with large veins eventually growing up the leg toward the groin.

Pathophysiology

When venous valves are working correctly, every movement of the leg causes blood to be pumped inward and upward past a series of valves. During ambulation, the normal pressure in the venous system of the lower leg is nearly zero. Immediately after ambulation, the early standing pressure in the normal leg remains low. Arterial inflow fills the leg veins slowly, and the only source of venous pressure is the hydrostatic pressure of a column of blood as high as the nearest competent valve. In venous insufficiency, after prolonged standing, the veins are completely filled, and all the venous valves float open. At this time, high hydrostatic venous pressure results from the unbroken column of fluid that extends from the head to the foot.

Failed valves cause the column of standing blood in the vein to remain high even when during ambulation. The hydrostatic pressure increases during and immediately after ambulation, which cause venous congestion.

High venous pressure is directly responsible for many aspects of venous insufficiency syndrome, including edema, tissue protein deposition, perivascular fibrin cuffing, red cell extravasation, impaired arterial inflow, and other locally mediated disturbances.

Not all of the sequelae of venous insufficiency are related to venous hypertension, and not all patients with venous hypertension develop ulceration. Some patients with venous ulceration do not have marked venous hypertension.

The poor clearance of lactate, carbon dioxide, and other products of cellular respiration also contribute to the development of the syndrome. A defect in the clearance of extraneous substances can be quantified: If albumin labeled with a radioactive tracer is injected into the foot tissues, the clearance rate is markedly slowed by deep venous obstruction or by deep or superficial venous incompetence. Although this effect is referred to as venous stasis, the reduced clearance of cellular metabolites is not always due to true venous stasis. In many cases, the venous blood is moving at a normal speed, but a local recirculation of this venous blood upward through normal veins and downward through varicosities prolongs the average transit time for the blood to pass from the heart and lungs through the legs and back to the central circulation.

The time required for an aliquot of radiolabeled blood to pass from the femoral artery through the leg and back to the central circulation is highly correlated with the development of leg ulcers. The aliquot transit time and the clearance time for an extremity are closely related to the volume of retrograde flow through refluxing veins. Superficial varicosities always produce venous recirculation and can result in prolonged clearance that may be localized or affect the whole leg. Experimental evidence shows that if the peak retrograde flows in the greater and short saphenous veins and popliteal vein add to less than 10 mL/s, progressive visible stasis dermatitis and ulceration do not occur. If the sum is greater than 15 mL/s, the incidence of ulceration is high. In some cases, purely superficial local reflux with a pressure of more than 7 mL/s can cause local ulceration.

Chronic nonhealing wounds of the lower extremity have many different potential causes, but most chronic lower-extremity ulcers are of venous etiology. Most venous ulcers are caused by venous reflux that is purely or largely confined to the superficial venous system. Only a minority are caused by chronic DVT or by valvular insufficiency in the deep veins.

Chronic nonhealing leg ulceration can be debilitating. Approximately 1 million Americans have an ulceration due to superficial venous disease, and approximately 100,000 are disabled because of their condition.

As many as 50% of patients with untreated varicose veins develop superficial thrombophlebitis at some time. This is of grave concern, because unrecognized DVT is present in as many as 45% of patients with what appears to be purely superficial phlebitis. The risk of DVT is 3 times higher in patients with superficial varicosities than in the general population.

Bed rest and intercurrent illness place patients with venous insufficiency at higher risk for DVT. Phlebitis develops in 60% of hospitalized patients with clinically evident superficial venous insufficiency, and in nearly one half of cases, the condition progresses to DVT. Approximately one half of patients with DVT have detectable pulmonary embolism, and the mortality rate in this group exceeds 1 in 3.

Bleeding from lower-extremity varicosities can be fatal.2 Twenty-three such fatalities were reported in England and Wales in 1971, and although there is no central registry to tabulate the frequency with which it occurs, such cases are not unusual in the United States. Bleeding is not a rare problem, but often is managed incorrectly.

Sex

The incidence and prevalence of deep and superficial venous disease depend on the age and sex of the population, but the prevalence in women exceeds that of men at any age.

In younger men, the incidence is less than 10%, compared with 30% in similarly aged women. In men over 50 years of age, the incidence is 20%, compared with 50% in similarly aged women.3

Age

The prevalence of venous insufficiency increases with age.

Reticular veins usually appear or are first noticed in adolescence and young adulthood, with only a small number of new cases developing after the childbearing years. Truncal varicosities and telangiectatic webs, on the other hand, are relatively less common in youth and can appear throughout life.

The Basle III study included a large number of children aged 10-12 years at one point and again 4 years later. The study revealed that symptoms and abnormal venous test results occur before any abnormal veins are visible at the surface. Abnormal reticular veins appear first and are followed by incompetent perforators and truncal varicosities, which appear several years later.

Clinical History

Patients with venous insufficiency often report subjective symptoms that are typically bothersome early in the disease, become less severe in the middle phases, and then worsen again with advancing age.

Even small telangiectasias are often symptomatic. More than one half of patients who present with telangiectasias smaller than 1 mm in diameter report symptoms that abate after treatment. Common symptoms include the following:

- Burning

- Swelling

- Throbbing

- Cramping

- Aching

- Heaviness

- Restless legs

- Leg fatigue

Subjective complaints are also common in patients with truncal varices; 18% of patients with varicosities report frequent or continuous symptoms, while almost 50% complain of episodic symptoms.

Patients with deep system insufficiency nearly always are symptomatic. Leg aching, heaviness, and soreness are the most common subjective symptoms.

Episodic pain and other symptoms associated with superficial venous disease may be temporally related to hormonal changes, both physiologic and pharmacologic.

One half of all pregnant women with varicose veins complain of pain, and 17% are unable to remain upright for more than 1-2 hours at a time because of its severity.

Pain caused by venous insufficiency often is improved by walking or by elevating the legs. Warmth tends to aggravate the symptoms of venous insufficiency, and cold tends to relieve them. Compression stockings usually ameliorate or prevent the pain of venous insufficiency.

In many ways, the behavior of the pain caused by arterial insufficiency is the opposite to the behavior of the pain caused by venous insufficiency.

The pain of arterial insufficiency usually is worse with walking and worse when the legs are elevated.

Cold tends to aggravate the symptoms, whereas warmth tends to relieve them. Compression stockings usually aggravate the pain of arterial insufficiency.

The pain of venous obstruction is worse with walking or warmth but better with elevation of the legs. Compression stockings usually improve the pain of venous obstruction.

Physical

The visual appearance of the lower extremities is a useful but not always reliable guide to the peripheral venous condition.4 Clinical findings in venous disease are also common to many other entities that affect the lower extremities. Physical examination alone is not a reliable means of assessing the venous system. Diagnostic testing nearly always is necessary to rule out deep venous obstruction, to assess the paths of reflux, and to guide treatment planning. The Trendelenburg test is traditionally part of the physical examination and may be helpful in making the differential diagnosis (see Procedures).

Swelling may result from acute venous obstruction (as in DVT) or deep or superficial venous reflux. Alternatively, swelling may be completely unrelated to the venous system.

Lower-extremity pitting edema is common in patients with venous insufficiency.

Hepatic insufficiency, renal failure, cardiac decompensation, infection, trauma, and environmental effects can also cause lower-extremity pitting edema that may be indistinguishable from the edema due to venous obstruction or venous insufficiency.

Lymphatic edema may be a sign of primary lymphatic outflow obstruction, or it may be secondary to the overproduction of lymph due to severe venous hypertension (a so-called venolymphatic syndrome).

Skin discoloration may be a sign of venous stasis, arterial insufficiency, chronic infection, prior injury, or a host of other conditions

Superficial venous insufficiency with skin changes.

Nonhealing ulcerations may be due to deep or superficial venous insufficiency. Other causes include arterial insufficiency, rheumatologic disorders, local trophic effects, unrecognized cancer, or other more exotic causes.

The most common physical signs of venous insufficiency are those attributed to the progressive syndromes of chronic venous stasis and chronic venous hypertension. These signs include the following:

- Edema

- Hyperpigmentation

- Venous dermatitis

- Chronic cellulitis

- Cutaneous infarction (atrophie blanche)

- Ulceration

A long-standing venous ulcer rarely converts to a basal cell carcinoma or squamous cell carcinoma. The venous ulcer may develop collision lesions (eg, basal cell carcinoma and stasis ulceration) at the same site.

Normal veins are visibly distended at the foot and ankle and, occasionally, in the popliteal fossa.

Normal veins are usually not visibly distended in the rest of the leg. Translucent skin may cause the normal veins to become visible in a bluish subdermal reticular pattern.

A dilated vein above the ankle is usually evidence of venous pathology.

Darkened, discolored, and stained skin is often a sign of chronic venous stasis, particularly if it is localized along the medial part of the ankle or the medial aspect of the lower leg.

These areas are especially prone to venous hypertension because their drainage largely depends on the competence and patency of the entire length of the greater saphenous vein and all of the perforating veins attached to it.

Nonhealing ulcers on the medial part of the ankle are most likely due to underlying venous stasis.

Skin changes or ulcerations that are localized to the lateral aspect of the ankle are more likely to be related to prior trauma or arterial insufficiency than to pure venous insufficiency.

Causes

The sequelae of venous insufficiency are caused by reflux through superficial or deep veins or by venous outflow obstruction. Most cases of venous insufficiency are related to reflux through the superficial veins.

Superficial venous insufficiency is most often caused by the failure of a valve in the superficial venous system. Greater than 80% of varicose veins seen on the leg are caused by venous insufficiency or a leaky valve in the great saphenous vein, which terminates near the inguinal ligament as it joins the common femoral vein.

The initial valve failure may occur at any level between the groin and the ankle, but the saphenofemoral junction is the high point of reflux in most patients with severe superficial venous insufficiency.

Valve failure can be spontaneous in patients with congenitally weak valves.

Congenitally normal valves can fail due to direct trauma, thrombosis, hormonal changes, or chronic environmental insult (eg, prolonged standing).

Deep venous insufficiency can be due to congenital valve or vessel abnormalities, but DVT is the most common cause of deep system valve injury.

A less common cause of venous insufficiency is Klippel-Trenaunay-Weber (KTW) syndrome, which involves port-wine stains, varicose veins, and bony or soft-tissue hypertrophy. Patients with pure Klippel-Trenaunay syndrome have only venous involvement, whereas those with the Parkes Weber variant also have arteriovenous malformations.

Like those of other forms of venous insufficiency, the capillary hemangiomas (port-wine stains) of KTW syndrome can lead to local skin breakdown and ulceration, bleeding, and secondary infection. This can occur in any organ system of the body.

The KT, or sciatic vein, is a large superficial vessel that is present during fetal development, but it usually does not persist. In patients with KTW syndrome, this vein may be noticed at birth, or it may become apparent later in life. The vein extends along the posterolateral aspect of the leg from the foot to the gluteal region. When present, it is invariably a reflux pathway rather than a pathway for antegrade flow.

Patients with KTW syndrome may have atresia of the deep veins as well as many abnormal venous pathways involving the deep and superficial venous systems.

Surgical attempts to treat the abnormal refluxing veins in KTW syndrome are fraught with peril because postoperative worsening of venous abnormalities is common.

KTW syndrome can produce such severe venous insufficiency that the otherwise normal lymphatic system becomes overwhelmed by the amount of lymph production, which leads to secondary lymphedema.

emedicine.medscape.com/article/1085412 Sep 25, 2020

Peripheral Vascular Disease

What is peripheral vascular disease (PVD)?

Peripheral vascular disease (PVD) is a slow and progressive circulation disorder. It may involve disease in any of the blood vessels outside of the heart and diseases of the lymph vessels - the arteries, veins, or lymphatic vessels. Organs supplied by these vessels such as the brain, heart, and legs, may not receive adequate blood flow for ordinary function. However, the legs and feet are most commonly affected, thus the name peripheral vascular disease.

Conditions associated with PVD that affect the veins include deep vein thrombosis (DVT), varicose veins, and chronic venous insufficiency. Lymphedema is an example of PVD that affects the lymphatic vessels.

When PVD occurs in the arteries outside the heart, it may be referred to as peripheral arterial disease (PAD). However, the terms "peripheral vascular disease" and "peripheral arterial disease" are often used interchangeably. In the US, 10 million people have peripheral artery disease. PAD occurs in 5 percent of adults older than 50 and in 20 percent of adults older than 70. It is frequently found in people with coronary artery disease, because atherosclerosis, which causes coronary artery disease, is a widespread disease of the arteries.

Conditions associated with PAD may be occlusive (occurs because the artery becomes blocked in some manner) or functional (the artery either constricts due to a spasm or expands). Examples of occlusive PAD include peripheral arterial occlusion and Buerger's disease (thromboangiitis obliterans). Examples of functional PAD include Raynaud's disease and phenomenon and acrocyanosis.

What causes peripheral vascular disease?

PVD is often characterized by a narrowing of the vessels that carry blood to the leg and arm muscles. The most common cause is atherosclerosis (the buildup of plaque inside the artery wall). Plaque reduces the amount of blood flow to the limbs and decreases the oxygen and nutrients available to the tissue. Clots may form on the artery walls, further decreasing the inner size of the vessel and potentially blocking off major arteries.

Other causes of peripheral vascular disease may include trauma to the arms or legs, irregular anatomy of muscles or ligaments, or infection. Persons with coronary artery (arteries that supply blood to the heart muscle) disease are frequently found to also have peripheral vascular disease.

What are conditions associated with peripheral vascular disease?

The term "peripheral vascular disease" encompasses several different conditions. Some of these conditions include, but are not limited to, the following: atherosclerosis - the build-up of plaque inside the artery wall. Plaque is made up of deposits of fatty substances, cholesterol, cellular waste products, calcium, and fibrin. The artery wall then becomes thickened and loses its elasticity.

Symptoms may develop gradually, and may be few, as the plaque builds up in the artery. However, when a major artery is blocked, a heart attack, stroke, aneurysm, or blood clot may occur, depending on where the blockage occurs.

Buerger's disease (thromboangiitis obliterans) - a chronic inflammatory disease in the peripheral arteries of the extremities leading to the development of clots in the small- and medium-sized arteries of the arms or legs and eventual blockage of the arteries. Buerger's disease most commonly occurs in men between the ages of 20 and 40 who smoke cigarettes. Symptoms include pain in the legs or feet, clammy cool skin, and a diminished sense of heat and cold.

Chronic venous insufficiency

A prolonged condition in which one or more veins do not adequately return blood from the lower extremities back to the heart due to damaged venous valves. Symptoms include discoloration of the skin and ankles, swelling of the legs, and feelings of dull aching pain, heaviness, or cramping in the extremities. Deep vein thrombosis (DVT) - a clot that occurs in a deep vein, and has the potential to dislodge, travel to the lungs, occlude a lung artery (pulmonary embolism), and cause a potentially life-threatening event. It is found most commonly in those who have undergone extended periods of inactivity, such as from sitting while traveling or prolonged bed rest after surgery. Symptoms may be absent or subtle, but include swelling and tenderness in the affected extremity, pain at rest and with compression, and raised vein pattern. Raynaud's phenomenon - a condition in which the smallest arteries that bring blood to the fingers or toes constrict (go into spasm) when exposed to cold or as the result of emotional upset. Raynaud's most commonly occurs in women between the ages of 18 and 30. Symptoms include coldness, pain, and pallor (paleness) of the fingertips or toes. Thrombophlebitis - a blood clot in an inflamed vein, most commonly in the legs, but it can also occur in the arms. The clot can either be close to the skin (superficial thrombophlebitis) or deep within a muscle (deep vein thrombosis). It may result from pooling of blood, venous wall injury, and altered blood coagulation. Symptoms in the affected extremity include swelling, pain, tenderness, redness, and warmth. Varicose veins - dilated, twisted veins caused by incompetent valves (valves that allow backward flow of blood) allowing blood to pool. It is most commonly found in the legs or lower trunk. Symptoms include bruising and sensations of burning or aching. Pregnancy, obesity, and extended periods of standing intensify the symptoms.

What are the risk factors for peripheral vascular disease?

A risk factor is anything that may increase a person's chance of developing a disease. It may be an activity, diet, family history, or many other things. Risk factors for peripheral vascular disease include factors which can be changed or treated and factors that cannot be changed.

Risk factors that cannot be changed include the following:

- Age (especially older than 50)

- History of heart disease

- Male gender

- Diabetes mellitus (type 1 diabetes)

- Postmenopausal women

- Family history of dyslipidemia (elevated lipids in the blood, such as cholesterol), hypertension, or peripheral vascular disease

Risk factors that may be changed or treated include:

- Coronary artery disease

- Impaired glucose tolerance

- Dyslipidemia

- Hypertension (high blood pressure)

- Obesity

- Physical inactivity

- Smoking or use of tobacco products

Those who smoke or have diabetes mellitus have the highest risk of complications from peripheral vascular disease because these risk factors also cause impaired blood flow.

What are the symptoms of peripheral vascular disease?

Approximately half the people diagnosed with peripheral vascular disease are symptom free. For those experiencing symptoms, the most common first symptom is intermittent claudication in the calf (leg discomfort described as painful cramping that occurs with exercise and is relieved by rest). During rest, the muscles need less blood flow, so the pain disappears. It may occur in one or both legs depending on the location of the clogged or narrowed artery.

Other symptoms of peripheral vascular disease may include:

- Changes in the skin, including decreased skin temperature, or thin, brittle shiny skin on the legs and feet

- Diminished pulses in the legs and the feet

- Gangrene (dead tissue due to lack of blood flow)

- Hair loss on the legs

- Impotence

- Non-healing wounds over pressure points, such as heels or ankles

- Numbness, weakness, or heaviness in muscles

- Pain (described as burning or aching) at rest, commonly in the toes and at night while lying flat

- Pallor (paleness) when the legs are elevated

- Reddish-blue discoloration of the extremities

- Restricted mobility

- Severe pain

- Thickened, opaque toenails

The symptoms of peripheral vascular disease may resemble other conditions. Consult your physician for a diagnosis.

How is peripheral vascular disease diagnosed?

In addition to a complete medical history and physical examination, diagnostic procedures for peripheral vascular disease may include any, or a combination, of the following:

1. Angiogram - an x-ray of the arteries and veins to detect blockage or narrowing of the vessels. This procedure involves inserting a thin, flexible tube into an artery in the leg and injecting a contrast dye. The contrast dye makes the arteries and veins visible on the x-ray.

2. Ankle-brachial index (ABI) - a comparison of the blood pressure in the ankle with the blood pressure in the arm using a regular blood pressure cuff and a Doppler ultrasound device. To determine the ABI, the systolic blood pressure (the top number of the blood pressure measurement) of the ankle is divided by the systolic blood pressure of the arm.

1. Blood lipid profile - a blood test to measure the levels of each type of fat in your blood: total cholesterol, Ldl cholesterol, Hdl cholesterol, triglycerides, and others.
2. Doppler ultrasound flow studies - uses high-frequency sound waves and a computer to create images of blood vessels, tissues, and organs. Doppler technique is used to measure and assess the flow of blood. Faintness or absence of sound may indicate an obstruction in the blood flow.
3. Magnetic resonance angiography (MRA) - a noninvasive diagnostic procedure that uses a combination of a large magnet, radiofrequencies, and a computer to produce detailed images of organs and structures within the body. An MRA is often used to examine the heart and other soft tissues and to assess blood flow.
4. Treadmill exercise test - a test that is given while a patient walks on a treadmill to monitor the heart during exercise.
5. Photoplethysmography (PPG) - an examination comparable to the ankle brachial index except that it uses a very tiny blood pressure cuff around the toe and a PPG sensor (infrared light to evaluate blood flow near the surface of the skin) to record waveforms and blood pressure measurements. These measurements are then compared to the systolic blood pressure in the arm.
6. Pulse volume recording (PVR) waveform analysis - a technique used to calculate blood volume changes in the legs using a recording device that displays the results as a waveform.
7. Reactive hyperemia test - a test similar to an ABI or a treadmill test but used for people who are unable to walk on a treadmill. While a person is lying on his or her back, comparative blood pressure measurements are taken on

the thighs and ankles to determine any decrease between the two sites.

8. Segmental blood pressure measurements - a means of comparing blood pressure measurements using a Doppler device in the upper thigh, above and below the knee, at the ankle, and on the arm to determine any constriction in blood flow.

What is the treatment for peripheral vascular disease?

There are two main goals for treatment of peripheral artery/vascular disease: control the symptoms and halt the progression of the disease to lower the risk of heart attack, stroke, and other complications.

Specific treatment will be determined by your physician based on:

• Your age, overall health, and medical history

• Extent of the disease

• Your signs and symptoms

• Your tolerance for specific medications, procedures, or therapies

• Expectations for the course of the disease

• Your opinion or preference

Treatment may include:

1. Lifestyle modifications to control risk factors, including

regular exercise, proper nutrition, and smoking cessation

2. Aggressive treatment of existing conditions that may aggravate pvd, such as diabetes, hypertension, and hyperlipidemia (elevated blood cholesterol)

3. Medications for improving blood flow, such as antiplatelet agents (blood thinners) and medications that relax the blood vessel walls

1. Angioplasty - a catheter (long hollow tube) is used to create a larger opening in an artery to increase blood flow. Angioplasty may be performed in many of the arteries in the body. There are several types of angioplasty procedures, including:
2. Balloon angioplasty - a small balloon is inflated inside the blocked artery to open the blocked area
3. Atherectomy - the blocked area inside the artery is "shaved" away by a tiny device on the end of a catheter
4. Laser angioplasty - a laser used to "vaporize" the blockage in the artery
5. Stent - a tiny coil is expanded inside the blocked artery to open the blocked area and is left in place to keep the artery open
6. Vascular surgery - a bypass graft using a blood vessel from another part of the body or a tube made of synthetic material is placed in the area of the blocked or narrowed artery to reroute the blood flow
7. With both angioplasty and vascular surgery, an angiogram is often performed prior to the procedure.

What are the complications of peripheral vascular disease?

1. Complications of peripheral vascular disease most often occur because of decreased or absent blood flow. Such complications may include:
2. Amputation (loss of a limb)
3. Heart attack
4. Poor wound healing
5. Restricted mobility due to pain or discomfort with exertion

6. Severe pain in the affected extremity
7. Stroke (three times more likely in persons with PVD)
8. By following an aggressive treatment plan for peripheral vascular disease, complications such as these may be prevented.

Prevention of peripheral vascular disease:

Steps to prevent PVD are primarily aimed at management of the risk factors for PVD. A prevention program for PVD may include:

1. Smoking cessation, including avoidance of second hand smoke and use of tobacco products
2. Dietary modifications including reduced fat, cholesterol, and simple carbohydrates (such as sweets), and increased amounts of fruits and vegetables
3. Treatment of dyslipidemia (high blood cholesterol levels) with medications as determined by your physician
4. Weight reduction
5. Moderation in alcohol intake
6. Medications as determined by your physician to reduce your risk of blood clot formation
7. Exercise plan of a minimum of 30 minutes daily
8. Control of diabetes mellitus
9. Control of hypertension (high blood pressure)

A prevention plan for PVD may also be used to prevent or lessen the progress of PVD once it has been diagnosed. Consult your physician for diagnosis and treatment.

Lymphedema and Chronic Venous Insufficiency Comparison:

	Chronic Venous Insufficiency	Lymphedema
Pain:	Yes	Can be severe due to nerve compression
Swelling:	Yes, may even include brawny edema.	Yes, can affect all or part of limb
Infections:	Yes, from ulcerations	Yes, typically cellulitis, see below
Fluids:	Hematolgic Fluids	Protein rich lymphatic fluids
Skin:	Discolorations ,	Discolorations ,growths, hardening
Leg Ulcers:	Yes ,	Yes also wounds from skin changes
Fibrosis:	No	Yes, extending into subcutaneous tissue

Treatment for swelling from chronic venous insufficiency:

Manual decongestive therapy (Complex or Complete Decongestive Therapy) is often prescribed. Follow up by usage of compression garments. Compression bandages such as short-stretch bandages and long-stretch may also be used. Treatment will also focus on the cause of the chronic venous insufficiency

Treatment for swelling from lymphedema:

Manual decongestive therapy ((Complex or Complete Decongestive Therapy) is the gold standard treatment. After decongestive therapy, compression bandages, custom fitted compression garments, compression sleeves, are used. Other treatment modalities may include the use of compression pumps, and surgery. Treatment focus will be on the control and management of lymphedema not the cause. There is no known cure for the cause of lymphedema.

Venous ulcers

Venous ulcers (stasis ulcer or varicose ulcers) are wounds that are thought to occur due to improper functioning of venous valves, usually of the legs. They are the major cause of chronic wounds, occurring in 70% to 90% of chronic wound cases. Venous ulcers develop mostly along the medial distal leg, and can be very painful.

Pathophysiology

The exact etiology of venous ulcers is not certain, but they are thought to arise when venous valves that exist to prevent backflow of blood do not function properly, causing the pressure in veins to increase. The body needs the pressure gradient between arteries and veins in order for the heart to pump blood forward through arteries and into veins. When venous hypertension exists, arteries no longer have significantly higher pressure than veins, blood is not pumped as effectively into or out of the area, and it pools.

Venous hypertension may also stretch veins and allow blood proteins to leak into the extravascular space, isolating extracellular matrix (ECM) molecules and growth factors, preventing them from helping to heal the wound. Leakage of fibrinogen from veins as well as deficiencies in fibrinolysis may also cause fibrin to build up around the vessels, preventing oxygen and nutrients from reaching cells. Venous insufficiency may also cause white blood cells (leukocytes) to accumulate in small blood vessels, releasing inflammatory factors and reactive oxygen species (ROS, free radicals) and further contributing to chronic wound formation. Buildup of white blood cells in small blood vessels may also plug the vessels, further contributing to ischemia. This blockage of blood vessels by leukocytes may be responsible for the "no reflow phenomenon," in which ischemic tissue is never fully reperfused. Allowing blood to flow back into the limb, for example by elevating it, is necessary but also contributes to reperfusion injury. Other comorbidities may also be the root cause of venous ulcers.

It is in the crus that the classic venous stasis ulcer occurs. Venous stasis results from damage to the vein valvular system in the lower extremity and in extreme cases allows the pressure in the veins to be higher than the pressure in the arteries. This pressure results in transudation of inflammatory mediators into the subcutaneous tissues of the lower extremity and subsequent breakdown of the tissue including the skin.

Classification

A clinical severity score has been developed to assess chronic venous ulcers. It is based on the CEAP (clinical, etiology, anatomy, and pathophysiology) classification system developed by an expert panel. A high score gives a poor prognosis.

Treatment

Venous ulcers are costly to treat, and there is a significant chance that they will recur after healing; one study found that up to 48% of venous ulcers had recurred by the fifth year after healing.

A review by Clinical Evidence concluded that several beneficial treatments exist. Bisgaard regimen

Most venous ulcers respond to a regimen called Bisgaard regimen for treating ulcers. Best remembered as a mnemonic 4E's - education, elevation, elastic compression and evaluation.

Compression therapy

Non-elastic, ambulatory, below knee (BK) compression aggressively counters the impact of reflux on venous pump failure. Compression therapy is used for venous leg ulcers and can decrease blood vessel diameter and pressure, which increases their effectiveness, preventing blood from flowing backwards. Compression is also used to decrease release of inflammatory cytokines, lower the amount of fluid leaking from capillaries and therefore prevent swelling, and prevent clotting by decreasing activation of thrombin and increasing that of plasmin.

Compression is applied using elastic bandages or boots specifically designed for the purpose. It is not clear whether non-elastic systems are better than a multilayer elastic system. Patients should wear as much compression as is comfortable. The type of dressing applied beneath the compression does not seem to matter, and hydrocolloid is not better than simple low adherent dressings.

Pentoxifylline

A meta-analysis of randomized controlled trials by the Cochrane Collaboration found that "Pentoxifylline is an effective adjunct to compression bandaging for treating venous ulcers and may be effective in the absence of compression".

Artificial skin

Artificial skin, made of collagen and cultured skin cells, is also used to cover venous ulcers and excrete growth factors to help them heal. A meta-analysis of randomized controlled trials by the Cochrane Collaboration concluded "Bilayer artificial skin, used in conjunction with compression bandaging, increases the chance of healing a venous ulcer compared with compression and a simple dressing".

Surgical correction of superficial venous reflux

A randomized controlled trial found that surgery "reduces the recurrence of ulcers at four years and results in a greater proportion of ulcer free time".

Anatomic and Hemodynamic Changes in the Venous Vascular Bed in the Lower Extremities With Chronic Venous Insufficiency

D Musil, J Herman

Abstract

The authors paid attention to revealing as precisely as possible anatomical and haemodynamic conditions in venous vascular bed in the course of ultrasonographic examination of 309 lower extremities with clinical manifestations of chronic venous insufficiency (CVI). A combined reflux in the superficial and deep venous system (53.7%) or isolated reflux in superficial veins (25.9%) proved to be the most frequent pathogenic bases of CVI. Pathophysiology of varices was mostly based on the venous reflux and the primary idiopathic CVI was mostly present (98.1%). The post- thrombotic partial obstruction of the deep venous system (post-thrombotic venous changes on the walls) was demonstrated exceptionally (1.9%). A high coincidence of reflux in the deep and superficial venous system points out to s.c. secondary reflux in the deep veins originating on the basis of primary reflux in the large or small saphena. An attempt was made to clarify, whether the development and frequency of incompetent perforators is directly connected with the presence and seriousness of reflux in the large and small saphena. The presence and severity of large saphena insufficiency does not univocally indicate the presence of dilated or insufficient perforators on the medical side of the crus, where these anastomoses are present most frequently. The large saphena is a long vein typically suffering from segmental insufficiency, i.e. reflux affecting a certain portion, whereas other parts of the vein may be fully competent. Anatomical venous variability and abnormalities on lower extremities were demonstrated in every fifth extremity (62 extremities, 20.1%). Most of them concerned large saphena (39 extremities, 62.8%), small saphena being second (15 extremities, 25.2%). Other anatomical deviations occurred sporadically as solitary findings. In the large saphena, duplication was present most frequently (54.8%). Insufficient variable superficial veins and anatomical venous anomalies were mostly not the only pathogenic basis of CVI, but were predominantly associated with insufficiently in the area of deep veins and perforators (84%). In our cohort there were altogether 55 extremities (17.8%) after the operation on superficial venous system, where relapses of varices were found. The causes of post-operation relapse of varices may be divided into three groups: 1. insufficiency of the large saphena, 2. insufficiency of the small saphena and 3. insufficiency of the deep veins. A combined simultaneous insufficiency in several venous systems was found most frequently (27 extremities,

49.1%). Even though the reflux in the deep veins was demonstrated in 50.9% of these extremities, a combination with the reflux in superficial veins and perforators (49.1%) was present with the exception of one case of isolated insufficiency. The insufficiency of the large and small saphena was clearly the leading single causes (15 extremities, 27.3%) of varix relapses. The patients should never be operated on the venous system of lower extremities without previous detailed ultrasonographic examination. It is the only way to increase probability of the operation success and to decrease the risk of relapses of CVI manifestations.

Vnitr Lek. 2003 Aug;49(8):610-7

The Venous Wall and Valvular Function in Chronic Venous Insufficiency

O Thulesius

Abstract

The present paper is an overview taking into account the four most important etiological factors which can be involved in the development of chronic venous insufficiency (CVI): (1) weakness of the vascular wall including connective tissue and smooth muscle, (2) dysfunction and damage of the venous endothelium, (3) damage of the venous valves and (4) disturbancies of the microcirculation. The first three can be implicated in the development of reflux and venous hypertension and it is difficult to pin-point one single factor as being the most important. Disturbancies of the microcirculation eventually lead to the typical complications of CVI. With better understanding of the disease process it is possible to attack the causative factors leading to CVI and prevent and heal complications.

Int Angiol. 1996 Jun;15(2):114-8.

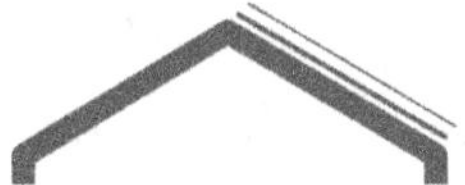

Chronic venous insufficiency (CVI) - a study of 100 cases

Mm Shahin-Ul-Islam Md. Zahirul Haque, Saki Md. Jakiul Alam, Mesbahuddin Noman, Fm Siddiqui

Abstract:

This study was carried out in the outpatient department of Dhaka Medical College Hospital. 100 patients presented with chronic venous insufficiency during the period of January 2005 to June 2005 were studied to find out the various modes of presentation, risk factors and relationship of symptoms with age, sex and Body Mass Index of the patients. It was found that, maximum patients presented with heaviness in the leg (87%), followed by aching leg pain (75%), leg swelling (70%),cramping leg pain (68%), tiredness (48%), burning pain (43%), engorged leg vein (39%), restless leg at night (21%), throbbing leg pain (18%), itching (13%), various skin changes without active ulceration (7%) and active leg ulceration only 3% of cases. Increasing age of the patients, obesity, increasing number of pregnancies, prolonged standing and sitting position at work were found to be positively correlated with CVI. Advanced age is associated with more advanced stage of CVI according to clinical CEAP classification. There is almost equal sex distribution among the stages of CVI except in advanced stage, in stage C4, C5 and C6 there is 10 patients out of them 9 are male and only 1 is female. Relationship of symptoms with BMI of the patients were also sort out and found that, in C3 group of CEAP classification out of 61 patients 46 are obese according to BMI, of which 32 are female and 14 are male and only 17 patients have BMI within normal range, but in other group there is no significant difference in incidence between two groups.

Journal of Medicine, (1970), 20-26, 9(1)

Varicose Veins and Chronic Venous Insufficiency

H Partsch

Abstract

Varicose veins are a very frequent disorder with prevalence in our adult population between 14% for large varices and 59% for small teleangiectasias. Subjective symptoms may be very non- specific. The term "chronic venous insufficiency (CVI)" defines functional abnormalities of the venous system producing advanced symptoms like oedema, skin changes or leg ulcers. Both entities, varicose veins and CVI, may be summarized under the term "chronic venous disorders" which includes the full spectrum of morphological and functional abnormalities of the venous system. A classification system to describe chronic venous disorders regarding clinical appearance, etiology, anatomical distribution and pathophysiology has been proposed under the acronym of CEAP. The revised version of the CEAP classification contains also definitions of clinical signs and suggests three levels of apparative investigations adjusted to the clinical stage. Concerning the etiology of venous disorders controversial theories exist leading to different therapeutic concepts. As a matter of fact, there is a vicious circle between structural changes in valves and venous wall and hemodynamic forces leading to reflux and venous hypertension. Different methods for treating varicose veins are available producing satisfactory early outcome in most cases, but followed by a high recurrence rate after years. Chronic venous insufficiency requires "chronic management". Compression therapy by bandages for initial treatment of severe stages and maintenance therapy using medical compression stockings is essential. In addition, correction of venous refluxes by surgery or endovenous procedures including echo-guided foam sclerotherapy should be considered in every single case.

Vasa. 2009 Nov;38(4):293-301.

Chronic Venous Insufficiency and Varicose Veins of the Lower Extremities

Young Jin Youn Juyong Lee

Abstract

Chronic venous insufficiency (CVI) of the lower extremities manifests itself in various clinical spectrums, ranging from asymptomatic but cosmetic problems to severe symptoms, such as venous ulcer. CVI is a relatively common medical problem but is often overlooked by healthcare providers because of an underappreciation of the magnitude and impact of the problem, as well as incomplete recognition of the various presenting manifestations of primary and secondary venous disorders. The prevalence of CVI in South Korea is expected to increase, given the possible underdiagnoses of CVI, the increase in obesity and an aging population. This article reviews the pathophysiology of CVI of the lower extremities and highlights the role of duplex ultrasound in its diagnosis and radiofrequency ablation, and iliac vein stenting in its management.

Korean J Intern Med. 2019 Mar;34(2):269-283

The Peculiarities of Diagnosis and Treatment of Chronic Venous Insufficiency and Venous Forms of Lower Extremity Dysplasia

S V Sapelkin, V N Dan, G Karmazanovskĭ, G I Kuntsevich

Abstract

The authors present the modern viewpoint concerning the problem of chronic venous insufficiency in the cases of venous forms of dysplasia. The treatment of patients with of venous forms of dysplasia should be based on the principles of interdisciplinary approach, which stipulates both the careful diagnosis on the basis of mainly non-invasive methods and integration of surgical and conservative treatment methods. Today such treatment should be combined and conducted within the multi-purpose highly specialized institution. Only the combination of all treatment methods will allow achieving the best functional and esthetic results. In the cases when indications are absent and conduction of surgical or any other treatment method is impossible it is necessary control the venous anomaly (dynamical follow-up, compression as a basic variant of conservative therapy). It will allow minimizing the unfavorable influence on vital functions and improving the patient's life quality.

Voenno-meditsinskiĭ zhurnal, (2006), 327(12)

ANATOMY

Role of saphenous vein wall in the pathogenesis of primary varicose veins

Mohamed A. Elsharawya,, Magda M. Naimb, Eiman M. Abdelmaguidc and Abdulmohsen A. Al- Mulhima

Primary varicose vein disease is a widely prevalent condition. It affects about 10–40% of 30–70- year-old people. Varicose veins were regarded as a secondary manifestation of valvular incompetence and exposure of the vein wall to pressures that it cannot withstand, i.e. the hydrostatic head of pressure from the right auricle in the upright position. Recently, it has been reported that varicose veins can develop without valvular incompetence. The theory of primary venous dilatation leading to secondary valvular incompetence has received more attention nowadays. This venous dilatation may be due to weakness of the vein wall as a result of structural problems.

Seventy specimens of long saphenous veins (LSV) were obtained from 35 patients admitted to the Vascular Unit, King Fahd Hospital of the University, Saudi Arabia and Suez Canal University Hospital, Egypt. The study was agreed by the local Ethical Committee and informed consent was taken from each patient. All patients had proximal thigh LSV excised. The LSV specimens were divided into two groups: normal vein group and varicose vein group. Two specimens were taken from each vein, approximately 3–4 cm from the saphenofemoral junction.

Normal vein group (11 patients) these were eight males and three females with mean age (years) 30±6.5. None of the patients had clinical evidence of chronic venous insufficiency in both lower limbs

Varicose vein group (24 patients) those included 16 females and eight males with mean age (years) 31.6±4.3. They had full history, preoperative physical examination and whole leg duplex mapping. All patients had a history of varicose veins for less than one year. All patients had primary class 2 (uncomplicated) chronic venous insufficiency affecting the LSV. The saphenofemoral valve (SFV) was competent in five and incompetent in 19 patients

Vein wall distensibilty is controlled by SMCs, collagen and elastin. Smooth muscles in the tunica media are responsible for wall tone, which is influenced by autonomic nerves and circulating stimulants. Passive tone is provided by collagen and elastin. Loss of tone in varicose veins could be due to defects in this wall. The present study agreed with most of the previous ones that there was an increase in intimal thickness in varicose veins compared to normal. This increased thickness could be due to increase in collagen content of intima and migration of SMCs from media to intima. In the current study, there was insignificant increase in muscle thickness in media of varicose veins when compared to normally components. Therefore, the pathological abnormalities in varicose veins were not due to deficiency of smooth muscles, but could be referred to the inability of muscle cells to provide the necessary tone in the vessel wall leading to vein wall dilatation. Many studies including the present one has shown that LSV contained a significantly higher amount of collagen in varicose veins compared to normal. This increase was more evident in tunica media causing separation of SMCs. some studies, including ours, have shown ultra-structural changes in SMCs of varicose veins compared to normal veins. These changes included abnormality in shape, conversion into fiber-like material, degeneration, vacuolization and break up of SMCs. Another important finding, in this study, as well as others, was that the abnormally shaped SMCs (which contain vacuoles most probably lysosomal) would have the ability to form pseudopodia and phagocytose other SMCs. Moreover, SMCs were seen to convert into fiber-like material, in this study and a previous one, which could be sequelae of its degeneration. Because of these muscle abnormalities, some authors considered that the primary defect might be in the SMCs of the vein wall and this defect could be genetically determined. The present study and others have demonstrated that elastic fibers were significantly decreased in internal elastic lamina of varicose veins when compared to normal. Moreover, there was loss of normal elastin/collagen lattice network. These morphological alterations of elastin may explain the functional finding of reduced strength and elasticity of varicose veins.

The present study has shown that there was no significant difference in the vein wall structural changes between varicose veins with and without valve incompetence. This supports the theory of primary weakness in the vein wall leading to dilatation of the vein with resultant separation of valve cusps.

In conclusion, studying the histopathological changes of varicose veins in comparison to normal ones, revealed that varicose veins showed intimal changes, disturbance in connective tissue components and smooth muscles. These findings supported the theory of primary weakness of the vein wall as a cause of varicosity.

Interact Cardiovasc Thorac Surg. 2007 Apr;6(2):219-24

Superficial Venous Disease

K *ellie R Brown, Peter J Rossi*

Abstract

S uperficial venous disease is a common clinical problem. The concerning disease states of the superficial venous system are venous reflux, varicose veins, and superficial venous thrombosis. Superficial venous reflux can be a significant contributor to chronic venous stasis wounds of the lower extremity, the treatment of which can be costly both in terms of overall health care expenditure and lost working days for affected patients. Although commonly thought of as a benign process, superficial venous thrombosis is associated with several underlying pathologic processes, including malignancy and deep venous thrombosis.

Surg Clin North Am. 2013 Aug;93(4):963-82, ix-x

CLASSIFICATION

Cross-sectional Study on Heredity and Venous Disorders: The End of the Dominant Maternal Heredity Dogma?

V Crebassa, T Roucaute, J J Guex, F A Allaert

Abstract

Objective: To evaluate the heredity factor of the chronic venous disorders and odds ratio linked to maternal or paternal heredity.

Methods: Cross-sectional epidemiological study conducted in daily practice of medical practitioners on all patients consulting them. The practitioners described the venous status of all patients consulting them and recorded the familial past history of venous disease.

Results: Among 21319 patients, 60.4% have a familial history of chronic venous disorder: unilateral paternal 7.5%, unilateral maternal 40.9% and bilateral: 12.0%. Chronic venous disorder prevalence is 58.8% in the global population, 38.2% in the absence of parental history, 67.0% for unilateral paternal, 71.3% for unilateral maternal and 79.2% for bilateral ($p < 0.0001$). After adjustment on age and sex, results show significant ($p < 0.0001$) odds ratio of 3.2 for unilateral paternal, of 3.4 for unilateral maternal and of 5.6 for a history in both parents. In the context of a history in both parents, the odds ratio increased to 5.6 for women and 8.4 for men.

Conclusion: This large cross-sectional study confirms the association between heredity and venous disease, but its results could call into question the maternal predominant character of the chronic venous disorder heredity.

Phlebology. 2016 Feb;31(1):42-9.

Diagnosis of chronic venous disease of the lower extremities: the "CEAP" classification.

Kistner RL, Eklof B, Masuda EM.

Abstract

Objective: To test a new classification of chronic venous disease (CVD)—based on clinical, etiologic, anatomic, and pathophysiologic data (the CEAP system)—in a series of patients by using objective tests to establish all diagnoses.

Material and Methods: The CEAP classification was applied to 102 extremities in 70 consecutive patients with CVD. Diagnoses were based on objective testing with continuous-wave Doppler studies, duplex scanning, plethysmography, venous pressure, and phlebography, which were applied selectively (the more invasive methods were reserved for cases of greater severity).

Results: Use of this classification provided an organized categorization of the key elements of the venous abnormalities in each case and clarified the interrelationships among the clinical manifestations, cause of the process, and anatomic distribution of involvement. For example, in this series of 102 extremities, 79% had primary venous disease, 18% had secondary disease, and 3% had congenital abnormalities. Ulcers were found in 7% of extremities with primary CVD and 44% with secondary CVD. Of the cases with ulceration, 43% were due to primary incompetence and 57% to post thrombotic disease. Reflux was the pathophysiologic problem in 86% of the total series and in 80% of ulcer cases. Similar relationships can be delineated for cases with varicose veins, edema, or skin changes. Study of the specific facets of the CEAP classification provided precise information about the cause and the effect of venous abnormalities that could be compared with cases in other series.

Conclusion: Use of the CEAP classification with diagnoses determined by objective testing accurately identifies categories of CVD. The objective date provides a clear description of the abnormalities in each case and may be used for analyses of meaningful relationships between categories of CVD. Adoption of this objective method of classifying CVD will facilitate inter institutional studies.

Mayo Clin Proc. 1996 Apr;71(4):338-45

EPIDEMIOLOGY

Epidemiology of Chronic Venous Diseases

Eberhard Rabe, Gabriele Berboth, Felizitas Pannier

Abstract

Aim: Overview of the recent knowledge in epidemiology of chronic venous diseases.

Methods: Systematic search and discussion of recent studies concerning epidemiology of chronic venous diseases.

Results: The more recent epidemiologic studies of venous diseases in which the CEAP classification was used showed a prevalence of 60-70 % CEAP clinical class C0 and C1, app. 25 % for C2 and C3 and up to 5 % for C4 to C6 with skin changes or venous ulcers. The incidence of varicose veins is app. 2 % per year.

Conclusions: Chronic venous diseases like varicose veins and chronic venous insufficiency belong to the most frequent diseases in our adult population.

Wien Med Wochenschr. 2016 Jun;166(9-10):260-3

Prevalence, Presentation and Occupational Risk Factors of Chronic Venous Disease in Nurses

A I Diken, A Yalçınkaya, E Aksoy, S Yılmaz, K Özşen, T Sarak, K Çağlı

Abstract

Objective: In this study involving a group of nurses employed in a number of different medical services with relatively well-defined working conditions, the presence and symptoms of chronic venous insufficiency were screened and their association with work burden and physical working conditions was explored.

Methods: Of the 294 actively employed nurses during the study period, 232 (79%) were recruited on the basis of their willingness for participation and fulfilment of the inclusion criteria.

Results: Among the study subjects, 62.9% had at least one symptom of chronic venous insufficiency, and 50.4% were found to have chronic venous insufficiency according to Clinical- Etiology-Anatomy-Pathophysiology classification criteria. A significant association was found between the diurnal ankle circumference difference in the left-right ankles and the mean duration of hospital stay.

Conclusions: Our results have shown that the average duration of hospital stay, which is among the variables used to estimate the work burden of nurses, is associated with an increased frequency of the signs and symptoms of chronic venous insufficiency.

Phlebology. 2016 Mar;31(2):111-7

The Epidemiology of Chronic Venous Insufficiency and Varicose Veins

Jennifer L Beebe-Dimmer, John R Pfeifer, Jennifer S Engle, David Schottenfeld

Abstract

Chronic venous disease is a common condition presenting to physicians in Western Europe and the United States. This article provides a comprehensive review of the published literature in the English language, from 1942 to the present, and focuses on the prevalence of chronic venous insufficiency and varicose veins, as well as the involved risk factors. Prevalence estimates vary widely by geographic location, with the highest reported rates in Western countries. Reports of prevalence of chronic venous insufficiency vary from < 1% to 40% in females and from < 1% to 17% in males. Prevalence estimates for varicose veins are higher, <1% to 73% in females and 2% to 56% in males. The reported ranges in prevalence estimations presumably reflect differences in the population distribution of risk factors, accuracy in application of diagnostic criteria, and the quality and availability of medical diagnostic and treatment resources. Established risk factors include older age, female gender, pregnancy, family history of venous disease, obesity, and occupations associated with orthostasis. Yet, there are several factors that are not well documented, such as diet, physical activity and exogenous hormone use, which may be important in the development of chronic venous disease and its clinical manifestations.

Epidemiol. 2005 Mar;15(3):175-84.

Epidemiology of Chronic Venous Insufficiency

G. De Backer, and G. De Backer

Abstract

In contrast to the knowledge on the frequency and determinants of arterial diseases, little epidemiologic research has been carried out on venous diseases; this may be partly due to methodological problems in defining chronic venous insufficiency and in measuring these conditions with sufficient validity.

Epidemiologic studies that were published after 1965 and that are not based on clinical series are reviewed; prevalence and incidence rates are reported. Studies of risk factors for varicose veins have largely resulted in inconsistent results; the sex difference is universal while the large geographical differences suggest strong environmental influ ences. For all other determinants much of the variation between studies is probably related to differences in definition, in population-sampling techniques, and in assess ment methods. Several plausible etiologic theories on the causes and development of chronic venous insufficiency are supported or refuted by the epidemiologic studies. Further research is needed, whenever possible cross-cultural, with particular emphasis on clear definitions, valid methods, and a prospective study design.

Angiology. 1997;48(7):569-576.

Late Incidence of Chronic Venous Insufficiency After Deep Vein Harvest

J Gregory Modrall, Jennie A Hocking, Carlos H Timaran, Eric B Rosero, Frank R Arko 3rd, R James Valentine, G Patrick Clagett

Abstract

Background: The deep veins (DV) of the thigh have proven to be versatile autogenous conduits for arterial reconstruction. Harvesting DV poses a theoretical risk of compromising venous outflow of the limb, which could predispose to chronic venous morbidity. The purpose of this study was to define the late incidence of chronic venous insufficiency (CVI) and to characterize the long-term alterations in venous physiology after DV harvest.

Methods: Since 1991, 269 patients have undergone arterial reconstructions using DV at our facility. Patients with DV harvest at least 43 months prior to the study (n = 151) were eligible for inclusion. Eighty-nine patients were excluded (deceased = 70; lost to follow-up = 19). Forty-six patients who declined formal testing were queried by phone for signs and symptoms of CVI. The current study presents a case-control series of 16 patients (27 limbs) after DV harvest and six age- and gender- matched control patients (12 limbs) who underwent examination and venous testing.

Results: At a mean follow-up of 70.1 +/- 5.6 months, 23 of 27 limbs (85.2%) had no significant CVI (CEAP C(0) to C(2)). Four limbs (14.8%) had significant venous morbidity (C(3) to C(6)), including edema alone (C(3); n = 2 limbs), edema with skin changes (C(4); n = 1 limb), and a healed venous ulceration (C(5); n = 1 limb). APG testing confirmed relative venous outflow obstruction after DV harvest (mean outflow fraction: harvested limbs = 38.4 +/- 3.9% vs control limbs = 51.7

+/- 4.3%; P = .04). Despite the relative outflow obstruction, the mean VFI was not significantly different between harvested and control limbs (harvested limbs = 1.08 +/- 0.15% vs control limbs =

0.77 +/- 0.16%; P = .19). DV harvest resulted in no significant changes in calf ejection fraction (harvested limbs = 67.4 +/- 6.4% vs control limbs = 86.8 +/- 9.5%; P = .09) or residual volume fraction measured (harvested limbs = 32.3 +/- 6.4% vs control limbs = 47.7 +/- 11.6%; P = .22). Of the 46 patients interviewed by phone, five (10.9%) reported bilateral amputations, seven (15.2%) reported chronic edema in their harvested limbs (C(3)), and 34 (73.9%) reported no signs of CVI in their harvested limbs (C(0)).

Conclusions: Deep vein harvest produces few symptoms of chronic venous insufficiency, and venous ulceration is infrequent. Despite relative venous outflow obstruction, noninvasive indices of chronic venous insufficiency on APG are often normal, suggesting that the risk of developing venous ulceration is low in the majority of patients after DV harvest.

J Vasc Surg. 2007 Sep;46(3):520-5

Characteristics of Venous Insufficiency in Western Turkey: VEYT-I Study

B Akbulut, H I Uçar, M Oç, M Ikizler, C Yorgancioglu, S Dernek, E Böke

Abstract

Objectives: Syndromes of venous hypertension and reduced venous clearance are important causes of morbidity and disability in patients with varicose venous disease. Published estimates of the prevalence of varicosities range from 7% to 55% in the adult population, with most studies demonstrating clinical varicose reflux in about 40% of the population where the frequency of venous insufficiency is believed to be higher in Westernized and industrialized nations, most likely due to differences in lifestyle and activity. Unfortunately, the prevalence in a Turkish population is not known. The goal of the VEYT-I study was to determine the characteristics of venous insufficiency in a Turkish population.

Method: Randomized patients who applied to a health-care centre were included in this study. The Tübingen questionnaire was used to evaluate the signs and symptoms of venous insufficiency and their seriousness in a Turkish population. Patients were additionally questioned on demographic data, education, working, living habits, quality of life and actual health status.

Results: A total of 2167 patients were involved in this study. Four patients with chronic renal failure and 40 patients with congestive heart failure were excluded. In patients with venous insufficiency, 90.1% did not receive any therapy. In all, 51.53% of patients with venous insufficiency were men, and mean age was 56.9 ± 9.4.

Conclusion: The prevalence of venous insufficiency seems to be somewhat higher when compared with Western populations. One of the most prominent facts is that about 90% of patients with venous insufficiency did not receive any therapy. Therefore, disease-related complications or discomfort might emerge soon, and so more importance should be given to venous insufficiency. The VEYT-I study is a continuing database study and the target is to enlarge the study population.

Phlebology. 2012;27(7):374-377. https://doi.org/10.1258/phleb.2011.011100

Chronic Venous Insufficiency-Epidemiology

R *Staffa*

Abstract

Chronic venous insufficiency (CVI) of lower limbs is one of the most widespread diseases occurring in developed countries worldwide. Literature data concerning its prevalence and incidence differ depending on evaluation criteria or on the definition of CVI. By comparing the available epidemiological literature published in the last decade, the authors point out the fact that the disunity in evaluation criteria of CVI is the weakness of all comparative studies. In spite of this, it is evident that, in addition to age and sex, the main risk factors of CVI include also the influence of working environment, genetic influences and geographic factors. Solely the acceptance of a unified classification of CVI and multinational collaborative studies could bring new information on epidemiology, etiology, prevention and therapy of this chronic disease, as in the case of coronary heart diseases in the past.

Bratisl Lek Listy,. 2002;103(4-5):166-8.

Epidemiology of Chronic Venous Insufficiency

P Carpentier, P Priollet

Abstract

From an epidemiological point of view, at least three different entities of chronic venous insufficiency (CVI) can be defined: heavy legs syndrome is experienced by about half the working people of industrialized countries. It is most frequently linked to varicosis, nevertheless, in one case out of three, no venous incompetence is associated. Female sex, prolonged standing position and overweight are other significant risk factors; varicosis comes with modern civilization. Its prevalence is very low in African and Asian or Australasian aborigen populations although immigrant subjects from these regions have the same risk as the population of their host country. Sedentarity, overweight, tight clothing may provide part of the explanation. But the main factor is probably linked to the low fiber diet in industrialized countries through induced constipation and increased abdominal pressure, or because of the associated low vitamin F intake. Varicosis is rarely seen before adulthood, and its prevalence increases with aging. Sex ratio is unbalanced (F/M estimates: 1.5 to 3.5), that is mainly explained by childbearing and hormonal Factors. A familial factor has also been evidenced, with a relative risk of 2, when one parent has varicosis, and about 3 when both are involved; epidemiological data regarding cutaneous trophic changes in CVI are restricted to leg ulcers: 1% of the general population, and 4 to 5% of people aged 80 and more are afflicted. Leg ulcers are frequently found in the post-thrombotic syndrome, but female sex and varicosis are other significant risk factors. Up to now, epidemiological data are too scarce for a definite demonstration of the natural history of the different subsets of CVI. On the other hand, they clearly show that major medical, social and economical problems are involved.

Presse Med. 1994 Feb 10;23(5):197-201.

The natural history and epidemiology of venous thrombosis

Cedric J. Carter

Abstract

Epidemiologic studies over the past 30 years have provided much of the basis for the understanding of venous thromboembolic disease. There has been an evolution from simple descriptive studies using clinical diagnosis to various forms of comparative studies using objective diagnoses.

Identification of high-risk cases in the hospitalized population has led to the development of both general and specific antithrombotic prophylactic regimens. This has occurred against a background of an increased understanding of the pathophysiology of venous thrombosis. Inhospital case interventions have allowed direct questions concerning pathophysiology to be addressed. Examples would include the use of certain types and dosages of anticoagulants and the use of mechanical devices to avoid stasis.

Despite these advances, there are still areas that require further attention. One aspect of importance is to evaluate the thrombotic risk of new procedures. The possibility that a new procedure may be either less or more thrombotic than its predecessor should be addressed. In the case of the former, additional antithrombotic measures are needed. An example of this is the relatively disappointing results of regular low-dose heparin treatment in some orthopedic procedures. In the case of the latter, less severe measures may be indicated. Current antithrombotic methods are not without risks and may not be necessary with some of the new endoscopic surgical procedures.

Another area of importance relates to the monitoring of compliance. The information on antithrombotic methods has been available for two decades, yet surveys of the application of these methods consistently show that antithrombotic protocols are used less in North America relative to their use in equivalent institutions in Europe.

A third area that still needs further epidemiologic study is the incidence and effects of venous thrombosis in the general community. Despite the two recent descriptive studies cited above, relatively little, as compared with the in-patient perspective, is known about community risk factors and their prevention. With respect to the natural history of hospital-based cases it seems unlikely that much is to be gained from surveying the efficacy of heparin or heparin-like treatment for mortality end points. However, a large and still unsatisfactorily examined area is the true frequency and impact of the postphlebitic syndrome. This aspect is germane to both hospital- and community-acquired DVT and, with an aging population, clearly deserves a lot more attention.

Prog Cardiovasc Dis. 1994 May-Jun;36(6):423-38

ETIOLOGY

The Influence of Environmental Factors in Chronic Venous Insufficiency

A *rkadiusz Jawien*

Abstract

The present article focuses on the prevalence and risk factors for varicose veins and the severe stage of chronic venous insufficiency (CVI). The evaluation was made by reviewing the results of specific well-designed studies performed on the general population (case-control studies, cross-sectional studies, and large case series). Data from the literature were compared with the results of a recent multicenter cross-sectional study in Poland, in which 40,095 individuals from 803 registers of primary care physicians were clinically examined and assigned a clinical CEAP class. Analysis of the associations between varicose veins or severe CVI prevalence and factors that are usually considered as representing a risk for the development of CVI was performed. In Poland, a prevalence of varicose veins and severe CVI (skin changes, leg ulcer) similar to that observed in the other developed countries was reported. It was more common in women, but female sex was not found to be a strong risk factor. Among the risk factors most closely associated with CVI were age, family history of varicose veins, and constipation, whatever the sex. This is in keeping with findings from recent epidemiologic studies. Obesity and lack of physical activity were strongly associated with CVI in women, more so than in men. The number of pregnancies (more than 2 pregnancies) significantly distinguished between women with and without CVI. Regarding these latter risk factors, the Polish results do not contradict the commonly held beliefs that are found in the literature. A modest association was found with female sex, previous injury in legs (DVT), and remaining in the standing position for a long time, although these parameters are usually among those mostly agreed as being risk factors. The role of the prolonged sitting position was not established. The Polish epidemiologic survey provided updated figures on the prevalence of and risk factors for varicose veins and severe CVI, using clear and globally accepted clinical definitions for the venous disease based on the CEAP classification.

Angiology. Jul-Aug 2003;54 Suppl 1:S19-31.

Venous Outflow Obstruction: An Underestimated Contributor to Chronic Venous Disease

P*eter Neglén, Tara L Thrasher, Seshadri Raju*

Abstract

Objective: To assess the importance of iliac venous outflow obstruction in limbs with and without concomitant deep or superficial reflux, we performed a retrospective analysis of data contemporaneously entered into a set time-stamped electronic medical records program.

Material and method: Four hundred forty-seven limbs underwent iliac vein stenting of chronic, nonmalignant obstruction when greater than 50% morphologic stenosis was found at transfemoral venography or intravascular ultrasonography. Group 1 (female-male ratio, 3.4:1; left limb-right limb, 2.7:1; nonthrombotic-thrombotic, 1.8:1) included 187 stented limbs in 176 patients with absence of deep and superficial reflux as identified at erect duplex Doppler scanning. Group 2 (female-male, 1.7:1; left-right, 1.9:1, nonthrombotic-thrombotic limb, 1:2.1) included 260 limbs in

253 patients with combination obstruction and reflux. Reflux was left untreated during the observation period. Clinical outcome (ulcer healing and recurrence rate, degree of pain per visual

analog scale, swelling grade) and hemodynamic effects (ambulatory venous pressure, venous refilling time, venous filling index at 90 seconds) of iliac venous stenting were assessed.

Result: Patients with reflux and obstruction had more severe disease (clinical class 4-6, 53% in group 2 vs 24% in group 1; P <.001). Similarly, rate of active ulcer was low in limbs with obstruction only (3% vs 24%, groups 1 and 2, respectively). Mean clinical follow-up was 13 +/- 12 months (SD) in 86% of limbs. Because of the presence of reflux in group 2, venous pressure was higher, venous filling time was shorter, and venous filling index at 90 seconds increased, compared with group 1. Multisegment scores were 2.6 +/- 1.6 and 0, respectively. Of greater interest, there was no deterioration in venous hemodynamics in group 2 after stenting. There was substantial clinical improvement in both groups after stenting. Approximately half of patients were completely relieved of pain after stenting, and a third were completely relieved of swelling. In addition, 55% of ulcerated limbs healed.

Conclusion: Iliac venous outflow obstruction appears to have an important role in clinical expression of chronic venous insufficiency, particularly in producing pain, and is easily overlooked, mainly because of diagnostic difficulty. The combination of reflux and obstruction is seen more frequently with severe clinical disease than is obstruction alone. Ulcer prevalence is clearly associated with reflux, with a low incidence in patients with obstruction alone. Removal of iliac vein outflow obstruction does not result in increased axial reflux, with clinical deterioration in limbs with combined reflux and obstruction.

J Vasc Surg. 2003 Nov;38(5):879-85.

Somatic Risk Factors for Chronic Venous Insufficiency in Women

Aleksandra Karch, Janusz Kasperczyk

Abstract

Chronic venous insufficiency is a major social problem. The nature of this illness lies in disturbances of the dynamic pressure balance in venous vessels, which leads to difficulties in venous reflux. As a consequence, teleangiectasia and varices are formed, and they are the basis for the development of trophic skin changes. The causes of the illness have not been fully recognised. It is suggested that genetic factors, body mass, past pregnancies, mode of life, or sex hormones may play an important role in the pathogenesis. The occurrence of this illness has been estimated to reach between 9 and 58% of the developed countries of North America and Europe's population; and women are suffering from it more often than men do. We decided to check the frequency of occurrence of the chronic venous insufficiency in the population of women inhabiting Zabrze-Rokitnica. In addition to this we tried to evaluate the influence of various factors on the occurrence and intensity of the illness. The research included women between 18 and 60 years of age, patients of the NZOZ "Therapeutica" in Zabrze. The occurrence of teleangiectasia and varices according to CEAP was appreciated. The height and body mass were measured as well as a short history was made concentrating on the chronic venous insufficiency risk factors. In the so-far surveyed population of women 49.7% had symptoms of chronic venous insufficiency, and 27.0% of the whole group had teleangiectasia and 22.7%—varices. The frequency of occurrence of chronic venous insufficiency correlated with BMI, age and the number of pregnancies.

Wiad Lek. 2002;55 Suppl 1:212-6

Heterotopic Ossificans in Chronic Venous Insufficiency: A New Consideration for Clinical, Aetiology, Anatomy and Pathophysiology Staging

D E Cafasso, D K Bowen, S A Kinkennon, M D Stanbro, D C Kellicut

Abstract

Objectives: Heterotopic ossification is defined as the abnormal formation of true bone within extra- skeletal soft tissues. It may be associated with a variety of clinical conditions, but is most frequently seen with musculoskeletal trauma, neurologic injury or genetic abnormalities. It has also been described in patients with chronic venous insufficiency; however, it often goes underdiagnosed due to chronic ulceration that masks exam findings. To date, few reports of heterotopic ossification due to chronic venous disease exist within the literature with the most recent dating back to the 1970s.

Methods: We present a case study of a man presenting with extensive leg ulceration and a history of chronic venous insufficency. He had a large non-healing venous stasis ulcer of the left lower extremity with extensive heterotopic ossification discovered intraoperatively.

Results: The patient was managed with serial wound debridement, innovative woundcare and eventual split thickness skin grafting that achieved limb salvage despite the complexity of his wound.

Conclusions: Our discussion focuses on the epidemiology, pathophysiology, diagnostic work-up and management of heterotopic ossification in the setting of chronic venous insufficiency. We propose that heterotopic ossification be included in any future modifications of the clinical, aetiology, anatomy and pathophysiology system classification as a complication of chronic venous disease.

Phlebology. 2013 Oct;28(7):361-5.

Chronic Venous Insufficiency and Microcirculation. Physiopathologic and Therapeutic Reflections

P *Carpentier, J L Magne, F Sarrot-Reynauld, A Franco*

Abstract

In patients with chronic venous insufficiency, tissular damage occurs as a consequence of microcirculatory disturbances. Venular distension, venulo-arteriolar reflex and probably valves in collecting venules are the only microcirculatory protective mechanisms against venous pressure overload. Edema is primarily a consequence of increased capillary hydrostatic pressure. However, the increase of endothelial macromolecular transport and a true lymphatic microangiopathy are important contributive factors. Venous ulceration is hypoxic although the amount of total blood flow is normal in the surrounding tissue. Several hypotheses were proposed for explaining this nutritional steal: arterio-venous shunt vessels have never been shown consistently, peri-capillary fibrin deposition might block oxygen diffusion, and last but not least, the abnormal geometrical arrangement of the capillary bed is facilitating functional shunting. On a therapeutic point of view, behind the classical hemodynamic therapy, the microvascular approach to chronic venous insufficiency supports the use of lymphatic manual drainage for controlling edema and rheologic therapy for improving skin capillary perfusion.

J Mal Vasc. 1987;12(3):280-4.

The Role of Perforators in Chronic Venous Insufficiency

T F O'Donnell

Abstract

The treatment of incompetent calf perforating veins (ICPVs) has been ascribed an important role in the therapeutic strategy for reducing superficial venous hypertension in patients with advanced chronic venous insufficiency (C4-C6). Since the open approach to ligation of ICPVs was developed by Linton over 70 years ago, there has been an evolution toward less invasive techniques with lower morbidity. This paper will review the evidence for interruption of ICPVs through a series of systematic analyses of (1) subfascial endoscopic perforating surgery (SEPS) and (2) percutaneous thermal ablation techniques (PAPS). The effectiveness and morbidity of each approach will be discussed as well as the strength of evidence supporting that technique. While there are numerous case series that suggest that SEPS is beneficial for ulcer healing and for the prevention of ulcer recurrence, the sole two RCTs that have compared either open division or SEPS for ICPVs have failed to show a statistical advantage for ICPV ablation. The results of these studies are clouded by the inclusion of patients who received concomitant treatment of their great saphenous vein (GSV). The evidence for PAPS is based on a few (n

= 5) case series in peer-reviewed journals, which are limited by small patient populations, limited follow-up, and a focus on surrogate outcomes (occlusion of the perforator) rather than clinical or functional outcomes. Moreover, most of these series were carried out in patients with mild disease. Sclerotherapy of ICPVs, by either liquid or foam, shows promise, but requires greater evidence. Our current approach for limbs with C4-C6 disease is to treat the GSV first and limit treatment of ICPVs to those with high volume flow and large-diameter ICPVs.

Phlebology. 2010 Feb;25(1):3-10.

The Involvement of Genetic Factors in Chronic Venous Insufficiency

Cristina Hoţoleanui, Cristina Jurj

Abstract

Chronic venous insufficiency (CVI) represents an important medical and social problem with a significant impact on the quality of life. Although the mechanisms of occurrence and development of chronic venous insufficiency became better understood in the last decades, the contribution of genetic risk factors is not precisely established. Many factors are involved in the etiopathogenesis of CVI, such as age, sex, heredity, sedentary life style. The impact of genetic factors is variably estimated. Genes polymorphisms associated with hyperhomocysteinemia, coagulation abnormalities, genetic factors involved in venous thrombosis leading to secondary CVI, represent the genetic background of this complex disease.

Rom J Intern Med. 2008;46(2):119-23

Causes of Severe Chronic Venous Insufficiency

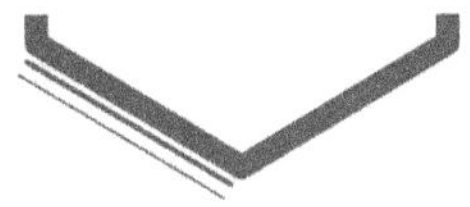

Peter J Pappas, Brajesh K Lal, Joaquim J Cerveira, Frank T Padberg Jr, Walter N Duran

Abstract

A large number of adults in this country have some form of chronic venous insufficiency and a significant percentage of these have venous ulcers. The past decade has refined understanding of leukocyte-mediated injury and has elucidated the role of inflammatory processes in the dermal pathology of chronic venous insufficiency. Understanding of these pathologic cellular functions and molecular regulation of these processes is increasing.

Seminars in Vascular Surgery, 18(1 SPEC. ISS.).

Microcirculatory Dysfunction in Chronic Venous Insufficiency (CVI)

M *Jünger, A Steins, M Hahn, H M Häfner*

Abstract

The elevated ambulatory pressure in the peripheral venous system of chronic venous insufficiency (CVI) patients manifests itself not only in the form of disturbed macrocirculation but also and particularly in microangiopathic changes. For this reason, it is closely correlated with trophic disorders of the skin and can ultimately lead to ulceration. Using microcirculation research techniques, we are able to provide clear evidence of a typical microangiopathy in chronic venous insufficiency. Fifty CVI in Widmer stages I, II, and III were examined with fluorescence video microscopy, intravital video capillaroscopy, transcutaneous oxygen partial pressure measurement, TcpO2 and laser Doppler flowmetry. The effects of compression therapy with individually fitted compression stockings on capillary morphology were studied over a period of 4 weeks in 20 CVI patients in Widmer stages I and II. The capillary pressure was measured during simulated muscle contraction using a servo-null micropressure system. We periodically drew blood from the dorsalis pedis vein and a brachial vein of 11 healthy test persons and 8 patients with stage III CVI during experimental venous hypertension in order to evaluate the expression pattern of leukocyte adhesion molecules involved in inflammation: LFA-1 (CD11a), Mac-1 (CD11b), p150,95 (CD11c), CD18, VLA-4 (CD49d), and L-selectin (CD62L). In the same patients, we used immunohistochemical methods to examine clinically unaffected skin and the skin near an ulcer, focusing on the adhesion molecules ICAM-1, VCAM-1, and E-selectin. The microangiopathic changes observed with worsening clinical symptoms include a decrease in the number of capillaries, glomerulus-like changes in capillary morphology, a drop in the oxygen content (tcpO2) of the skin, increased permeability of the capillaries to low-molecular-weight substances, increased laser Doppler flux reflecting elevated subcutaneous flow, and diminished vascular reserve. These microangiopathic changes worsen in linear proportion to the clinical severity of chronic venous insufficiency. In patients with venous ulcerations, the baseline expression of LFA-1 and VLA-4 on lymphocytes, Mac-1 expression on the myeloid cell line, and L-selectin expression on all three cell lines was not significantly different form that in healthy controls. During orthostatic stress, there was a significant reduction in the expression of L-selectin in blood cells collected at foot level in the controls (p=0.002), but not in the patients. Clinical improvement by compression therapy was accompanied by an increase in the number of nutritive capillaries, while the diameter of the capillaries and the dermal papillae was reduced. When ulcers healed in a short period (<6 weeks), we observed a concomitant increase in the number of capillaries (p<0.05). Microangiopathy appears before tropic disorders of the skin develop. Even trophically normal skin areas may have dilated nutritive capillaries, an early sign of disturbed skin perfusion. These changes represent a plausible explanation for the development and to recurrency tendency of venous ulcers. The reduced expression of lymphocytic L-selectin in healthy controls during the orthostatic stress test may be an indication that the cells are activated by venous stasis. Clinically effective therapeutic measures improve the impaired microcirculation of the skin in the ankle area.

Microcirculation. 2000;7(6 Pt 2):S3-12

Glycosaminoglycan Sulodexide Modulates Inflammatory Pathways in Chronic Venous Disease

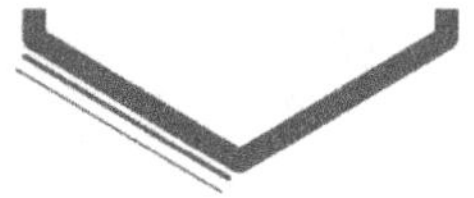

F Mannello, D Ligi, J D Raffetto

Abstract

Inflammation represents an important epiphenomenon in the etiopathogenesis of chronic venous disease, a worldwide debilitating condition affecting millions of subjects. The pathophysiology of chronic venous disease (CVD) is based on the hemodynamic abnormalities in conjunction to alterations in cellular and extracellular matrix biocompounds. The endothelial dysfunction results from early perturbation in the endothelium linked to glycocalyx injury and promoted by inflammatory cells and mediators (such as matrix metalloproteinases and interleukins), which lead to progressive dilation of the vein resulting in chronic venous insufficiency. Activated leukocytes during the inflammatory process release enzymes, free radicals, chemokines and inflammatory cytokines in the vessel microenvironment, which are responsible for the changes of the venous wall and venous valve, reflux and venous hypertension, and the development/progression of tissue destruction and skin changes. Sulodexide, a highly purified mixture of glycosaminoglycans composed by 80% fast moving heparin and 20% of dermatan sulphate, exhibits anti-thrombotic and profibrinolytic properties, restoring also the essential endothelial glycocalyx. Glycosaminoglycan sulodexide has been also characterized to reduce the release of inflammatory cytokines/chemokines and to inhibit the matrix metalloproteinases-related proteolytic cascades, counteracting endothelial dysfunctions. The pleiotropic effects of sulodexide set the basis for a very promising agent in treating the spectrum of CVD.

Int Angiol. 2014 Jun;33(3):236-42.

Pathophysiology of Chronic Venous Disease

J D Raffetto, F Mannello

Abstract

Chronic venous disease (CVD) is a debilitating condition with a prevalence between 60-70%. The disease pathophysiology is complex and involves genetic susceptibility and environmental factors, with individuals developing visible telengiectasias, reticular veins, and varicose veins. Patient with significant lower extremity symptoms have pain, dermal irritation, swelling, skin changes, and are at risk of developing debilitating venous ulceration. The signature of CVD is an increase in venous pressure referred to as venous hypertension. The various symptoms presenting in CVD and the clinical signs that are observed indicate that there is inflammation, secondary to venous hypertension, and it leads to a number of inflammatory pathways that become activated. The endothelium and glycocalyx via specialized receptors are critical at sensing changes in shear stress, and expression of adhesion molecules allows the activation of leukocytes leading to endothelial attachment, diapedisis, and transmigration into the venous wall/valves resulting in venous wall injury and inflammatory cells in the interstitial tissues. There is a complex of cytokines, chemokines, growth factors, proteases and proteinases, produced by activated leukocytes, that are expressed and unbalanced resulting in an environment of persistent inflammation with the clinical changes that are commonly seen, consisting of varicose veins to more advanced presentations of skin changes and venous ulceration. The structural integrity of protein and the extracellular matrix is altered, enhancing the progressive events of CVD. Work focusing on metabolic changes, miRNA regulation, inflammatory modulation and the glycocalyx will further our knowledge in the pathophysiology of CVD, and provide answers critical to treatment and prevention.

International Angiology 2014, Jun: (Vol. 33, Issue 3) 212-21.

The Microvascular Pathophysiology of Chronic Venous Insufficiency

P *F McDonagh*

Abstract

Severe chronic venous insufficiency (CVI) demonstrates as chronic, hard-to-heal wounds of the lower extremity. The wound is the result of poor skin perfusion due to a complex series of pathologic events, often initiated by a deep vein thrombosis (DVT). As years pass, the DVT causes venous valvular damage and incompetence. The calf muscle pump fails to augment venous return, and venous blood pressure is chronically elevated upon standing. Mechanisms that normally prevent the transmission of venous hypertension back upstream to the dermal microcirculation are lost. Early dermal microvascular responses include increased fluid filtration and edema. An inflammatory response induces white cell activation and adhesion. It is thought that activated white cells are trapped in dermal capillaries and increase microvascular permeability. Plasma proteins leak into the tissue space, increasing the edema. Ischemic damage to the epidermis leads to epithelial cell necrosis and ulceration. The ulcer is often slow to heal, due to inadequate perfusion and delivery of substrates required for proper wound healing. Current treatments aim to improve calf pump function, reduce edema, improve perfusion, and enhance wound healing.

Yale J Biol Med. 1993 Jan-Feb; 66(1): 27–36.

Possible Ramifications of Prolonged Standing at the Workplace and Its Association with the Development of Chronic Venous Insufficiency

Avi Shai, Isabella Karakis, David Shemesh

Abstract

The issue of working conditions and their health ramifications have recently been raised on the public agenda in Israel with special emphasis on occupations requiring prolonged standing. This review article discusses the physiological and medical aspects of prolonged standing in the workplace. Searching the literature, 19 studies were found which specifically examined the effect of prolonged standing versus prolonged sitting at work. Most of these studies suggested that prolonged standing may result in the development and aggravation of chronic venous insufficiency. The association between prolonged standing and venous insufficiency was found to be more pronounced in women than in men.

Harefuah. 2007 Sep;146(9):677-85, 734

Frequency and Significance of Perforating Venous Insufficiency in Patients with Chronic Venous Insufficiency of Lower Extremity

I smet Tolu , Mehmet Sedat Durmaz

Abstract

Objective: The aim of this study was to reveal the frequency and impact of perforating venous insufficiency (PVI) in chronic venous insufficiency (CVI) of lower extremity (LE).

Materials and Methods: Between 2012 and 2017, a total of 1154 patients [781 females (67.68%)

and 373 males (32.32%), 228 (19.76%) unilateral and 926 (80.24%) bilateral LE] were examined using Doppler ultrasound (US). A total of 2080 venous systems of LEs [31.4% male (n=653) and 68.6% female (n=1427); 1056 left LEs (50.77%) and 1024 right LEs (49.23%)] were examined. All patients had symptoms of venous insufficiency (VI).

Results: PVI was revealed in 27.5% (n=571) of LEs. Varicose veins (VVs) related with perforating vein (PV) were revealed in 44.7% of LEs (n=929). PVI was observed in 50.91% of patients with chronic deep venous thrombosis (DVT), 64.41% with deep venous insufficiency (DVI), 59.81% with great saphenous vein (GSV) insufficiency, 68.49% with small saphenous vein (SSV) insufficiency, 58.65% with accessory GSV insufficiency, and 58.77% with PV associated with VVs. There was a statistically significant relationship between PVI and chronic DVT, DVI, GSV, SSV, and accessory GSV insufficiency (p<0.001). A significant relationship was observed between the increase in PV diameter and the presence of PVI (p<0.001).

Conclusion: PVI is quite common in combined VI, and PV evaluation should be a part of LE venous system examination.

Eurasian J Med 2018; 50: 99-104

CLINICAL

Edemas in Chronic Lower Extremity Venous Insufficiency: Clinical Manifestations, Medical and Surgical Treatments

G N Gorokhovskaia, V L Iun

Abstract

The review presents data on the causes and pathogenesis of lower extremity (LE) edemas with special emphasis on the edemas occurring in chronic LE venous insufficiency. It discusses the possibilities of noninvasive and surgical treatments for LE edemas in venous insufficiency. Particular attention is given to the possibilities of phlebotonic therapy.

Ter Arkh. 2013;85(4):93-7.

Chronic Venous Insufficiency in Postthrombotic Syndrome and Varicose Veins

Jürg Hafner, D Mayer, B Amann, L E French, S Läuchli, T Hofer, A-A Ramelet, Ch Jeanneret

Abstract

Venous disorders have a high prevalence and require approximately 1% of health budgets of industrialized countries. The postthrombotic syndrome (PTS) is defined by subjective symptoms and morphologic trophical skin changes following deep venous thrombosis. Prevention of venous thromboembolism in risk situations, easy availability of diagnostic tools (D-dimers, colour-coded duplex sonography) and early detection of deep venous thrombosis, as well as immediate therapeutic anticoagulation along with leg compression during the acute phase and over a two year period of time significantly reduce the incidence of PTS. Chronic venous insufficiency (CVI) includes trophical skin and soft tissue pathologies of the lower leg due to venous hypertension in the distal venous system of the lower extremity. Roughly, two main causes can be distinguished. (A) Deep venous insufficiency (A1 in postthrombotic syndrome; A2 in primary deep venous insufficiency) and (B) superficial venous reflux, usually varicose veins. Compression therapy, surgical ablation of superficial venous reflux, and tangential ablation with split skin graft (shave treatment) of refractory venous ulcers are the mainstays in the treatment of CVI.

Praxis (Bern 1994). 2010 Oct 6;99(20):1195-202

Chronic Venous Insufficiency: Clinical Assessment and Patient Selection

S hyam Krishnan, and Stephen C. Nicholls

Abstract

C hronic venous insufficiency is a complex condition, with widely varied clinical manifestations, etiologies, and underlying pathophysiology. An orderly workup is mandatory to assess the nature of a patient's underlying venous disease. This begins in the office setting with a careful medical history, physical examination, and bedside diagnostic tests. These are augmented by confirmatory diagnostic testing, including duplex ultrasonography, venography, plethysmography, and ambulatory venous pressure measurement. Based upon the results of these examinations, the patient's venous disease can be classified according to standardized classification schemes, which in turn leads to the selection of an appropriate treatment strategy. This article outlines the steps in the clinical assessment and classification of patients with chronic venous insufficiency.

Objectives: Upon completion of this article, the reader should be able to understand the proper steps in the clinical assessment of patients with chronic venous insufficiency, including history, physical examination, bedside diagnostic tests, additional outpatient diagnostic tests, and appropriate patient classification; and utilize the patient classification system to select appropriate patients for intervention.

Historically, the condition known as chronic venous insufficiency has suffered from a lack of detailed, objective investigation into its pathophysiology and treatment. With current technology, however, specific investigations can clearly delineate the cause of chronic venous insufficiency in a particular patient and help guide the clinician to appropriate therapeutic interventions. An orderly and objective diagnostic workup is mandatory. The following steps in diagnosis and clinical assessment of the patient with chronic venous disease have been proposed1:

1. Determine the nature of the problem.
2. Determine the severity of the problem.
3. Perform diagnostic testing.
4. Determine CEAP classification.
5. Weigh treatment alternatives. **INITIAL CLINIC EVALUATION** History

Initial evaluation begins in the office setting with a thorough history and physical examination. Typical symptoms of venous insufficiency include aching, pain, tightness, skin irritation, pruritus, heaviness, tingling, muscle cramps, and cosmetically unsatisfying varicose veins.2 Symptoms often worsen during the course of the day and with prolonged standing. Patients with more severe insufficiency can present with complaints of edema, skin changes, or ulceration.3 Several clinical entities can mimic the symptoms of chronic venous insufficiency, including osteoarthritis, sciatica, osteomyelitis, tendonitis, ligamentous injuries, arthritis, peripheral neuropathy, and arterial insufficiency. Specific features of the pain that should be noted include the degree to which the pain interferes with the patient's occupation or lifestyle as well as the amount of time that the patient can stand before the onset of pain or swelling. The age of onset of varicose veins should be recorded, as an early onset may suggest a congenital abnormality such as Klippel-Trenaunay syndrome. A family history of varicose veins is present in over one third of patients. It is crucial to note whether there has been a personal history of deep vein thrombosis or pulmonary embolism. Some patients may not be able to provide this information directly, and it may be elicited only by asking specific questions regarding a history of leg swelling, previous operations, lower extremity injuries, prolonged bed rest, chest pain, hemoptysis, or anticoagulant use. Finally, a careful history of past treatments for varicose veins, including operative and percutaneous procedures, should be recorded.

Physical Examination

Physical examination of the patient should include a general examination in addition to a detailed examination of the lower extremities. The patient should be examined in the standing position and suitably un- dressed to permit complete examination of the entire extremity from the groins to the toes. The examination should be performed in a warm and well-lit room that respects the privacy of the patient.

The examination begins with careful inspection and palpation of the legs. The location and distribution of all major subcutaneous varicosities should be noted and recorded in the chart; this is facilitated by outline drawings of each limb that show both anterior and posterior surfaces. Varicosities of the main saphenous trunk and spider veins should be noted. The limb is also inspected for the presence or absence of edema and angiomatous malformations. Large varicosities over known sites of perforating veins should be identified. Palpation of the limbs may detect additional varicosities that are not readily apparent by inspection. This is especially true of the terminal segments of the greater saphenous vein (GSV) and lesser saphenous vein (LSV) where they join the femoral and popliteal veins, respectively. Careful palpation of the inner thigh and leg as well as the posterior calf may detect saphenous trunk varicosities that may be missed by visual inspection alone. Palpation of the legs should also be performed to detect temperature differences between the legs, areas of induration, and the presence of firm subcutaneous cords, which may be the sequelae of prior episodes of superficial thrombophlebitis.

Several tests can be performed in the outpatient setting during the initial evaluation that often give clues to the source of venous hypertension. The cough impulse test is performed by palpating the thigh at the fossa ovalis over the saphenofemoral junction (SFJ) while the patient is standing. The patient is asked to cough, and a palpable thrill at the SFJ, which is a result of turbulent retrograde flow, indicates reflux at the SFJ. The cough impulse test is difficult to perform in obese patients or in patients who jerk or cough vigorously. The tap test, or percussion test, is also performed while palpating the SFJ of a standing patient. The GSV is tapped at the level of the knee. A palpable transmitted impulse at the SFJ suggests that the GSV is distended with blood. The SFJ is then tapped while the GSV is palpated at the knee. A palpable transmitted pulse at the knee with this maneuver indicates incompetence of GSV valves be- tween the SFJ and the knee. These clinical tests are largely of historical interest in the modern era and have been supplanted by more sophisticated diagnostic imaging tests. When compared with Doppler ultrasonography, clinical tests (cough impulse test and percussion test, combined with palpation) were falsely negative in 28% of incompetent SFJs and 36% of incompetent saphenopopliteal junctions (SPJs).

The Brodie-Trendelenburg test is used to detect venous incompetence and to differentiate between perforator and GSV incompetence. The test is performed by initially draining the superficial lower extremity veins by elevating the lower limbs to 45 degrees and gently stroking the limb from the foot along the course of the major veins. A tourniquet is then placed as close to the groin as possible and applied tightly enough to prevent superficial vein reflux. The patient is asked to stand and the limb is examined. If the distal veins remain collapsed for 15 to 30 seconds after standing, the tourniquet is released. SFJ incompetence is diagnosed if the distal veins fill rapidly upon release of the tourniquet. If the caudal veins fill rapidly when the patient stands with the tourniquet in place, perforator incompetence is suggested. The location of the incompetent perforator can then be determined by varying the position of the tourniquet. Rapid filling of the varices with a tourniquet in the suprapatellar position can identify an incompetent midthigh perforator, and rapid filling with the tourniquet below the knee suggests incompetent lower leg perforators. In the case of combined SFJ incompetence and perforator incompetence, direct palpation of the varix during tourniquet release may detect an increase in venous distention.4 The Brodie-Trendelenburg test is highly sensitive for the identification of superficial and perforator reflux (91%), although poorly specific (15%).

The Perthes test is performed with the patient in the standing position with a tourniquet positioned below the knee. The patient is asked to activate the calf muscle pump by performing 10 heel raises. Emptying of the varicose veins signifies a site of reflux cranial to the tourniquet, namely the SFJ, SPJ, or thigh perforators. Persistence of distended varicose veins signifies a site of reflux caudal to the tourniquet, that is, calf perforators. Pain associated with heel raising suggests the possibility of deep venous obstruction. As with the Trendelenburg test, the Perthes test is highly sensitive but poorly specific.

Perhaps the most commonly performed maneuver in the office setting is hand-held continuous - wave Doppler ultrasound examination of the saphenous vein. With the patient in the standing position, the SFJ is insonated while an assistant performs compression of the caudal calf. GSV incompetence can be demonstrated by eliciting reflux with the release of calf compression. Similar interrogation of the SPJ can be performed to detect LSV incompetence. Doppler examination of the

SFJ to diagnose incompetence has a sensitivity and specificity of 97% and 73%, respectively, when compared with duplex ultrasonography as the "gold standard.

Additional Diagnostic Studies Venography

The historical gold standard for the diagnosis of venous insufficiency, in terms of both anatomic localization and hemodynamic quantification, has been venography. Although there are still situations in which venography is necessary for planning treatment, it has several draw- backs that have reduced its once widespread use. Venography is an invasive procedure and carries with it attendant risks. Extravasation of contrast material into the foot can cause a chemical cellulitis and, rarely, this can progress to tissue necrosis, ulceration, or gangrene.7 Other complications include postphlebographic thrombosis (reported in up to 13% of patients8) and the postphlebographic syndrome, characterized by pain, tenderness, and erythema around the ankle joint not associated with thrombosis. There are other limitations of venography besides potential technical complications. Competent valves in the upper leg can obscure valvular reflux in the lower leg, and pressurized contrast injection can create false-positive results. Finally, the venographically observed severity of reflux does not necessarily correlate with the clinical severity of the disease. Contra- indications to venography are few and include known contrast allergy and local infection.

Ascending venography is typically performed to determine the degree of patency of the deep venous system and to identify the presence of incompetent perforators. It is performed with the patient in reverse Trendelenburg position with the limb to be examined in a relaxed non–weight-bearing position. A superficial vein on the lateral aspect of the dorsum of the foot is selected and cannulated with a 21-gauge butterfly needle directed caudally. A tourniquet is inflated above the ankle or the knee to improve deep venous filling (as opposed to filling of the saphenous veins) and assess for perforator incompetence. Then 50 to 100 cm3 of nonionic contrast material is slowly injected by hand and the calf veins are examined under fluoroscopy. The injection site should be visualized intermittently to ensure that there is no extravasation of contrast or immediately if there is any local swelling or pain. If contrast extravasation occurs, the injection should be immediately terminated and the extravasated contrast dispersed by means of saline dilution, massage, and/or warm compresses. After examination of the calf veins, the popliteal, femoral, and iliac veins are sequentially imaged. Opacification of the more cranial veins can be enhanced by raising the calf, having the patient lie supine, and releasing the tourniquet. Distorted veins and valve cusps, excessive collaterals (especially around the thigh, knee, and iliofemoral region), and intraluminal filling defects are pathognomonic for post-thrombotic disease, and their absence suggests primary valvular incompetence.

Descending venography is used to document the presence and extent of reflux, to define valvular anatomy, and to identify specific incompetent valves. It is also performed with the patient in reverse Trendelenburg position and with the limb to be examined in a relaxed non–weight-bearing position. A catheter is positioned in the common femoral vein, either by direct puncture or by advancement from an arm or the contralateral femoral vein. A slow hand injection of contrast material is performed under fluoroscopy and the patient is instructed to breathe normally. If reflux is identified, individual incompetent valves in the common femoral vein, profunda femoris vein, superficial femoral vein, and GSV are noted. Contrast injection is then repeated while the patient is instructed to perform a sustained Valsalva maneuver. This increases resistance to prograde flow and causes valve closure. Incompetent valves are noted to allow leakage and retrograde flow of contrast material. Individual valve function can be classified as normal (no leakage despite Valsalva), minimal abnormality (wisp of contrast reflux with Valsalva), moderate abnormality (contrast reflux with Valsalva), and severe abnormality (contrast material pours through valve).[10] In addition to valve function, the caudal extent of reflux through incompetent valves should be noted.

Ambulatory Venous Pressure Measurement Along with venography, ambulatory venous pressure (AVP) measurement was a historical gold standard for the diagnosis of chronic venous insufficiency. It is performed by introducing into a dorsal foot vein a 21-gauge needle, which is then connected to a pressure transducer. Baseline measurement is obtained with the patient relaxed and bearing weight on the contralateral limb. In this position, venous pressure approximates the hydrostatic pressure exerted by the column of blood extending from the right atrium to the foot. The patient is then asked to perform 10 tiptoe movements at the rate of one per second. The AVP is then measured as the lowest pressure achieved at the end of exercise. The recovery time is defined as the time required for the pressure to rise to 90% of the baseline value after the cessation of exercise. A modification of this technique involves manual calf compression instead of tiptoe movements. This modification has been shown to produce identical results while avoiding the potential difficulties of the patient's cooperation and reactive hyperemia.11

In healthy limbs, calf muscle contraction forces blood up the leg and competent valves prevent retro- grade flow.8 During AVP measurement, the venous blood pressure falls rapidly (typically to less than 30 mm Hg) and recovery, which is through capillary inflow, is slow (typically more than 20 seconds). In limbs with incompetent valves, reflux occurs between contractions and the measured pressure remains proportionately high while recovery, which occurs by rapid filling through incompetent valves, is fast. In limbs with deep venous obstruction, the AVP may rise during exercise and produce a bursting pain related to calf vein congestion (akin to a positive Perthes test). AVP has been correlated with the clinical severity of disease. The incidence of ulceration increases in a linear fashion with an increase in the AVP, and ulceration never occurs at AVP less than 30 mm Hg and always occurs at AVP greater than 90 mm Hg.12

Like venography, AVP measurement is an invasive procedure that is not ideally suitable for screening or for repeated examinations to monitor the results of therapy.

Plethysmography

Air plethysmography is a noninvasive test that can quantify venous insufficiency and is reported to correlate with AVP measurements.13 It is performed with a 35-cm-long polyvinyl chloride air chamber that sur- rounds the lower leg and is connected to a pressure transducer and chart recorder. The pressure transducer is calibrated with 100 mL of air. A baseline reading is obtained with the patient supine and with the leg elevated to 45 degrees to empty the veins. The patient is then asked to stand upright with weight supported on the opposite leg until the veins are full. This change in volume represents the functional venous volume, and the venous filling index (VFI) is calculated by dividing 90% of the venous volume by the time required for filling to 90% of the venous volume. The patient is then asked to perform a heel-raise maneuver and the volume displaced by this maneuver is recorded as the ejection volume. The ejection fraction (EF) is calculated by dividing the ejection volume by the venous volume. Finally, 10 heel- raise maneuvers are performed to reach a residual volume plateau. The residual volume fraction (RVF) is calculated by dividing the residual volume by the venous volume. The VFI is an index of global venous reflux, the EF is a reflection of calf muscle pump function, and the RVF is a reflection of AVP.

The limitations of air plethysmography are that it is imprecise in the localization of segmental reflux and the RVF correlates only loosely with disease severity. A VFI of 2.67 mL/s has been proposed as a cutoff point between normal limbs and limbs with chronic venous insufficiency, with a positive predictive value of 96%.1

Duplex Scanning

Duplex ultrasonography is arguably the most useful initial diagnostic evaluation in the workup of chronic venous disease. Its advantages include that it is non- invasive, can be repeated as often as necessary, gives reproducible results, and allows anatomic, physiologic, and hemodynamic evaluation of the venous system. The study is performed with both B-mode imaging and spectral Doppler analysis. It can identify the underlying pathophysiology (reflux, obstruction, or both) and localize the disease to specific venous segments (deep system, superficial system, perforators). A 5- to 7.5-MHz linear transducer is used to evaluate the limb below the inguinal ligament, and a 2- to 3.5-MHz phased array transducer is used to evaluate the iliac system and the inferior vena cava.

Duplex examination of the veins must be systematic and orderly. The deep venous system is evaluated first, with the patient in the supine position with the hip externally rotated and the knee flexed. The linear transducer is initially placed longitudinally just below the inguinal ligament to visualize the common femoral vein and the confluence of the superficial and deep femoral veins. Proper imaging of the popliteal vein is best performed in the prone position with the calf supported on pillows, although a lateral approach can suffice if the patient is unable to lie prone. Patency of the deep veins is evaluated both by assessing compressibility by the transducer during B-mode imaging and by evaluating flow patterns. Venous flow patterns in patent deep veins are spontaneous and phasic with respiration, although flow augmentation with foot compression may be required to document patency in the crural veins. After assessing patency, venous valvular competence is evaluated with a Valsalva maneuver for upper thigh segments (Fig. 1) and limb compression for lower limb segments (Fig. 2). Normal valve closure time is less than 2 seconds when the patient is in the supine position. For patients in mild reverse Trendelenburg position, valve closure time of greater than 0.5 seconds has a sensitivity of 90% and specificity of 84% for diagnosing valve incompetence when compared with descending venography.15 An alternative to the Valsalva maneuver for assessing valve competence is the rapid cuff deflation technique, which has the benefit of providing a single method for studying all of the veins of the limb without relying on the presence of a more cephalad incompetent valve.16

After evaluation of the deep venous system is performed, the superficial system is examined. This portion of the examination is ideally performed with the patient in the standing position while bearing weight on the contralateral limb. This position produces maximal venous distention while relaxing the calf pump, which allows provocative maneuvers to identify incompetent segments. The transducer is angled medially in the groin to visualize the SFJ. The GSV is examined for patency and competence throughout its length. Vein diameter is recorded and major tributaries are followed and similarly evaluated for patency and competence. Reflux is identified and documented with pulse wave Doppler imaging during and after an abrupt compression and release of the distal limb. The patient is then turned around, and similar investigation of the LSV is performed. The LSV has a more variable termination in the deep system and significant reflux may exist in the vein of Giacomini.17 Finally, the locations of known perforators should be evaluated for incompetence.

Classification

After obtaining a thorough history, performing a careful physical examination, and obtaining additional diagnostic imaging studies, a final classification of the patient's chronic venous disease can be made. Traditional classification systems were fairly simplistic and categorized disease on the basis of etiology. Examples include classification of disease as primary (idiopathic) or secondary (post-thrombotic) or as reflux due to greater saphenous reflux, lesser saphenous reflux, or perforator incompetence. Other more descriptive systems included Widmer's classification and Porter's classification.18

In the early 1990s, advances in the diagnosis and understanding of the complex pathophysiology of venous disorders led to development of the CEAP classification system. The first CEAP consensus document was developed at the sixth annual meeting of the American Venous Forum in 1994 and was recently revised, including the introduction of a basic CEAP version. The CEAP classification (Table 1) consists of four parameters: the clinical manifestation (C), the etiologic factors (E), the anatomic distribution of disease (A), and the underlying pathophysiology (P).

The C class consists of six levels of clinical manifestations. In the basic form of the CEAP, the single highest applicable descriptor is used, whereas in the advanced form of the CEAP, every applicable descriptor is used. Each clinical class is further subdivided by a subscript for the presence of symptoms (S, symptomatic) or absence of symptoms (A, asymptomatic). The E class consists of four levels of etiologic factors, and the A class consists of four levels of anatomic distribution. The P class consists of four levels of underlying pathophysiology. In the basic form of the CEAP, no further subdivision is performed. In the complete (advanced) form of the CEAP, the underlying pathophysiology is further categorized according to 18 named venous segments.

In addition to the actual classification, it is recommended that the level of investigation that led to the classification be added, according to the following levels:

Level I: Office visit with history and physical examination, with or without hand-held Doppler scanning Level II: Noninvasive vascular laboratory testing, including duplex color scanning and plethysmography, as indicated

Level III: Invasive or complex imaging studies, including ascending and descending venography, venous pressure measurements, computed tomography, or magnetic resonance imaging.

Superficial Veins

1. Telangiectasias or reticular veins
2. Greater saphenous vein above the knee
3. Greater saphenous vein below the knee
4. Lesser saphenous vein
5. Nonsaphenous vein Deep Veins
6. Inferior vena cava
7. Common iliac vein

8. Internal iliac vein
9. External iliac vein
10. Pelvic (gonadal veins, broad ligament veins, other)
11. Common femoral vein
12. Deep femoral vein
13. Femoral vein
14. Popliteal vein
15. Crural (paired peroneal, anterior tibial, posterior tibial veins)
16. Muscular (gastrocnemial veins, soleal veins, other)

Perforating Veins

17. Thigh
18. Calf

The CEAP system has been widely published in several languages in journals around the world, making it a truly universal document. It is a complete classification system that accounts for all etiologies, pathophysiologies, and anatomic segments and, as such, has become the standard system used in most published clinical papers on chronic venous disease. Despite this, there are certainly limitations to the CEAP classification. It is rather complex and somewhat daunting for the new user and is difficult to use in everyday routine. This may be mitigated by the development of software packages to facilitate classification. Other limitations include the absence of strict hierarchy between the clinical classes, omission from the clinical classification of corona phle- bectasia (fan-shaped intradermal telangiectasias on the medial or lateral aspect of the foot, felt by many to be an early sign of chronic venous insufficiency), and lack of an accounting of the degree of reflux in the physiologic classification.

Venous Severity Scoring

Although the CEAP system is an excellent scheme for standardized classification of chronic venous disease, it is a relatively static system. The C (clinical) class of disease does represent a spectrum of disease severity, but it does not allow a practical assessment of change in response to treatment or adverse events. In response to this, the American Venous Forum's Ad Hoc Committee on Venous Outcomes proposed three different severity scoring systems to assess objectively an individual patient's response to treatment as well as to allow improved outcome assessment.

The Venous Clinical Severity Score (VCSS) consists of nine clinical descriptors, each graded on a scale of 0 to 3 representing the spectrum of absent, mild, moderate, and severe features. The nine descriptors are pain, varicose veins, edema, pigmentation, induration, inflammation, number of active ulcers, duration of active ulceration, and size of the largest current ulcer (Table 3). This scoring system is designed to be complementary to, rather than a replacement of, the C class of the CEAP. As such, VCSS takes advantage of the progressive order of severity intrinsic to the C class but also gives additional weight to some of the upper level attributes. The VCSS also includes only elements that are dynamic over a relatively short period of time. The VCSS has been shown to be valid in relation to the C class and also reliable, with acceptable intraobserver variability.

A second scoring system is the Venous Segmental Disease Score (Table 4). This system was designed to correlate pathophysiologic designations with specific venous segments. A major motivation for the development of this score was the ability to gather the necessary information for accurate scoring by duplex scanning. The third scoring system is the Venous Disability Score

(Table 5), which is a simpler system that classifies patients on the ability carry out usual activities with or without compressive therapy or limb elevation.

CONCLUSION

Current evaluation of patients with chronic venous insufficiency benefits from improved understanding of the etiology and pathophysiology of the disease as well as precise diagnostic tests. Evaluation of these patients begins in the office with a careful history and physical examination. Bedside diagnostic tests can be performed, although these have essentially been replaced by more accurate imaging modalities. All patients who are likely to require intervention should first undergo duplex scanning, with additional tests such as venography, plethysmography, and venous pressure measurement reserved for equivocal findings. On the basis of these studies, the patient's disease can be classified according to the CEAP system and venous severity scoring systems, which then serves as the basis for appropriate selection of patients for treatment or interventions, or both.

Semin Intervent Radiol. 2005 Sep;22(3):169-77.

Clinical Characteristics of Pain in Chronic Venous Insufficiency

J M Coget, J P Millien

Abstract

Since the report of the 1st International Conference of Phlebology at Chambéry, devoted to venous pain, the subject has scarcely attracted attention apart from the meeting of the Benelux Society of Phlebology devoted to "pain in the legs". Pain due to superficial venous insufficiency has scarcely changed in nature for 30 years and remains one of the major presenting symptoms in phlebology. Acute or chronic, punctate or diffuse, modifications in this functional symptomatology have been accentuated, or have varied in their aspects under the influence of certain fashions or certain habits of modern life, i.e.: sedentary behaviour, underfloor heating, the use of oral contraceptives or of menopausal hormone replacement therapy. However, the distribution of the various aspects of venous pain remains in the same proportions as those described by the authors cited previously. While the etiological diagnosis must essentially eliminate all other causes: arterial, neurological, muscular, articular, it is essential not to neglect deep venous insufficiency of the gemellar veins, often responsible for a wide range of symptomatology and still all too often neglected. The pathogenesis of this pain not only involves the concept of pain receptors but also the appearance of algogenic metabolites at the site of the microcirculatory unit, to which endothelial cells are particularly sensitive during stasis. In fact, pain is the expression of disorders concerning local exchanges, whether thermal, pressure, metabolic or hemorheological. It is the alarm bell of venous insufficiency and merits the attention of the phebologist who must thus undertake active treatment before problems become irreversible.

Phlebologie. Jan-Mar 1992;45(1):9-16.

Is the Pigmentation a Characteristic Sign for Chronic Venous Insufficiency?

N Klüken, M Zabel

Abstract

In epidemiological studies pigmentations were declared a decisive criterium of stadium II of chronic venous insufficiency. It is discussed in this work if it is possible as the pigmentation is sometimes absent in advanced stages of chronic venous insufficiency. On the other hand it has got to be considered that there are many other possibilities of pigment building on the legs without chronic venous insufficiency. Pigmentation may be of actinic, endocrine, atrophic or especially of inflammatory origin. These pigmentations cannot be differentiated from those caused by chronic venous insufficiency macroscopically, and therefore, in our opinion, the question if pigmentation is a specific sign for chronic venous insufficiency has to be negated. Further, it is examined if the histomorphology of the pigmentation caused by chronic venous insufficiency offers a different aspect from that caused by other diseases. Special attention is given to the pigments containing melanin and iron. Melanin, as an example, is increased in skin inflammation whether there is chronic venous insufficiency or independent of any edematous changes, in subfascial chronic venous insufficiency without any inflammatory component, only the pigment containing iron increased.

Phlebologie. Oct-Dec 1983;36(4):315-20.

Chronic Venous Insufficiency: Mechanisms and Management

S Ibrahim, D R MacPherson, S Z Goldhaber

Abstract

CVI is a common disease with significant morbidity that results from venous hypertension of the extremities. Increased perfusion pressure probably traps excessive numbers of white blood cells in the capillaries. Activated leukocytes subsequently damage capillary endothelium, increase capillary permeability, and cause ischemia of the overlying skin as a result of leakage of fibrinogen and formation of a fibrin cuff. Diagnosis of CVI is not difficult because its clinical manifestations are usually evident. Vascular compression therapy remains the foundation of medical management for CVI. Refractory cases may require a combined medical and operative approach.

Am Heart J. 1996 Oct;132(4):856-60

Chronic Venous Insufficiency

W *L Miller*

Abstract

The consequences of chronic deep venous insufficiency are a major medical concern and result in significant loss of human productivity in addition to a significant compromise of lifestyles. The postphlebitic syndrome of chronic venous stasis and ulceration is a result of chronic venous hypertension and reflects a sequela of events occurring secondary to venous valvular insufficiency and reflux. Diagnostic techniques have advanced considerably; however, the prevention and management of this entity continue to be inadequate. Many new areas are being explored, both from a medical and a surgical perspective, and it is hoped that as clinical investigation proceeds, new conceptual approaches and techniques will arise to combat this difficult medical problem. The literature reviewed in this article reflects a spectrum of research attempting to understand the basic underlying hemodynamic as well as cellular and tissue changes that contribute to the development of postphlebitic signs and symptoms. More investigation is needed to enable us to proceed from the descriptive understanding of this entity to the mechanisms that result in this disease state. Preventive and curative management needs to succeed the current palliative approach to therapy.

Cardiovasc Clin. 1992;22(3):67-80

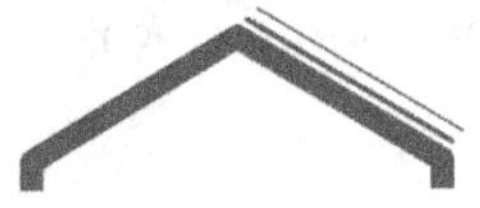

Chronic Venous Insufficiency

J CJM Veraart

Abstract

Chronic venous insufficiency (CVI) is a complex of symptoms occurring on the lower leg, which includes varicose veins, oedema, pigmentation and venous leg ulceration. Most patients have severe complaints, which result in a high medical consumption, mainly due to venous leg ulceration. CVI is caused by a decompensation of the venous system together with reflux in the superficial, deep and/or perforating veins of the lower leg in supine position. The exact pathogenesis of the skin symptoms is still largely unclear. An increased walking venous pressure induces macrocirculatory and microcirculatory changes such as dermal pericapillary fibrin cuffs, leukocyte accumulation and the activation of cytokines. CVI can be treated in several ways: compression therapy, if needs be combined with sclerotherapy or surgery, or with supportive medication.

Ned Tijdschr Geneeskd. 2002 Feb 2;146(5):199-203

Chronic Venous Insufficiency

G Hauer, J Staubesand, Y Li, V Wienert, A Lentner, G Salzmann

Abstract

In severe chronic venous insufficiency (CVI) the fascia cruris is increasingly involved in the pathological process. The resulting loss of compliance as a consequence of altered fascia texture leads to increased pressure in the compartments of the lower extremity, followed by reduced circulation. Arteries and nerves, which penetrate the fascia along with insufficient perforating veins, are damaged through the increased pressure and are therefore functionally impaired. Accordingly many pathological changes in the crural ulcer have their anatomical substrate here. The microcirculation is distributed by either primary varicosis with secondary insufficiency of the deep veins or by primary insufficiency of the deep venous system as seen in a post-thrombotic syndrome. Subsequent therapy should be based on this knowledge and therefore consists of medication and basic physical therapy along with dissection of the perforating veins-fasciotomy and fasciectomy combined with plastic surgery. All of the therapeutic measures have to take the stage of the CVI into consideration. In order to eliminate the insufficient perforating veins and to perform fasciotomy the endoscopic approach is considered the state of the art. In extreme cases, only fasciectomy combined with plastic surgery can lead to durable healing.

Chirurg. 1996 May;67(5):505-14

Secondary Chronic Venous Disorders

Mark H Meissner, Bo Eklof, Phillip Coleridge Smith, et al

Abstract

Secondary chronic venous disorders (CVD) usually follow an episode of acute deep venous thrombosis (DVT). Most occluded venous segments recanalize over the first 6 to 12 months after an episode of acute DVT, leading to chronic luminal changes and a combination of partial obstruction and reflux. Such morphological changes produce venous hypertension with the highest levels of ambulatory venous pressure occurring in patients with combined outflow obstruction and distal reflux. The clinical manifestations of secondary CVD, including pain, venous claudication, edema, skin changes, and ulceration are commonly referred to as the post-thrombotic syndrome. Such sequelae are best avoided by early and aggressive treatment of proximal DVT. The diagnostic evaluation of secondary CVD is similar to primary CVD and is based upon duplex ultrasound. However, the definition of hemodynamically significant venous stenosis remains obscure and there are no reliable tests to confirm the presence of such lesions. Diagnosis depends more on anatomic rather than hemodynamic criteria, and IVUS is superior to venography in estimating the morphological degree and extent of iliac vein stenosis. The fundamental role of compression in the treatment of

CVD is well recognized. Compliance with compression is essential to heal ulcers and minimize recurrence. The efficacy of various adjuncts to ulcer treatment, including complex wound dressings and medications have been variable. Although superficial venous surgery has not been demonstrated to improve ulcer healing rates, it does decrease ulcer recurrence. Deep venous valve reconstruction is performed in only a few specialized centers, and the results are better for primary than for secondary CVD. Treatment of incompetent perforating veins remains controversial. Although artificial venous valves are promising, most early experimental models have failed. With respect to venous obstruction, iliocaval angioplasty and stenting has emerged as the primary treatment for proximal iliofemoral venous obstruction with surgical bypass assuming a secondary role.

J Vasc Surg. 2007 Dec;46 Suppl S:68S-83S.

DOPPLER

Ultrasound Is the First Choice When Chronic Venous Disease in the Lower Extremities Is Suspected

Thor Bechsgaard, Kristoffer Lindskov Hansen, Charlotte Strandberg, Lars Lönn, Jørgen Arendt Jensen, Michael Bachmann Nielsen, Niels Bækgaard

Abstract

Chronic venous disease affects one quarter of the population and is routinely examined with Doppler ultrasound. The veins are evaluated in terms of diameter, compressibility and blood flow. The examination is performed with the patient in the standing position but can be complemented in the supine position, if disease of the deep veins is suspected. New angle-independent ultrasound techniques may contribute with more complex visualization of the blood flow and may in the future replace Doppler ultrasound in some areas of vein diagnostics.

Ugeskr Laeger. 2016 Oct 31;178(44):V05160380.

Duplex Evaluation of Venous Insufficiency

Nicos Labropoulos, Luis R Leon Jr

Abstract

Duplex ultrasound is the most useful examination for the evaluation of venous valvular incompetence. Multi-frequency 4 to 7-MHz linear array transducers are typically used for this assessment of superficial and deep reflux. The examination is done with the patient standing and manual compression maneuvers are used to initiate reflux. Automatic rapid inflation and deflation cuffs may be used when a standard stimulus is needed. Cutoff values for reflux have been defined. Perforating veins must be identified and flow direction during compression recorded. When ulcers are present, duplex ultrasound is used to investigate veins of the ulcerated legs. Venous outflow obstruction is also studied by duplex ultrasound and chronic changes in deep and superficial veins following deep venous thrombosis noted. The main drawback in evaluation of chronic obstruction is inability to quantify hemodynamic significance. Anatomic variations in superficial and deep veins are common and their identification is necessary. Reporting results of duplex ultrasound studies must take into consideration the proper classification of venous disease as well as the new anatomic terms that have been accepted.

Vasc Surg. 2005 Mar;18(1):5-9.

Quantification of Venous Reflux by Means of Some Duplex Scanner and Light Reflection Rheography Parameters and Its Correlation With Chronic Venous Insufficiency Symptoms

G Mosti, M L Iabichella, P Picerni, G De Marco

Abstract

Background: The quantification of venous reflux is rarely made but it is valuable for studying the natural history of CVI, its prognostic implications and the therapy effectiveness. We have evaluated some parameters of chronic venous insufficiency, caused by valvular incompetence, by means of duplex scanner and light reflection rheography searching for a better correlation with the clinical stages of vein disease.

Methods: We have examined 107 patients (35 males, 72 females; aged 22-78, mean 61.5 +/- 14.3) with long saphenous insufficiency in different clinical stages and measured the venous reflux, the reflux duration, the reflux grade, the vein diameter near the saphenofemoral junction with the duplex scanner and the refilling time with the light reflection rheography. The reproducibility of the studied techniques has been determined by examining 20 legs four times each in the same day or on different days. Statistical analysis of the data was performed by means of the variance analysis followed by the Waller-Duncan test.

Results: The venous reflux, the venous diameter and the refilling time can easily range between mild and severe insufficiency: reflux is 6.3 +/- 2.5 ml/sec at stage I; 27.5 +/- 10.1 at stage III; venous diameter is

6.04 +/- 1.4 at stage I; 10.6 +/- 2.2 at stage III; refilling time is 23.6 +/- 9.6 at stage I; 5.4 +/- 2.4 at stage

III. The reflux time and reflux grade are unable to separate the various CVI stages.

Conclusions: The measurement of venous reflux, venous diameter and refilling time is simple, quick, reproducible; these indices are able to differentiate mild from severe CVI but unable to separate patients at the second stage of the venous disease from those at the third stage and then ineffective in the ulcer risk assessment but the reflux is highly predictable. The ulcer risk is practically absent for reflux < 12 ml/sec; highly probable for reflux > 15 ml/sec (20/46 cases; 43.4%).

Minerva Cardioangiol. 2000 Nov;48(11):331-9.

The Role of Ultrasound in the Diagnosis and Treatment of Chronic Venous Insufficiency

H*jalti M Thorisson, Jeffrey S Pollak, Leslie Scoutt*

Abstract

Chronic venous insufficiency (CVI) is an exceedingly common and underdiagnosed disorder with a wide range of symptoms and prognosis ranging from cosmetic issues to skin ulceration with tissue loss. Ultrasound plays a pivotal role in the diagnosis, classification, and guidance of percutaneous treatment of CVI. It is therefore of critical importance to the practicing radiologist to have a sound understanding of the pathophysiology, pertinent venous anatomy, and classification of CVI. We review the superficial and deep venous anatomy of the lower extremity, introduce a pattern recognition approach for mapping of varicosities, and review the protocol for ultrasound evaluation for CVI. In addition, we discuss the pathophysiology of CVI and the role of ultrasound in guidance for and follow-up of percutaneous treatment.

Ultrasound Q. 2007 Jun;23(2):137-50.

PPG, APG, Duplex: Which Noninvasive Tests Are Most Appropriate for the Management of Patients with Chronic Venous Insufficiency?

William A Marston

Abstract

Numerous noninvasive tests have been described for assistance in the diagnosis and treatment of patients with chronic venous insufficiency (CVI). These tests include venous duplex ultrasound examination in the supine and standing positions, photoplethysmography (PPG), and air plethysmography (APG). The goal of these studies is to provide accurate information describing the anatomic or the hemodynamic characteristics of the patient with CVI, precluding the need for invasive studies. These tests will be reviewed including the typical information obtained, the usefulness of this information, and the relevance for clinical management of patients with CVI. Based on the clinical class, recommendations for a noninvasive testing protocol are outlined.

Semin Vasc Surg. 2002 Mar;15(1):13-20.

Experimental Venous Hypertension in Legs with Chronic Venous Insufficiency and in Healthy Legs, Measured Using a Double-Wavelength Laser Doppler Technique Ken Malanin, Pekka Vilkko, Pertti J. Kolari

Abstract

The venoarteriolar response (VAR) of the skin in legs caused by experimental venous hypertension was measured using a new, double-wavelength laser Doppler probe technique (543 nm and 780 nm). This enables the measurement of the laser Doppler flux in the superficial and deep layers of the skin simultaneously. The recordings were obtained from the leg with the patient in a recumbent position with a sphygmo manometer cuff around the thigh. The VAR was recorded at the cuff pressures of 30 mmHg and 60 mmHg. Ten patients with chronic venous insufficiency (CVI) and 20 control subjects with healthy legs were investigated.

The VAR increased in relation to the increase of cuff pressure at both wavelengths. There were no significant differences in the VAR between the cuff pressures within or between the legs with CVI and healthy legs. The VAR measured at 780 nm was very significantly greater than the VAR measured at 543 nm in legs with CVI ($p<0.005$), as well as in healthy legs ($p<0.001$).

Method

The recordings were obtained from the leg with the patient in a recumbent position with a sphygmomanometer cuff around the thigh.

The VAR was recorded at the cuff pressures of 30 mmHg and 60 mmHg. 10 patients with chronic venous insufficiency (CVI) and

20 control subjects with healthy legs were investigated.

RESULTS:

1. The VAR increased in relation to the increase of cuff pressure at both wavelengths.
2. There were no significant differences in the VAR between the cuff pressures within or between the legs with CVI and healthy legs.
3. The VAR measured at 780 nm was very significantly greater than the VAR measured at 543 nm in legs with CVI (p<0.005), as well as in healthy legs (p<0.001).

Conclusion:

1. The VAR depends both

a. on the wavelength of the laser Doppler light used and
b. on the degree of venous hypertension.

1. The VAR is not impaired in legs with CVI compared with healthy legs. Angiology. 1998 Sep;49(9):729-33

Expert Assessment of Chronic Venous Insufficiency

K Grossmann, P Thiele, H Voigt, J Mühlan

Abstract

In the expertise of a chronic venous insufficiency kind and stage of the venous disease must be proved as objectively as possible. The diagnostic demands in the individual step programmes serve for the exact assessment of the remaining part of efficiency. The criteria of valuation are summarized, in which case we also deal with several possibilities of combination with other vascular diseases. The expert opinion of an accident is discussed. References to the inability to work, rating of nursing money, and increased material benefit in impairments of health and to the acknowledgement of an identity card for injured persons supplement the statements.

Z Gesamte Inn Med. 1990 Feb 15;45(4):115-21.

Imaging of Venous Insufficiency

Neil M. Khilnani, Robert J. Min

Abstract

Duplex ultrasonography (DUS) is an essential part of the evaluation of patients with most forms of superficial venous insufficiency. DUS has also become an important tool in directing and assessing the results of a variety of minimally invasive treatments of this disease. In this article, we review the salient aspects of performing an adequate DUS evaluation and the utility of this technique in guiding treatment. *Semin intervent Radiol 2005; 22(3): 178-184*

EVALUATION

Modern Diagnostic Methods of Chronic Venous Insufficiency

Gabriele Menzinger

Abstract

A number of different instrument-based examination methods are available for assessing the various phlebological disorders and planning therapeutic measures. These tools can help identify insufficient vein sections and evaluate functional outcomes. The most important analysis methods and their use, depending on the respective clinical stage of the illness, are represented.

Wien Med Wochenschr. 2016 Jun;166(9-10):275-7

Pulse oximetry index: a simple arterial assessment for patients with venous disease.

B ianchi J, Zamiri M, Loney M, McIntosh H, Dawe RS, Douglas WS.

Abstract

O bjective:
    To provide additional safety data comparing ankle brachial pressure index (ABPI) and pulse oximetry (Lanarkshire Oximetry Index, LOI) as measures of arterial circulation in patients with venous disease of the leg.

Method: A total of 107 (195 legs) attending hospital leg ulcer clinics participated in this prospective open study. We attempted to measure brachial and foot arterial pressures in all patients using both the handheld Doppler method (ABPI) and pulse oximeter method (LOI). Features of patients with limbs in which either the ABPI or LOI could not be assessed were documented. ABPI and LOI values were compared, and agreement between the two assessment methods was assessed.

Results: We found the LOI measurement to be a simpler technique than Doppler ABPI measurement, with an endpoint less prone to the subjective variability associated with the Doppler method. Of the 195 legs assessed, we obtained LOI in 10 in which an ABPI could not be recorded. LOI could not be recorded in only one leg. There was a linear association (p<0.001) and fair agreement (kappa=0.303) between LOI and ABPI in the 184 legs in which both ratios could be measured. There was no evident tendency for LOI to read either low or high compared with ABPI.

Conclusion: Pulse oximetry LOI is a simple alternative to Doppler ABPI in the screening of patients for arterial disease that could be a contraindication to, or require modification of, compression therapy. It can be measured in some legs that cannot be assessed by Doppler ultrasound.

J Wound Care. 2008 Jun;17(6):253-4, 256-8, 260

Gait and Calf Muscle Endurance in Patients with Chronic Venous Insufficiency

C J T van Uden, C J M van der Vleuten, J G M Kooloos, J H
Haenen, H Wollersheim

Abstract

Objective: To gain insight in gait and calf muscle endurance
in patients with severe chronic venous insufficiency.

Methods: Fifteen patients with severe chronic venous
insufficiency (healed or active ulcers) and 19 healthy controls were
selected for this study. Subjects had to perform eight trials at
preferred walking speed and eight trials at instructed walking speed
(1.25 m/s) during which the gait parameters were recorded. The
calf muscle endurance was tested by use of the heel-rise test.

Results: Patients had a significantly lower preferred walking speed (1.25 m/s +/- 0.31) compared with healthy controls (1.44 m/s +/- 0.0.15) (p = 0.039). During preferred walking speed patients had a wider base of support (p = 0.003), a bigger step time (p = 0.005), and a bigger stride time (p = 0.004) compared with healthy controls. At instructed walking speed only base of support was different between the two groups (p = 0.016). Patients had a significantly (p = 0.003) smaller number of heel rises (14.6 +/- 7.34), indicating decreased calf muscle endurance compared with controls (23.5 +/- 6.54).

Conclusion: This study indicates a disturbed gait and decreased calf muscle endurance in patients with severe chronic venous insufficiency. The results of this study point to a possible role for gait and strength training in the rehabilitation process of patients with severe chronic venous insufficiency.

Clin Rehabil. 2005 May;19(3):339-44.

Prospective Evaluation of Chronic Venous Insufficiency Based on Foot Venous Pressure Measurements and Air Plethysmography Findings

Masato Fukuoka, Takaki Sugimoto, Yutaka Okita

Abstract

Purpose: The purpose of this study was to evaluate lower extremity venous function in patients with chronic venous insufficiency, with foot venous pressure (FVP) measurements and air plethysmography (APG).

Methods: Eighty-five limbs of 63 patients with a history of chronic venous insufficiency (CVI) from 1995 to 1999 were studied. FVP parameters studied included ambulatory venous pressure (AVP), percent decrease in FVP with manual calf compression (%drop), ratio of increase in FVP over 4 seconds after release of compression (4SR%), and time to 90% recovery of FVP were measured. APG parameters studied included functional venous volume, 90% refilling time (VFT90), venous filling index, ejection fraction, and residual volume fraction.

Results: Venous filling index and 90% refilling time were significantly decreased in limbs with stasis syndrome compared with the control group. AVP, %drop, and 4SR% also showed significantly decrease in limbs with stasis syndrome compared with those without it. AVP, %drop, and 4SR% were significantly different for the primary group compared with the secondary group, whereas no differences were found with regard to any APG parameter.

Conclusions: APG enables prediction of the presence of CVI, whereas FVP measurements are more useful for evaluation of clinical severity of CVI.

J Vasc Surg. 2003 Oct;38(4):804-11.

Continuous intrathoracic pressure monitoring with a new esophageal microchip catheter in sleep-related upper airway obstructions.

Berg S, Hybbinette JC, Gislason T, Hawke M.

Abstract

A new small-diameter microchip catheter, especially developed for continuous intrathoracic pressure monitoring to assess the degree of respiratory obstruction and effort in patients with sleep- related upper airway obstructions, was investigated. The technical performance and clinical applicability of the catheter was tested in a simplified screening study comprising 122 sleep recordings in patients with varying complaints of snoring and daytime tiredness. In six obese snorers, sensitivity of the catheter to apneas, hypopneas, and nonapneic snoring was compared to the traditional assessment of respiratory events by conventional polysomnography. The catheter was found to be easy to handle and introduce, with technical qualities meeting the demands for overnight recordings of intrathoracic pressure variations. Patient tolerance was high (93%), and sensitivity to apneas and hypopneas was equivalent to that of traditional polysomnography. Periods with upper airway obstruction and increased respiratory effort on the borderline between asymptomatic obstructions and obstructions resulting in significant blood-gas changes could be detected primarily with intrathoracic pressure monitoring. Monitoring the intrathoracic pressure variations in the esophagus has been shown previously to reflect respiratory effort. Increased respiratory effort might be one of the explanations for the fragmented sleep patterns and sleep related daytime symptoms sometimes seen in patients without a pathologic respiratory index. In addition to being applicable for the detection of apneas and hypopneas, continuous nocturnal monitoring of the intrathoracic pressure variations also detects small increases in respiratory effort and thus may constitute a valuable tool for the understanding and diagnosis of upper airway resistance syndrome and obstructive sleep apnea syndrome.

J Otolaryngol. 1995 Jun;24(3):160-4

Photoplethysmography in Chronic Venous Insufficiency

P Barthélémy, S Schlama, C Juhan

Abstract

Venous photoplethysmography (P.P.G.) is a non-invasive diagnostic technique using reflection of infrared light on the skin. The record gives a curve analogous to venous pressure. Normally the venous pressure of the leg decreases in response to calf muscle exercise. We have affixed the P.P.G. transducer to the skin above the medial malleolus and have analyzed the recovery half time (T 1/2) on 170 limbs: 49 normal, 82 with superficial venous insufficiency and 39 with deep venous insufficiency. Reference tests were ascending and retrograde phlebography and venous Doppler evaluation. A tourniquet was used to occlude the superficial venous network. T 1/2 without tourniquet is useful to screen limbs with venous insufficiency. T 1/2 with tourniquet differentiates deep and superficial venous insufficiency. P.P. G. can document the rise of deep venous insufficiency in patients with varicose veins and or repermeation of deep veins or post phlebitic syndrome among patients who have had thrombophlebitis.

J Mal Vasc. 1985;10(4):303-7.

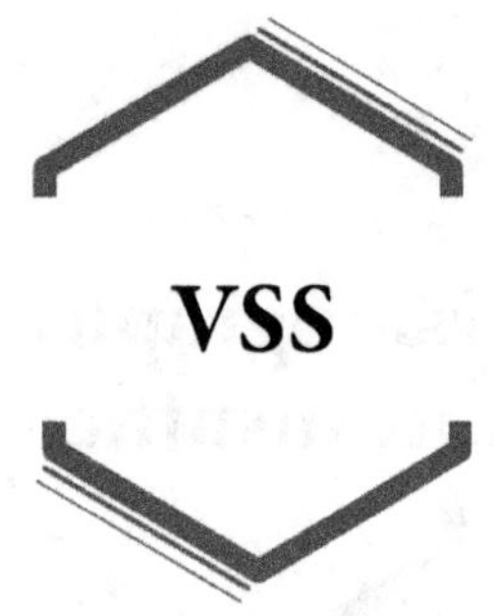

VSS

Clinical presentation and venous severity scoring of patients with extended deep axial venous reflux

LucGillet MD Michel R.Perrin MD François AndréAllaert MD, PhD

Abstract

The CEAP classification was conceived and created at the sixth annual meeting of the American Venous Forum in Maui, Hawaii, in 1994 by an international ad hoc committee. It is an internationally recognized classification. It has been published in 25 medical journals or books, has been translated into 8 languages, and was recently revised. This classification is only descriptive in scope and cannot quantify the severity of chronic venous disorders (CVD). The Venous Severity Score (VSS) has supplemented the original classification3 and was updated in 2000 (the VSS is also available online at http://www.jvascsurg.org; click on the Special Collection section and then the Reporting Standards section).4 With the CEAP classification and the VSS, we now have an instrument that is descriptive and can quantify CVD. However, although the CEAP has been widely circulated among physicians specializing in venous disease and is used in scientific research, an analysis of the literature shows that use of the VSS continues to be limited.

The objective of this study was to evaluate the prevalence of and profile of patients presenting with chronic venous insufficiency (CVI) and cascading deep postthrombotic or primary venous reflux involving the femoral, popliteal, and crural veins to the ankle5 (C3-C6; primary etiology, s; Ad, s, p).

Background: The objective of this study was to evaluate the prevalence and profile of patients presenting with chronic venous insufficiency (class C3-C6) and cascading deep venous reflux involving femoral, popliteal, and crural veins to the ankle.

Methods

From September 2001 to April 2004, 2894 patients were referred to our center for possible venous disorders. The superficial, deep, and perforator veins of both legs were investigated with color duplex scanning. The criterion for inclusion in this study was the existence of cascading deep venous reflux involving the femoral, popliteal, and crural veins to the ankle whose duration had to be longer than 1 second for the femoropopliteal vein and longer than 0.5 seconds for the crural vein. The advanced CEAP classification, the Venous Clinical Severity Score (VCSS), the Venous Segmental Disease Score (reflux; VSDS), and the Venous Disability Score (VDS) were used.

Results: Seventy-one limbs in 60 patients were identified. Eleven limbs (15.5%) were classified as C3, 36 (50.7%) as C4, 21 (29.6%) as C5, and 3 (4.2%) as C6. A primary etiology was identified in 11 (15.5%) limbs, and a postthrombotic etiology was identified in 60 limbs (84.5%). In the latter group, all but four patients were aware that they had had a previous deep venous thrombosis. In addition to femoropopliteal and calf veins, reflux was present in the common femoral vein in 60 (84.5%), the deep femoral vein in 27 (38%), and the muscular calf veins in 62 (87.3%). Incompetent perforator veins were identified in 53 (74.6%) limbs. Fifty-one (71.8%) limbs had a combination of superficial venous insufficiency (AS2, AS2, 3, AS4, or their combination) previously treated or present. Of these, 11 had primary etiology alone, and 40 had a secondary etiology with or without primary disease. Means and 95% confidence intervals of the VCSS, VSDS, and VDS were 9.72 (8.91-10.53), 7.2 (6.97-7.42), and 1.08 (0.83-1.32), respectively. A significant increase in the VCSS and in the VSDS (P < .0001) paralleled the CEAP clinical class. The VDS was higher in the C3 and C6 classes but did not reach significance. There was a significant link between the pain magnitude in the VCSS and the VDS (P < .0001). Severity of pain and high VDS did not depend on the wearing of elastic compression stockings. VCSS increased significantly according to the presence of an incompetent perforator vein (P < .05) and/or reflux in the deep femoral vein (P < .05).

Conclusions

This study confirmed the value of the Venous Severity Score as an instrument for evaluation of chronic venous insufficiency. A significant increase in the VCSS and VSDS paralleled CEAP clinical class; VDS was higher in classes C3 and C6 without reaching significance, probably because of the small size of the samples. Some clinical and anatomic features need to be clarified to facilitate scoring.

J Vasc Surg. 2006 Sep;44(3):588-94.

Evaluating chronic venous disease with a new venous severity scoring system

Michael A Ricci ,Joseph Emmerich, Peter W Callas, Shelly Naud, Carla Vossen,Edwin G Bovill

Abstract

Background: The Venous Clinical Severity Score (VCSS) has been proposed by the American Venous Forum as an objective means to clinically assess venous disease more completely than with the clinical CEAP classification. However, validation of the VCSS against an objective test is lacking. The purpose of this study was to test the VCSS against abnormalities found on venous ultrasound (US) scans.

Methods: As part of a screening project in a large kindred population with protein C deficiency, VCSS and venous US scanning were performed in 210 patients (420 limbs). A single examiner scored the VCSS (0-3) clinically for pain, varicose veins, edema, skin pigmentation, inflammation, induration, ulcer duration and size, and compressive therapy. Another experienced examiner, blinded to the subject's medical history, performed a US examination of the deep and superficial venous system, with a hand-carried US system. The relationship between US and VCSS scores was analyzed by calculating an odds ratio (OR) and its 95% confidence interval (CI).

Results: Of the 420 limbs screened, VCSS was 0 in 283 limbs, and VCSS was 1 or greater in the following categories: pain, 63 limbs; varicose veins, 70 limbs; edema, 51 limbs; skin pigmentation, 17 limbs; inflammation, 2 limbs; induration, 8 limbs; and compressive therapy, 9 limbs. The highest total score in any limb was 8. A clear association was seen with the VCSS and abnormalities found on US scans. When the score was dichotomized (0 = normal, 1 = any abnormality), it was a strong predictor of US scan abnormalities; limbs with VCSS greater than 0 had a 26-fold greater chance of US scan abnormalities than did limbs with VCSS = 0 (OR, 26.5; 95% CI, 11-64). With ultrasonography as the standard, sensitivity of VCSS compared with US scans was 89.3%, and specificity was 76.1%. Negative predictive value of VCSS = 0 was 97.9%, and positive predictive value for any positive score was 36.5%

Conclusions: The results of this study are based on a large kindred population with a higher risk for venous disease than found in the general population. Though the VCSS was devised to quantify the severity of chronic venous disease, this study found it a useful screening tool. The VCSS showed good association with abnormalities on US scans, and when VCSS = 0 there is a high likelihood that the patient does not have venous disease. This simple test may prove valuable in clinical practice.

In an attempt to standardize outcome assessment of venous interventions, an ad hoc committee of the American Venous Forum (AVF) developed a clinical scoring system, the Venous Clinical Severity Score (VCSS),1 meant to expand and supplement the existing CEAP classification system.2 In addition, the Venous Segmental Disease Score (VSDS) has been proposed to complement the VCSS, allow scoring with duplex ultrasound (US) scanning, and combine the anatomic and pathophysiologic components of CEAP.1 Meissner et al3 determined intraobserver variation with VCSS to be minimal, whereas interobserver variation in three of 10 categories (pain, inflammation, pigmentation) was significant. Interobserver agreement regarding presence or absence of disease (as defined by a score of ≤3 or ≥8) was good ($\kappa = 0.59$ and 0.65).3 However, the clinical aspects of VCSS have not been validated against an objective test such as venous US scanning. This study was designed to test the association of venous abnormalities detected with US scanning with the VCSS and the "C" (Clinical) component of the CEAP classification.

J Vasc Surg. 2003 Nov;38(5):909-15

Performance characteristics of the venous clinical severity score

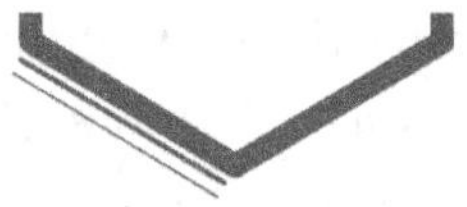

M*ark H. Meissner, Cynthia Natiello, Stephen C. Nicholls*

Abstract

Objective: To facilitate study of the natural history and management of venous disease, a 10- component venous clinical severity (VCS) score has been proposed as an objective measure of disease severity. The purpose of this study was to evaluate the validity and reliability of this instrument. **Methods**: VCS component scores (0 to 3) for pain, varicose veins, edema, pigmentation, inflammation, induration, stocking use, and ulcer size, duration, and number were measured in consecutive patients with chronic venous disease. Differences between observers (n = 3) and on serial evaluation by the same observer were determined. **Results**: One hundred twenty-eight limbs in 64 patients were evaluated. Mean VCS score increased from CEAP class 0 (1.7 ± 1.8) to class 6 (14.7 ± 3.0; R = .84; P < .0001). Scores in 68 limbs evaluated twice by the same observer differed by a mean of only 0.8 (P = .15), with a reliability coefficient of 0.6. Mean scores of 8.0 (± 5.1), 7.2 (± 5.1), and 8.0 (± 5.4) were obtained in 63 limbs evaluated by all three investigators (P = .02). Only the component scores for pain, inflammation, and pigmentation showed significant (P < .05) interobserver variability. Interobserver agreement on the absence of disease or presence of severe disease as defined by scores of 3 or less or 8 or more was good ($\kappa = 0.59$ and 0.65, respectively). **Conclusion**: The VCS score is a critically needed tool for evaluating changes in venous disease over time. The score is reliable and shows good correlation with CEAP clinical classification.

J Vasc Surg. 2002 Nov;36(5):889-95

Venous severity scoring: An adjunct to venous outcome assessment

Robert B. Rutherford, Frank T. Padberg Jr, Anthony J. Comerota, Robert L. Kistner, Mark H. Meissner, Gregory L. Moneta

Abstract

Some measure of disease severity is needed to properly compare the outcomes of the various approaches to the treatment of chronic venous insufficiency. Comparing the outcomes of two or more different treatments in a clinical trial, or the same treatment in two or more reports from the literature cannot be done with confidence unless the relative severity of the venous disease in each treatment group is known. The CEAP (Clinical-Etiology-Anatomic-Pathophysiologic) system is an excellent classification scheme, but it cannot serve the purpose of venous severity scoring because many of its components are relatively static and others use detailed alphabetical designations. A disease severity scoring scheme needs to be quantifiable, with gradable elements that can change in response to treatment. However, an American Venous Forum committee on venous outcomes assessment has developed a venous severity scoring system based on the best usable elements of the CEAP system. Two scores are proposed. The first is a Venous Clinical Severity Score: nine clinical characteristics of chronic venous disease are graded from 0 to 3 (absent, mild, moderate, severe) with specific criteria to avoid overlap or arbitrary scoring. Zero to three points are added for differences in background conservative therapy (compression and elevation) to produce a 30 point– maximum flat scale. The second is a Venous Segmental Disease Score, which combines the Anatomic and Pathophysiologic components of CEAP. Major venous segments are graded according to presence of reflux and/or obstruction. It is entirely based on venous imaging, primarily duplex scan but also phlebographic findings. This scoring scheme weights 11 venous segments for their relative importance when involved with reflux and/or obstruction, with a maximum score of

10. A third score is simply a modification of the existing CEAP disability score that eliminates reference to work and an 8-hour working day, substituting instead the patient's prior normal activities. These new scoring schemes are intended to complement the current CEAP system. (J Vasc Surg 2000;31:1307-12.)

Methods of outcomes assessment need to be able to gauge change in status after treatment in a meaningful and objective way, and for purposes of analysis and comparison, they should usually be quantitative rather than qualitative. They should result in a practical assessment of the success of a given treatment over time, whether applied to groups of patients of varying levels of severity or patients grouped into similar levels of severity. Both, but particularly the former, require a quantitative method of gauging the severity of disease. Properly comparing the outcomes of two or more treatments in the same institution, the reported results of the same treatment from different institutions, or the results of the same treatment using different adjunctive measures is not possible unless the relative severities of the underlying disease in the treatment groups are known.1 However, if the severity of the disease is uniformly quantified and the score changes with treatment, a disease severity score can not only serve as a background against which to view other outcome criteria in comparing treatment groups, but can itself reflect the degree of change in disease severity associated with treatment. As such, disease severity scores can be very useful in outcomes assessment. The widespread use of a properly designed disease severity scoring scheme should allow patient groups of similar degrees of severity to be selected for entry into clinical trials and to be compared in regard to outcome following different therapies. If generally adopted, the reported outcomes after a given treatment by different practices, groups, or institutions can also be compared knowing the relative severity of disease of the treated patients in each report. Thus, a venous severity scoring system can become a valuable adjunct in venous outcomes assessment.

The increasingly popular CEAP (Clinical-Etiology-Anatomic-Pathophysiologic2) classification system, particularly its clinical classes C1 to C6, does represent a progressive gradation of disease severity. It gauges the severity of disease at a given point in time, but because a number of its components are relatively static and do not change significantly in response to treatment and other components have alphabetic designations, it cannot be used for disease severity scoring in its current form. For example, the healing of an active ulcer would drop the patient from C6 to C5, but no further. Some of the elements of C4, particularly subcutaneous fibrosis and cutaneous atrophy, are unlikely to change significantly with treatment. The elimination of edema or varicose veins, or reticular veins and telangiectasias for that matter, conceivably could produce an improvement in clinical class, but the results of their treatment are not usually so absolute. Significant improvements short of complete elimination of the characteristic venous state would not result in categorical improvement.

The clinical class of CEAP does not allow a practical assessment of change in response to treatment or adverse events, but then it was not intended to do so. Nevertheless, the American Venous Forum's Ad Hoc Committee on Venous Outcomes believed that CEAP identifies most if not all the necessary components involved in comprehensive outcomes assessment, and many of its elements could be individually graded to produce a venous severity scoring system. This approach was selected, and the results of these deliberations are reported here.

It should be noted that a "Clinical Score" is included in the full CEAP document and is included in the most recent edition of the Handbook of Venous Disorders (see Table 38.3, page 656).2 It uses a 0 to 2 grading of a number of symptoms and signs, which include pain and venous claudication, as well as the characteristic elements of the C3 to C6 levels of CEAP, for a maximum score of 18. Varicose veins are not included in this clinical score, so a patient with successful removal of these could only be gauged by a change in pain, at the most two points. Although the approach used in this clinical score is conceptually sound, it is rather simplistic. Furthermore, the scores assigned can be rather arbitrary and subjective because many of the scoring levels are inadequately delineated by the descriptive terms associated with them. Also, some of the characteristics (e.g., number of ulcers, duration of ulcers, recurrence of ulcers) are not capable of improvement; the score can only remain unchanged or increase. It has not gained widespread acceptance or use and was not included in the current version of venous reporting standards.3

In the development of a severity scoring system based on CEAP, it was obvious that a clinical severity score could be primarily based on the C of CEAP, and that the E or etiology is fixed and could not be incorporated. However, both the anatomic (A) and pathophysiology (P) segments, which essentially involve the presence or absence of reflux and/or obstruction, could be combined and adapted into a grading scheme reflecting disease severity, and in some situations even gauge change with treatment, as in a comparison of anticoagulant therapy, thrombolysis, or thrombectomy for deep venous thrombosis (DVT). It was believed that such a scheme could be scored using duplex scan findings. Therefore, a Venous Segmental Disease Score was also developed, in addition to a Clinical Severity Score. These two elements of the proposed venous severity scoring system will thus be seen to be closely allied to CEAP.

Finally, it was considered important to avoid confusing or undermining the existing venous reporting standards, and particularly the CEAP classification system in developing new methods for venous outcomes assessment such as venous severity scores. The importance of the uniform classification framework provided by CEAP is acknowledged and seen in its increasing use. Thus, the goal of this report is not to replace or change any aspect of the classification scheme of CEAP, but to augment it with additional, closely related, and compatible methods, some of which are modifications of other features of CEAP (ie, the clinical score and the disability score), to further improve the ability to assess venous outcomes.

J Vasc Surg. 2000 Jun;31(6):1307-12.

VENOUS HYPERTENSION

Venous Hypertension Induces Increased Platelet Reactivity and Accumulation in Patients with Chronic Venous Insufficiency

XinWu Lu, YuJie Chen, YinHuang, WeiMin Li, MiEr Jiang

Abstract

The objective of this study was to determine whether there are changes in platelet activation and rheology in patients with chronic venous insufficiency (CVI) and what their impact is on this disease. Anticoagulated peripheral venous blood collected from 21 patients with CVI and 13 normal control subjects in different bodily positions was incubated either with 0.5 µmol/L adenosine diphosphate (ADP) or without agonist and analyzed by whole blood flow cytometry. Soluble P- selectin was analyzed in obtained sera by enzyme-linked immunosorbent assay. Platelet count was determined by a whole blood analyzer. Circulating platelets were more reactive to stimulation with

0.5 µmol/L ADP in patients with CVI compared with control subjects. There was no statistically significant change in platelet activation without ADP and the level of soluble P-selectin as a function of posture. Under simulated venous hypertension, platelet accumulation was observed in patients with CVI. Patients with

CVI had increased platelet reactivity and accumulation during orthostasis, suggesting this might be a contributory factor to CVI pathogenesis.

Angiology. May-Jun 2006;57(3):321-9.

Skin microcirculatory responses in chronic venous insufficiency: the effect of short- term venous hypertension.

Cheatle TR, Coleridge Smith PD, Scurr JH

Abstract

The purpose of this study was to examine the effects on the skin microcirculation of a short period of venous hypertension. 34 subjects (17 patients with lipodermatosclerosis and 17 controls) were studied. Laser-Doppler flowmetry was used to assess the hyperaemic responsiveness of the skin following three minutes of ischaemia. This was done by measuring the ratio of peak to basal flow, and the time taken to reach 95% of peak flow. The limb was then subjected to 30 minutes of venous hypertension, following which the hyperaemic responses were repeated. Normal controls demonstrated a significant reduction in hyperaemic response after venous hypertension. Liposclerotic skin had a much less pronounced response to ischaemia which was not significantly affected by 30 minutes of venous hypertension. The clinically normal skin in venous patients showed intermediate values. The results suggest that a short period of venous hypertension causes an immediate deficit in microcirculatory function. This short time scale is consistent with the white cell activation theory of skin damage in venous disease. The loss of vasodilatory capacity by liposclerotic skin may reflect either the constricting effect of pericapillary fibrin cuffs or a fixed degree of capillary occlusion.

Aim:

The purpose of this study was to examine the effects on the skin microcirculation of a short period of venous hypertension.

Methods:

1. 34 subjects

a. 17 patients with lipodermatosclerosis and

a.   17 controls were studied.

1.   Laser-Doppler flowmetry was used to assess the hyperaemic responsiveness of the skin following three minutes of ischaemia.
2.   This was done by measuring the ratio of peak to basal flow, and the time taken to reach 95% of peak flow.
3.   The limb was then subjected to 30 minutes of venous hypertension, following which the hyperaemic responses were repeated.

Results:

1.   Normal controls demonstrated a significant reduction in hyperaemic response after venous hypertension.
2.   Liposclerotic skin had a much less pronounced response to ischaemia which was not significantly affected by 30 minutes of venous hypertension.
3.   The clinically normal skin in venous patients showed intermediate values.

Conclusion:

The results suggest that.

1.   a short period of venous hypertension causes an immediate deficit in microcirculatory function.
2.   This short time scale is consistent with the white cell activation theory of skin damage in venous disease.
3.   The loss of vasodilatory capacity by liposclerotic skin may

reflect

a. either the constricting effect of pericapillary fibrin cuffs
b. or a fixed degree of capillary occlusion.

Vasa. 1991;20(1):63-9

The Microcirculation in Venous Hypertension

P$^{D\ Smith}$

Abstract

Objective: To review the factors that result in skin ulceration of patients with chronic venous insufficiency.

Data sources: Index Medicus was searched using an on-line computer system for years 1966-1995 to identify articles relating to venous ulceration and the microcirculation.

Data extraction: Articles and sections of articles relating to the mechanisms which cause venous ulceration and the efficacy of the treatment of venous ulceration have been included.

Data synthesis: It seems unlikely that venous ulceration is attributable to failure of diffusion of oxygen and other small nutritional molecules to the tissues of the skin. It is much more likely that neutrophils attach themselves to the cutaneous microcirculation, become activated and produce endothelial injury. Repeated over many months or years, this leads to the chronic inflammatory process of lipodermatosclerosis. The microvascular changes in the skin are characterised by activated endothelium and perivascular inflammatory cells.

Conclusion: There is evidence of leucocyte involvement in the pathogenesis of venous ulceration. The exact mechanisms remain to be resolved. Improved treatment for patients may be devised with a better understanding of the basic causes of this condition.

Vasc Med. 1997;2(3):203-13.

Venoarteriolar Response to Chronic Venous Insufficiency-Venous Hypertension

B^{-M Taute}

B-M Taute

Abstract

Chronic venous insufficiency is an advanced chronic venous disease, which as a result of venous hypertension leads to specific skin or subcutaneous tissue changes on the lower extremities.

The descriptive CEAP classification enables a standardized classification of chronic venous disorders.

Color-coded duplex ultrasonography is the center of diagnostic measures, which enable functional and morphological conclusions regarding specific venous changes and possible differential diagnoses.

Chronic venous insufficiency therapy targets the reduction or elimination of the underlying venous hypertension.

Due to their high prevalence and age-associated increase, chronic venous diseases represent a problem affecting the quality of life of persons concerned and representing a cost-intensive problem for public health care.

Internist (Berl). 2010 Mar;51(3):351-7

PATHOLOGY

Granulocytes Function in Patients with Chronic Venous Insufficiency Followed by Chronic Wounds

Y*u S Vinnik, G E Karapetyan, L V Kochetova, R A Pakhomova*

Abstract

Aim: To analyze efficiency of ozone therapy, ultrasound and cryotherapy for infected and purulent wounds due to chronic venous insufficiency.

Material and methods: There were 127 patients with chronic venous insufficiency followed by chronic wounds. Efficacy of systemic and local ozone therapy was assessed. De Sole method was used to analyze chemiluminescent and spontaneous activity of neutrophils of peripheral blood.

Results: Advanced generation of active forms of oxygen was revealed in patients with chronic wounds and chronic venous insufficiency. Complex ozone therapy including intravenous administration of ozonized autologous blood, oxygen-ozone and ultrasonic exposure of the wound and cryogenic stimulation reduce painful period up to 3.1±0.6 days, accelerate epithelialization of the wound and normalize release of active forms of oxygen.

Khirurgiia (Mosk). 2019;(1):37-42.

Pathogenesis of Varicose Veins and Implications for Clinical Management

J oseph J. Naoum; Glenn C. Hunter

Abstract

Varicose veins (VVs) classically result from venous hypertension owing to incompetence of the major communications between the superficial and deep veins of the lower extremity. In a significant number of patients, there is no demonstrable truncal saphenous reflux and varicosities are the result of isolated perforating and nonsaphenous vein incompetence. The clinical and histologic features of VVs are the result of disruption of the normal architectural structure of the venous wall as a consequence of remodeling of the extracellular matrix (ECM) in response to increased venous distention and altered hemodynamic shear stress. Although a number of genes, growth factors, proteases, and their inhibitors known to modulate the ECM have been implicated in the pathogenesis of VVs, their etiology remains unknown. The complex variations in venous anatomy in patients with VVs require detailed vein mapping to determine the source and drainage locations of reflux if the rates of residual and recurrent varicosities are to be reduced. The distinct pathogenic mechanisms involved in the development of VVs have important implications for the management of VVs that include a wide spectrum of treatment modalities ranging from reassurance, alternative medicines, conservative management or compression therapy, and surgical or endovascular therapy.

Vascular. 2007 Sep-Oct;15(5):242-9

Chronic Venous Insufficiency Pathogenesis and Modern Diagnostic Possibilities

Ts Bushkevich, A R Zubarev, N V Krivosheeva, E G Gradusov

Abstract

Ultrasound angioscanning is one of modern highly effective diagnostic techniques in trophic lesion stage of varicose disease. This technique allows for reliable determination of the levels and character of pathological venous refluxes, having significant impact on the course of the disease and leading to chronic venous insufficiency (CVI). The authors revealed the leading role of profound venous valvular insufficiency in the progress of CVI, stressing the necessity for its correction. They point out to the causes of low horizontal venous-venous refluxes and valvular insufficiency of gastrocnemius muscle-venous sinuses leading to isolated insufficiency in the distal segments of posterior tibial veins, which intensifies CVI progress at the account of disturbances in the functioning of tibial muscular-venous pump.

Klinicheskaia Meditsina, 2007, 85(10).

Platelet-monocyte aggregates in patients with chronic venous insufficiency remain elevated following correction of reflux.

Michael J Rohrer, R Brannon Claytor, Charles S C Garnette, Craig C Powell, Marc R Barnard, Mark I Furman, Alan D Michelson

Abstract:

An increased number of circulating platelet-monocyte aggregates (PMAs) is present in patients with all clinical classes of chronic venous insufficiency (CVI). The purpose of this study was to determine whether patients with CVI maintain elevated levels of PMAs following complete surgical correction of chronic venous insufficiency. Patients with superficial venous insufficiency and a normal deep venous system documented by duplex scan were included in the study. Venous blood was drawn from a superficial vein in the leg and an antecubital vein prior to vein stripping and again six weeks postoperatively. Control subjects without evidence of venous disease had blood drawn from an antecubital vein. Whole blood flow cytometry was used to analyze the samples for the presence of platelet-monocyte aggregates following incubation with buffer or 0.5 microM adenosine diphosphate (ADP). Postoperative duplex scanning demonstrated elimination of venous reflux in the superficial venous system and normal deep vein physiology in all nine patients. Preoperatively, patients with CVI had significantly elevated levels of circulating PMAs in both arm and leg samples without stimulation by an agonist compared to controls (15.2+/-1.1 and 14.3+/-1.3 vs 7.4+/-0.3 for controls, p<0.02 for each), and after stimulation by 0.5 microM ADP (33.7+/-4.7 and 34.3+/-5.2 vs 12.5+/-3.8 for controls, p<0.04 for each). There was no significant change in the number of PMAs in either patient arm or leg blood samples six weeks following correction of venous reflux by removal of the diseased veins. Complete correction of chronic venous insufficiency did not diminish the elevated circulating levels of platelet-monocyte aggregates. We conclude that the presence of an increased number of PMAs identified in patients with CVI is not secondary to the presence of venous reflux, but may be involved with the primary etiology of chronic venous insufficiency. This finding also suggests that a stimulus other than venous hypertension may be important in triggering the leukocyte activation seen in patients with chronic venous disease.

Aim: The purpose of this study was to determine whether patients with CVI maintain elevated levels of PMAs following complete surgical correction of chronic venous insufficiency.

Methods: 1. Patients with superficial venous insufficiency and a normal deep venous system documented by duplex scan were included in the study.

1. Venous blood was drawn from a superficial vein in the leg and an antecubital vein prior to vein stripping and again six weeks postoperatively.
2. Control subjects without evidence of venous disease had blood drawn from an antecubital vein.

3. Whole blood flow cytometry was used to analyze the samples for the presence of platelet- monocyte aggregates following incubation with buffer or 0.5 microM adenosine diphosphate (ADP).

Results:

1. Postoperative duplex scanning demonstrated elimination of venous reflux in the superficial venous system and normal deep vein physiology in all nine patients.
2. Preoperatively, patients with CVI had significantly elevated levels of circulating PMAs in both arm and leg samples without stimulation by an agonist compared to controls (15.2+/-1.1 and 14.3+/-

1.3 vs 7.4+/-0.3 for controls, p<0.02 for each), and after stimulation by 0.5 microM ADP (33.7+/- 4.7 and 34.3+/-5.2 vs 12.5+/-3.8 for controls, p<0.04 for each).

1. There was no significant change in the number of PMAs in either patient arm or leg blood samples six weeks following correction of venous reflux by removal of the diseased veins.

Complete correction of chronic venous insufficiency did not diminish the elevated circulating levels of platelet-monocyte aggregates.

Conclusion:

1. We conclude that the presence of an increased number of PMAs identified in patients with CVI is not secondary to the presence of venous reflux, but may be involved with the primary etiology of chronic venous insufficiency.
2. This finding also suggests that a stimulus other than venous hypertension may be important in triggering the leukocyte activation seen in patients with chronic venous disease.

Cardiovasc Surg. 2002 Oct;10(5):464-9

Update on Venous-Insufficiency-Induced Inflammatory Processes

P$^{D\ Smith}$

Abstract

The causes of venous ulceration remain unclear. Twentieth-century hypotheses concentrated on the possibility that this problem was caused by failure of oxygen delivery to the skin. However, it has been difficult to substantiate these predictions in practice. Although the presence of tissue hypoxia has been suggested by studies in which transcutaneous oxygen tension has been assessed with transducers heated to unphysiological temperatures, when oxygen measurements are made at room temperature there is little evidence of tissue hypoxia. This has led to the assessment of alternative mechanisms of ulcer development. There has been considerable interest in recent years in the inflammatory processes that surround venous ulceration. A complex sequence of events appears to surround the development of leg ulceration. Increased leukocyte activation has been shown in patients with venous disease as well as increased expression of soluble endothelial adhesion molecules. Histologic studies of the skin in patients with chronic venous disease show a perivascular infiltration of the capillaries of the papillary plexus (the most superficial part of the dermis) with monocytes, macrophages, and connective tissue proteins including fibrin. Fibrosis of the skin and subcutaneous tissues may be initiated by increased gene expression and production of transforming growth factor-beta1. Vascular endothelial growth factor may be involved in the capillary proliferation that has been reported in the skin by a number of authors. Increased expression of several tissue metalloproteinases has been reported both in liposclerotic skin and periulcer skin. The tissue inhibitors of metalloproteinases are also increased and the net result is unclear. Treatment of venous disease using micronized purified flavonoid fraction moderates some of the inflammatory markers, including leukocyte ligand expression and endothelial adhesion molecule shedding. These compounds have also been shown to reduce leukocyte-endothelial adhesion in animal models of ischemia-reperfusion injury. Many inflammatory processes have now been shown to be involved in the development of the skin changes in patients with chronic venous disease. However, the precise sequence of events that leads to leg ulceration is still unclear. Pharmacologic treatments aimed at moderating some of these inflammatory processes are now under investigation as potential ways of treating patients with the more advanced stages of venous disease.

Angiology (Vol. 52, Issue 8 SUPPL. 1).

Comparative Histopathological Study of the Venous Wall of Chronic Venous Insufficiency and Varicose Disease

Nisarat Dhanarak, Burapa Kanchanabat

Abstract

Objective: To investigate venous histopathology of chronic venous insufficiency and varicose patients (C2).

Methods: Retrospective review of venous histopathology of 52 patients (13, 8, 2, and 28 were C2, C4, C5 and C6).

Results: The intimal thickness, intimal fibrosis, total thickness and intimal/total thickness ratio were highest in venous clinical severity score 0, 1 chronic venous insufficiency (no or minimal varicosity) follow by Venous Clinical Severity Score 2,3 chronic venous insufficiency (trunkal varice) and C2 veins (mean intimal thickness 62, 36, 26 μm, mean intimal fibrosis 74%, 72%, 65%, mean total

thickness 184, 159, 133 μm, mean intimal/total thickness ratio 0.32, 0.20, 0.21). The statistical significances were found when comparing intimal thickness, intimal fibrosis, intimal/total thickness ratio and total thickness of Venous Clinical Severity Score 0, 1 chronic venous insufficiency veins and C2 veins. The medial changes are relatively constant among groups.

Conclusion: Compared with C2 vein, the intimal changes in chronic venous insufficiency venous wall differ, particularly in the VCSS 0, 1 chronic venous insufficiency.

Phlebology. 2016 Oct;31(9):649-53.

Microcirculation in Chronic Venous Insufficiency

ME Gschwandtner, H Ehringer

Abstract

In this review, the anatomy and physiology of the venous system and its pathophysiology are described. Theories regarding the possible causes of disturbances in venous microangiopathy are summarized. The theories concern the deoxygenation of red blood cells, arteriovenous shunts, fibrin cuffs, and the trapping of growth factors and/or white blood cells. Furthermore, microlymphatic, neurologic and hemorheologic disturbances in venous disease are outlined. Findings in venous microangiopathy obtained from histology, capillary microscopy, microlymphography, laser Doppler fluxmetry and transcutaneous oxygen partial pressure are detailed. Finally, the recently discovered pattern of perfusion in microcirculation within and around venous ulcers is discussed.

Vascular Medicine, (2001), 6(3)

Microangiopathy of Cutaneous Blood and Lymphatic Capillaries in Chronic Venous Insufficiency (CVI)

U K Franzeck, P Haselbach, D Speiser, A Bollinger

Abstract

The severity of microangiopathy in patients with chronic venous insufficiency (CVI) determines the extent of the trophic disturbances of the skin. Resulting from valvular incompetence of deep and/or perforating veins and the accompanying venous outflow obstruction caused by deep venous thrombosis (DVT), the increased ambulatory venous pressure heads are transmitted retrograde into the microvasculature of the skin at the ankle region. In the present study, we have assessed the changes in the cutaneous microvasculature by dynamic fluorescence video microscopy, fluorescence microlymphography, and transcutaneous oxygen tension (tcPO2) measurements. In mild forms of CVI, capillary density, morphologic characteristics, and tcPO2 are still normal. Fluorescent light intensity is, however, significantly increased, indicating an increased transcapillary diffusion of sodium fluorescein (NaF) as a marker for enhanced leakage of the capillaries in the early stage of the disease. The pericapillary halo diameters are significantly enlarged, compared to controls (p < 0.01). In the severe stages of CVI and in patients with venous ulcers, capillary thromboses, probably caused by endothelium-blood cell interactions, may lead to a reduced capillary density. In order to enlarge the exchange surface area, the remaining skin capillaries become tortuous (capillary tufts). Parallel to the reduced capillary number, tcPO2 decreases and can be extremely low at the ulcer rim or at white atrophy spots. Fibrin cuffs are not a specific finding for venous ulceration and do not significantly impair oxygen diffusion. Fluorescence microlymphography permits visualization of the lymphatic capillaries of the superficial skin. In severe stages of CVI, the lymphatic capillary network at the medial ankle area is destroyed, and the remaining lymphatic capillary fragments have an increased permeability to FITC-dextran with a molecular weight of 150,000. These findings demonstrate a special lymphatic microangiopathy in CVI, suggesting an additional lymphatic component in the edema formation.

Yale Journal of Biology and Medicine, 1993:66(1).

Significance of Cutaneous Microangiopathy for the Pathogenesis of Dermatitis in Venous Congestion Due to Chronic Venous Insufficiency

M Jünger, U Hahn, S Bort, T Klyscz, M Hahn, G Rassner

Abstract

Skin damage due to chronic venous insufficiency is preceded by severe microangiopathy of skin. With increasing clinical symptoms like edema, hyperpigmentation, induration, ulcer and atrophy blanche number of nutritive capillaries and transcutaneous oxygen-tension decreases, transcapillary, and interstitial leakage increases and cutaneous vascular reserve disappears. These congruent results were found by means of capillaroscopy, fluorescence-videomicroscopy, transcutaneously measured oxygen partial pressure and Laser Doppler Fluxmetry. Most of capillaries are elongated and tortuous, especially in ulcer stage they look glomerular. Compared to pin-shaped capillaries glomerular capillaries contribute less to nutrition because of functional AV-shunts. As dilated capillaries are already seen in skin areas without any trophic skin changes, cutaneous microangiopathy seems to be first consequence of venous hemodynamic disturbances which then is followed by skin disease. As severe microangiopathy still remains after healing of ulcer, it explains frequent recurrencies.

Wiener Medizinische Wochenschrift (1946), 144(10–11).

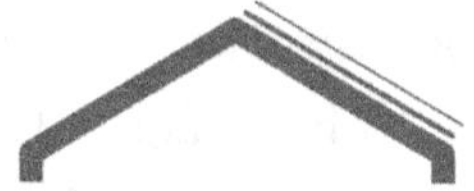

Current Aspects of Endothelial Protection in Treatment of Patients With Chronic Venous Insufficiency at the Stage of Trophic Disorders

Yu M Stoiko, V G Gudymovich, A V Tsyplyashchuk

Abstract

The authors analysed the results of comprehensive examination and treatment of a total of 40 patients presenting with lower limb chronic venous insufficiency at the stage of trophic disorders (class C6), including 28 (70%) patients with varicose disease of lower extremities and 12 (30%)

patients with post-thrombotic disease. Studying the microcirculatory blood flow by means of laser Doppler flowmetry showed a statistically significant ($p<0.05$) baseline decrease in the index of microcirculation in patients (12.2 ± 2.4 perf. units for varicose disease and 10.8 ± 1.8 perf. units for post-thrombotic disease) as compared with the control group of apparently healthy volunteers (20.4 ± 1.5 perf. units). All stages of treatment included the program of stimulation of reparative processes and normalization of microcirculation by means of sulodexide. Conservative measures were independent therapeutic procedures in 31 patients. Of these, trophic ulcers completely epithelialized in 9 patients and decreased by half of its initial surface in 22 patients. The study of the microcirculatory blood flow in dynamics suggested improvement of microcirculation during treatment. Hence, comprehensive therapy using sulodexide in patients with venous trophic ulcers is accompanied by an endothelium-protecting effect and leads to improvement of the indices of microcirculation of the skin of the crus.

Angiol Sosud Khir. 2016;22(4):109-114.

Neutrophil Activation and Mediators of Inflammation in Chronic Venous Insufficiency

S *mith P.D.*

Abstract

The effect of venous hypertension on the state of activation of leucocytes has been investigated in patients with venous disease and control subjects. Leucocytes become 'trapped' in the circulation of the leg during periods of venous hypertension produced by sitting or standing. This is greater in the limbs of patients with chronic venous disease than controls. Studies of the plasma levels of neutrophil granule enzymes show that these are increased during periods of venous hypertension, suggesting that this causes activation of the neutrophils. Investigation of the leucocyte surface ligand CD11b shows that the more activated neutrophils and monocytes are sequestered during venous hypertension. Measurement of plasma levels of the soluble parts of the vascular (VCAM), intercellular (ICAM) and endothelial leucocyte (ELAM) adhesion molecules show that these are all elevated in patients with chronic venous disease compared to controls. Following 30 min of venous hypertension produced by standing, these levels are further increased. These data suggest that venous hypertension causes neutrophil and monocyte activation, which in turn causes injury to the endothelium. I believe that this may be the mechanism that initiates the pathological processes which lead to venous ulceration. It has recently been shown that the venotonic drug Daflon 500 mg (450 mg diosmin, 50 mg hesperidin, Servier, France) influences these processes. Surface expression of CD62L is reduced in neutrophils and monocytes, and plasma levels of soluble endothelial adhesion molecules are reduced. These observations may explain the anti-inflammatory effects of Daflon 500 mg.

J Vasc Res. 1999;36 Suppl 1:24-36

Deleterious Effects of White Cells in the Course of Skin Damage in CVI

P*D Coleridge Smith*

Abstract

Venous ulceration remains a common problem and a significant challenge to the physicians treating it. Many theories have been advanced in the past to explain its causes but there is little evidence to support tissue hypoxia as the main factor, as was once thought. In recent years attention has focussed on the inflammatory events which attend venous disease and the development of venous ulceration. It has been proposed that these form a major contribution to the development of venous leg ulcers.

In the arterial system an analogous series of events appears to cause damage following severe ischemia. Massive neutrophil activation in the microcirculation following reperfusion of a tissue results in severe, ischemic damage to that tissue. A similar series of events is proposed to explain venous disease. During venous hypertension leukocytes are sequestrated in the microcirculation of the lower limb. It has been shown that these undergo activation whilst they are in the leg. The exact location of leukocyte sequestration is unclear but it is suggested that this may occur in the skin. The damage caused to the lower limb skin components can be identified by measuring plasma levels of endothelial adhesion molecules, which are shed into the circulation following a period of venous hypertension. In the long term this leads to a chronic inflammatory state in the skin in some patients where venous hypertension is sustained or there is susceptibility to venous hypertension. The resulting inflammatory process is referred to as "lipodermatosclerosis" and has a number of well-known clinical features. There is proliferation of the dermal capillaries eventually leading to a "glomerulus" like appearance. In the skin and subcutaneous tissues there is fibrosis. The microcirculation in the papillary dermis is surrounded by an inflammatory cellular infiltrate. The importance of understanding the mechanisms of the development of venous ulceration is in creating new treatments for this problem. Compression treatment has been effective in healing leg ulcers for thousands of years. Surgical treatment offers a possible cure in patients where superficial venous reflux is the main problem. Deep vein reconstruction is only suitable for a few patients. Many venous ulcers can be healed by compression, only to recur within a few months. Pharmacological treatments may offer the possibility of more rapid ulcer healing and the maintenance of an ulcer- free state if the correct pathophysiological mechanisms can be identified and addressed.

Int Angiol. 2002 Jun;21(2 Suppl 1):26-32.

THROMBOPHILIA

Protein C deficiency in a controlled series of unselected outpatients: an infrequent but clear risk factor for venous thrombosis (Leiden Thrombophilia Study)

T Koster, FR Rosendaal, E Briet, FJ van der Meer, LP Colly, PH Trienekens, SR Poort, PH Reitsma and JP Vandenbroucke

Abstract

A deficiency of protein C (PC), antithrombin, or protein S is strongly associated with deep-vein thrombosis in selected patients and their families. However, the strength of the association with venous thrombosis in the general population is unknown. This study was a population-based, patient- control study of 474 consecutive outpatients, aged less than 70 years, with a first, objectively diagnosed, episode of venous thrombosis and without an underlying malignant disease, and 474 healthy controls who matched for age and sex. Relative risks were estimated as matched odds ratios. Based on a single measurement, there were 22 (4.6%) patients with a PC deficiency (PC activity, less than 0.67 U/mL or PC antigen, less than 0.33 U/mL when using coumarins). Among the controls, the frequency was 1.5% (seven subjects).

Thus, there is a threefold increase in risk of thrombosis in subjects with PC levels below

0.67 or 0.33 U/mL (matched odds ratio, 3.1%; 95% confidence interval (CI), 1.4 to 7.0). When a PC deficiency was based on two repeated measurements, the relative risk for thrombosis increased to 3.8 (95% CI, 1.3 to 10); when it was based on DNA-confirmation, the relative risk increased further to 6.5 (95% CI, 1.8 to 24). In addition, there was a gradient in thrombosis risk, according to PC levels. The results for antithrombin are similar to those for PC, although less pronounced (relative risk, 2.2; 95% CI,

1.0 to 4.7). We could not find an association between reduced total protein S (relative risk, 0.7; 95% CI,

0.3 to 1.8) or free protein S levels (relative risk, 1.6; 95% CI, 0.6 to 4.0) and thrombosis risk. Although not very frequent, PC and antithrombin deficiency are clearly associated with an increase in thrombosis risk.

Blood, Vol 85, No 10 (May 15). 1995: 2756-2761

Venous Thromboembolism and Other Venous Disease in the Tecumseh Community Health Study

William W. Coon, M.D., Park W. Willis, Iii, M.D., And Jacob B. Keller, M.P.H.

Abstract

The prevalence and incidence of venous thromboembolism and other venous disease has been determined as part of a longitudinal study of health and disease in a Michigan community. When these data are extrapolated to 1970 U.S. census figures, a rough estimate of annual incidence of clinically recognized deep venous fhrombosis is over 250,000 cases while that of superficial thrombophlebitis is over 123,000. An estimated 24 million US citizens have "significant" varicose veins while 6 to 7 million have stasis changes in the skin of the legs and 400,000 to 500,000 have or have had a varicose ulcer. The relatively high frequency of these conditions in the adult population of Tecumseh, Michigan, indicates that they represent several of the more common medical problems encountered by the practicing physician.

The frequency of development and prevalence of venous thromboembolism and other interrelated venous conditions in the US population. Published estimates have been derived from data obtained from diagnoses of hospitalized patients. While figures extracted from a hospital population may provide a reasonable estimate of the frequency of recognized fatal pulmonary embolism, they probably represent a gross underestimate of the prevalence of deep and superficial venous thrombosis and nonfatal pulmonary embolism and provide no reliable approximation of the frequency of varicose veins, stasis skin changes, or varicose ulcers. The Tecumseh Community Health Study has provided the milieu required to determine the frequency of appearance of these conditions in a segment of the US population.

Circulation:. 1973 Oct;48(4):839-46.

How to work up hypercoagulability

Michael Laposata, MD, PhD, Elizabeth M. Van Cott, MD

This is the fifth in a periodic series of articles written by members of the CAP Coagulation Resource Committee and focusing on laboratory evaluation of coagulation disorders.

A 28-year-old man was repairing a sink in his home when he became acutely short of breath. He was taken to the emergency room, where medical personnel established a diagnosis of pulmonary embolism. Two years earlier, the patient had suffered a deep vein thrombosis and was anticoagulated with warfarin for six months. He was evaluated around the time of his deep vein thrombosis and found to have normal values for what his primary care physician believed was the full battery of laboratory tests appropriate for identifying acquired or congenital hypercoagulation risk factors. However, the patient was tested only for antiphospholipid antibodies, protein C, protein S, and antithrombin. He was not evaluated for factor V Leiden, the prothrombin G20210A mutation, or homocysteine. Because the patient's antiphospholipid antibody tests and protein C, protein S, and antithrombin levels were normal, his physician terminated his Coumadin therapy at six months, in accordance with published guidelines for treating a spontaneous venous clot in the absence of identifiable risk factors.1

After his second thrombotic event (the pulmonary embolism), the patient was referred to our practice for further evaluation. We tested for activated protein C resistance, the prothrombin G20210A mutation, and obtained a homocysteine level. In this evaluation, the patient was found to be heterozygous for the prothrombin G20210A mutation and heterozygous for factor V Leiden and had no evidence of hyperhomocysteinemia.

The published recommendation for patients with one spontaneous thrombosis and a congenital risk factor (such as factor V Leiden in combination with the prothrombin G20210A mutation) is lifelong warfarin therapy.1 Had the warfarin not been discontinued after his first thrombotic event, the second, more life-threatening clot may have been prevented.

Primary care physicians are now confronted with an array of new diagnostic tests at a faster rate than ever before, particularly in the area of thrombophilia. This poses an educational challenge to physicians. Featured in this area are six algorithms for selecting and interpreting tests that lead to a diagnosis of activated protein C resistance, the prothrombin G20210A mutation, hyperhomocysteinemia, protein C deficiency, protein S deficiency, and antithrombin deficiency. (Antiphospholipid antibodies were the focus of the coagulation case study published in the March 1999 issue of CAP TODAY, page 84.) These flowcharts are evolving rapidly. They represent one current approach to diagnosing hypercoagulable states associated with these six laboratory abnormalities. The current case illustrates the diagnosis of two of the more common risk factors for thrombosis. Future coagulation case studies published as part of this series will refer to the diagnostic algorithms in this article.

CAP Today. 2000 Jan;14(1):24-6

Hypercoagulable states: an algorithmic approach to laboratory testing and update on monitoring of direct oral anticoagulants

Megan O. Nakashima and Heesun J. Rogerscorresponding author

Abstract

Hypercoagulability can result from a variety of inherited and, more commonly, acquired conditions. Testing for the underlying cause of thrombosis in a patient is complicated both by the number and variety of clinical conditions that can cause hypercoagulability as well as the many potential assay interferences. Using an algorithmic approach to hypercoagulability testing provides the ability to tailor assay selection to the clinical scenario. It also reduces the number of unnecessary tests performed, saving cost and time, and preventing potential false results. New oral anticoagulants are powerful tools for managing hypercoagulable patients; however, their use introduces new challenges in terms of test interpretation and therapeutic monitoring. The coagulation laboratory plays an essential role in testing for and treating hypercoagulable states. The input of laboratory professionals is necessary to guide appropriate testing and synthesize interpretation of results.

Keywords: Hypercoagulability, Algorithmic approach, Antiphospholipid syndrome, direct oral anticoagulant, venous thromboembolism

Blood Res. 2014 Jun; 49(2): 85–94.

Hypercoagulability

B enjamin Senst; Prasanna Tadi; Amandeep Goyal; Arif Jan.

Abstract

Hypercoagulability or thrombophilia is the increased tendency of blood to thrombose. A normal and healthy response to bleeding for maintaining hemostasis involves the formation of a stable clot, and the process is called coagulation. Hypercoagulability describes the pathologic state of exaggerated coagulation or coagulation in the absence of bleeding. Different constituents of the blood interact to create a thrombus. Arterial thrombosis, such as in myocardial infarction and stroke, is different from venous thromboses, such as deep venous thrombosis (DVT) and pulmonary embolism (PE). Pathophysiology and treatment differ for arterial and venous thrombosis, but risk factors overlap. Thromboembolism describes the migration of a local thrombus to distant areas leading to luminal obstruction. Different hypercoagulable states and thrombophilic diseases cause hypercoagulability. As early as 1906 Wasserman et al., described the antiphospholipid syndrome. In 1965 Egeberg et al., discovered antithrombin III deficiency. During the 1980s protein C (Griffin, 1981) and protein S (Comp, 1984) deficiencies were introduced. Dahlbäck discovered activated protein C resistance in 1993, which is commonly caused by the factor V Leiden mutation.

Hypercoagulable States

Frequently, patients who have deep venous thrombosis or pulmonary embolism are labeled has having a hypercoagulable state. Labeling patients as hypercoagulable has implications in many aspects of their care. These include, but are not limited to, medications (life long warfarin treatment & careful selection of medications so as not to alter the bioavailability of warfarin) and diet (to limit ingestion of Vitamin K if on warfarin).

It is important to realize that clots develop for many reasons. The true Hypercoagulable States are only one category in this differential diagnosis. Therefore, before labeling a patient as hypercoagulable, these other causes must be ruled out.

Patient has had a recent surgical procedure. Surgery allows exposure of blood to tissue factor.

- Immobilization causing stastis of blood.

- Obesity

- Malignancy, especially adenocarcinoma

- Previous history of deep venous thrombosis (DVT) or pulmonary embolus (PE)

- Pregnancy (up to 2 months postpartum)

- Fracture

- Heart failure (causes stasis)

- Travel

- Oral contraceptive use

Therefore, all that clots is not hypercoagulable. When a person presents with a DVT, PE, or some other clot, the patient's history should be probed for the above risk factors. Then, one can pursue looking for a true hypercoagulable state. For someone to be labeled as having a hypercoagulable state, the following four criteria must be considered; usually any two will justify laboratory investigation:

- Thrombosis, first time at age < 40 y/o
- Recurrent thrombosis
- Family history of thrombosis

- Thrombosis in unusual sites (cerebral veins, hepatic veins, renal veins, IVC, mesenteric veins) There are several disease processes related to the clotting cascade that result in a hypercoagulable state. To be considered for such a disease, the patient should meet at least 1 or 2 of the above 4 criteria. Identifying these individuals is very important because of the necessity of instituting prophylactic anticoagulation as well as making dietary changes and providing genetic counseling. These diseases and their dates of discovery are the following:

- Antithrombin III deficiency (1965)
- Protein C deficiency (1981)
- Protein S deficiency (1984)
- Activated Protein C resistance (Factor V Leiden) (1993)
- Antiphospholipid syndrome (1970s-1980s)
- Prothrombin 20210 defect (1996)
- Dysfibrinolysis (1990s)
- Please click to get detailed information on each condition.

Congenital deficiency of a normal protein which in turn leads to thrombosis is a special hypercoagulable state termed thrombophilia. Therefore, the above disorders are more appropriately termed thrombophilic states. This is in contrast to hemophilia which results from the congenital deficiency of a procoagulant protein. The conditions listed above account for only about 50% of inherited thrombophilia, implying that we have more illnesses to discover. Also, some rare patients may be doubly or even triply heterozygous for the above disorders and therefore have additive risk for thrombosis.

StatPearls Publishing; 2023 Jan

Thrombophilia as a predictor of persistent residual vein thrombosis

Luca Spiezia, Daniela Tormene, Raffaele Pesavento, Laura Salmaso, Paolo Simioni, Paolo Prandoni

To compare the probability of leg vein recanalization between carriers and non-carriers of thrombophilia after an episode of deep vein thrombosis (DVT) of the lower extremities, we reviewed the clinical records of 472 patients with proximal DVT who were diagnosed with thrombophilia and had long-term ultrasound scanning.

One hundred and thirty-seven patients (29.0%) were carriers of thrombophilia. After adjusting for age, sex, DVT localization and modality of presentation,

the hazard ratio of vein recanalization in thrombophilic compared with non-thrombophilic patients was 0.49 (95% CI, 0.38 to 0.63).

These findings suggest that thrombophilia is an independent predictor of persistent residual vein thrombosis.

Haematologica March 2008 93: 479-480

Risk of recurrent venous thromboembolism in patients with common thrombophilia: a systematic review

Wai Khoon Ho, Graeme J Hankey, Daniel J Quinlan, John W Eikelboom

Abstract

The 2 most common genetic polymorphisms that predispose to a first episode of venous thromboembolism (VTE) are factor V Leiden (FVL) and prothrombin G20210A. However, the effect of these polymorphisms on the risk of recurrent VTE is unclear. We performed a meta-analysis to obtain best estimates of the relative risk of recurrent VTE associated with these genetic polymorphisms. Electronic and manual searches were used to identify cohort studies of patients with a first episode of VTE that reported the incidence of objectively confirmed recurrence following discontinuation of anticoagulation among those with or without heterozygous FVL or prothrombin G20210A polymorphism. Thirteen reports fulfilled our criteria for inclusion. Pooled results from 10 studies involving 3104 patients with first-ever VTE revealed that FVL was present in 21.4% of patients (95% confidence interval [CI], 20%-23%) and associated with an increased odds of recurrent VTE of 1.41 (95% CI, 1.14-1.75; P = .08 for heterogeneity). Pooled results from 9 studies involving 2903 patients with first- ever VTE revealed that prothrombin G20210A was present in 9.7% of patients (95% CI, 9%-11%) and associated with an increased odds of recurrent VTE of 1.72 (95% CI, 1.27-2.31; P = .19). The estimated population-attributable risk of recurrence for FVL was 9.0% (95% CI, 4.5%-13.2%) and for prothrombin G20210A was 6.7% (95% CI, 3.4%-9.9%). Heterozygous FVL and prothrombin G20210A are each associated with a significantly increased risk of recurrent VTE after a first event, but the magnitude of the increase in risk is modest and by itself is unlikely to merit extended-duration anticoagulation. These data call into question the cost-effectiveness of routine testing for these common inherited thrombophilic polymorphisms among patients with a first episode of VTE.

Arch Intern Med. 2006 Apr 10;166(7):729-36.

Thrombophilia, Clinical Factors, and Recurrent Venous Thrombotic Events

S *verre C. Christiansen, MD; Suzanne C. Cannegieter, MD, PhD ; Ted Koster, MD, PhD ; et al Jan P. Vandenbroucke, MD, PhD ; Frits R. Rosendaal, MD, PhD*

Abstract

Context: Data on the recurrence rate of venous thrombotic events and the effect of several risk factors, including thrombophilia, remain controversial. The potential benefit of screening for thrombophilia with respect to prophylactic strategies and duration of anticoagulant treatment is not yet known.

Objectives: To estimate the recurrence rate of thrombotic events in patients after a first thrombotic event and its determinants, including thrombophilic abnormalities.

Design, setting, and patients: Prospective follow-up study of 474 consecutive patients aged 18 to 70 years without a known malignancy treated for a first objectively confirmed thrombotic event at anticoagulation clinics in the Netherlands. The Leiden Thrombophilia Study (LETS) was conducted from 1988 through 1992 and patients were followed up through 2000.

Main outcome measures: Recurrent thrombotic event based on thrombophilic risk factors, sex, type of initial thrombotic event (idiopathic or provoked), oral contraceptive use, elevated levels of factors VIII, IX, XI, fibrinogen, homocysteine, and anticoagulant deficiencies.

Results: A total of 474 patients were followed up for mean (SD) of 7.3 (2.7) years and complete follow- up was achieved in 447 (94%). Recurrence of thrombotic events occurred in 90 patients during a total of 3477 patient-years. The rate of thrombotic event recurrence was 25.9 per 1000 patient-years (95% confidence interval [CI], 20.8-31.8 per 1000 patient-years). The incidence rate of recurrence was highest during the first 2 years (31.9 per 1000 patient-years; 95% CI, 20.3-43.5 per 1000 patient-years). The risk of thrombotic event recurrence was 2.7 times (95% CI, 1.8-4.2 times) higher in men than in women. Patients whose initial thrombotic event was idiopathic had a higher risk of a thrombotic event recurrence than patients whose initial event was provoked (hazard ratio [HR], 1.9; 95% CI, 1.2-2.9). Women who used oral contraceptives during follow-up had a higher thrombotic event recurrence rate (28.0 per 1000 patient-years; 95% CI, 15.9-49.4 per 1000 patient-years) than those who did not (12.9 per 1000 patient- years; 95% CI, 7.9-21.2 per 1000 patient-years). Recurrence risks of a thrombotic event by laboratory abnormality ranged from an HR of 0.6 (95% CI, 0.3-1.1) in patients with elevated levels of factor XI to an HR of 1.8 (95% CI, 0.9-3.7) for patients with anticoagulant deficiencies.

Conclusions: Prothrombotic abnormalities do not appear to play an important role in the risk of a recurrent thrombotic event. Testing for prothrombotic defects has little consequence with respect to prophylactic strategies. Clinical factors are probably more important than laboratory abnormalities in determining the duration of anticoagulation therapy.

JAMA. 2005;293(19):2352-2361

Pro CR Global: An Effective Screening Test for Thrombophilia

P. K. Gupta. Ahmed M. Kannan, S. N. Dwivedi, V. P. Choudhry, Renu Saxena

Abstract

In the present study, the Pro CR Global test was evaluated as a screening test for estimation of the activity of the main plasma components of the anticoagulant protein C (PC) / protein S (PS) pathway; 300 patients with a history of thrombosis were investigated for Pro CR Global. It was positive in 74 patients. Tests for estimation of PC, PS, activated protein C resistance (APCR), and lupus anticoagulant (LAC) were performed in all the patients with abnormal Pro CR Global and in 10 patients with normal Pro CR Global. In all, 66 of the 74 patients had a defect in PC/PS/ APCR or LAC; 18 patients had both PC and PS deficiency, 25 had PS deficiency alone, 10 had PC deficiency alone, one had APCR alone, eight had PS, PC deficiency with APCR, and four had PS deficiency with APCR. In the 10 patients who tested negative with the Pro CR Global test, PC, APCR, and LAC were negative in all. However, PS deficiency was seen in two of them. The sensitivity and specificity of Pro CR Global, calculated with respect to positivity of PC, PS, LAC, or APCR as the gold standard, were 97% and 50%, respectively. The diagnostic accuracy of the assay was 88.1%. It is thus recommended that Pro CR Global can be used effectively as a screening test to detect abnormality in the PC/PS/APCR/LAC pathway.

Am. J.Hematol. 74:208–210, 2003

Should patients with venous thromboembolism be screened for thrombophilia?

J*ames E Dalen*

Abstract

In the mid-19th century, Virchow identified hypercoagulability as part of the triad leading to venous thrombosis, but the specific causes of hypercoagulability remained a mystery for another century. The first specific cause to be identified was antithrombin III deficiency. Many other causes of thrombophilia, both genetic and acquired, have been discovered since then. The 2 most common genetic causes of thrombophilia are the Leiden mutation of factor V and the G20210A mutation of prothrombin. The most common acquired cause is antiphospholipid syndrome. These factors increase the relative risk of an initial episode of venous thromboembolism (VTE) by a factor of 2 to 10, but the actual risk remains relatively modest. Therefore, thrombophilia screening to prevent initial episodes of VTE is not indicated, except possibly in women with a family history of idiopathic VTE who are considering oral contraceptive therapy. Some physicians screen for thrombophilia to aid decision making concerning the duration of anticoagulant therapy. However, several studies have demonstrated that, with the exception of antiphospholipid syndrome, thrombophilia does not significantly increase the risk of recurrent VTE. On the other hand, idiopathic VTE significantly increases the risk of recurrence in patients with or without thrombophilia.

Am J Med. 2008 Jun;121(6):458-63.

THROMBOSIS

Association Between Superficial Vein Thrombosis and Deep Vein Thrombosis of the Lower Extremities

B *inder B, Lackner HK, Salmhofer W.*

Abstract

Superficial venous thrombosis (SVT), also termed superficial thrombophlebitis of the lower extremities is a common, generally benign condition characterized by tenderness, swelling, and induration occurring from thrombus formation within the superficial leg veins—most commonly the great saphenous vein (60%-80% of cases) and small saphenous vein (10%-20% of cases). Complications of SVT, such as pulmonary embolism, are extremely rare. However, according to one prevalence study, SVT may be associated with deep venous thrombosis (DVT) in up to 65% of cases. This suggests that the potential risk of thromboembolic complications stemming from SVTs may be underestimated.

In an informative prospective analysis, Binder and colleagues set out to determine the incidence of lower extremity DVT in patients with ultrasonography-confirmed SVT. They studied 46 outpatients (32 women and 14 men; mean age, 65 years) with clinical signs of lower extremity SVT. In this sample, risk factors for SVT included age older than 60 years (29 of 46 cases) and female gender (70%). All patients underwent color-coded duplex sonography and compression ultrasonography of all venous segments (groin to ankle) of both lower limbs. In addition, laboratory studies were conducted including a D-dimer assay and complete work-up for thrombophilic disorders (ie, protein C, protein S, antithrombin III deficiency, factor V Leiden mutation, and antiphospholipid antibodies).

In Binder and colleagues' SVT cohort, ultrasonography revealed concomitant, mostly asymptomatic DVT in 11 of 46 patients (24%). Although most of these cases (73%) occurred in the same leg as the SVT, 9% occurred in the contralateral leg, and 18% occurred in both legs. Five DVTs occurred in the ipsilateral leg through progression of the SVT into the deep venous system via perforating veins. D-dimer levels were elevated in 37 of 46 patients, and 8 patients had heterozygous mutations of factor V Leiden. The strongest risk factors for the development of DVT were SVT of the lower leg and increased D-dimer levels. In agreement with prior studies, additional DVT risk factors included age older than 60 years, female gender, and the presence of malignancy. [1,3] In contrast, SVTs located in the thigh region and the finding of normal D-dimer levels reduced the likelihood of concomitant DVT.

Primary risk factors for both SVT and DVT include the presence of varicose veins, a thrombophilic disorder (eg, factor V Leiden mutation), oral contraceptive use, immobilization, malignancy, trauma to the area, or history of thromboembolism.[1] In addition, much practical information can be gleaned from Binder and colleagues' recent analysis. As the investigators conclude:

SVT of the lower extremity may present a higher risk of associated DVT (24% in their cohort) than previously reported. As in the current study, DVT is often asymptomatic.

Although most DVT associated with SVT occurs in the ipsilateral leg (most commonly through propagation of thrombus through perforating veins into the deep venous system), DVT may also occur in noncontiguous sites of the same leg or even in the contralateral leg. This is likely due to an associated thrombophilic state.

In cases of SVT, elevated D-dimer levels predict a higher likelihood of concomitant DVT. Conversely, normal D-dimer levels reduce the risk of concomitant DVT.

On the basis of these observations, Binder and colleagues reasonably conclude that patients with SVT, especially of the lower leg, should be evaluated for the possibility of concomitant DVT; this should be done using ultrasonography to inspect the deep venous networks of both legs, from groin to ankle.

Assessment of both legs is especially crucial in patients with SVT and elevated D-dimer levels because such individuals are at high risk of developing concurrent DVT.

Arch Dermatol. 2009 Jul;145(7):753-7

Residual venous thrombosis as a predictive factor of recurrent venous thromboembolism

P *aolo Prandoni, Anthonie W.A., LensingMartin H.,et al*

Abstract

Background: The optimum duration of anticoagulant therapy after an episode of deep venous thrombosis (DVT) is controversial. Contributing to the controversy is uncertainty about whether residual venous thrombosis, as assessed by repeated ultrasonography over time, increases the risk for recurrent thromboembolism. **Objective**: To determine the risk for recurrent thromboembolism in patients who have persistent residual thrombosis compared with patients who have early vein recanalization. Design: Prospective cohort study. Setting: A university hospital in Padua, Italy. Patients: 313 consecutive symptomatic outpatients with proximal DVT who received conventional short-term anticoagulation. Measurements: Ultrasonographic assessment of the common femoral and popliteal veins was performed 3 months after acute DVT in all patients and at 6, 12, 24, and 36 months in patients found to have residual venous thrombosis. Veins were considered recanalized if they were 2.0 mm or less in diameter on a single test or 3.0 mm or less in diameter on two consecutive tests. Recurrent thromboembolism was assessed during a 6-year period. **Results**: The cumulative incidence of normal results on ultrasonography was 38.8% at 6 months, 58.1% at 12 months, 69.3% at 24 months, and 73.8% at 36 months. Of 58 recurrent episodes, 41 occurred while the patient had residual thrombosis. The hazard ratio for recurrent thromboembolism was 2.4 (95% CI, 1.3 to 4.4; P = 0.004) for patients with persistent residual thrombosis versus those with early vein recanalization. **Conclusion**s: Residual venous thrombosis is an important risk factor for recurrent thromboembolism. Ultrasonographic assessment of residual venous thrombosis may help clinicians modify the duration of anticoagulation in patients with DVT.

Br J Haematol. 2011 Apr;153(2):168-78.

The post-thrombotic syndrome

S usan R Kahn

Abstract

The post-thrombotic syndrome (PTS) is a frequent, sometimes disabling complication of deep vein thrombosis (DVT) that reduces quality of life and is costly. This article discusses risk factors for PTS after DVT and available means to prevent and treat PTS, with a focus on new information in the field. After DVT, PTS will develop in 20% to 50% of patients, and severe PTS, including venous ulcers, will develop in 5% to 10%. The principal risk factors for PTS are anatomically extensive DVT, recurrent ipsilateral DVT, persistent leg symptoms 1 month after acute DVT, obesity, and older age. By preventing the initial DVT and ipsilateral DVT recurrence, primary and secondary prophylaxes of DVT will prevent cases of PTS. Based on recent evidence from a large multicenter trial, routine use of elastic compression stockings (ECS) after DVT to prevent PTS is not advocated, but in patients with DVT-related leg swelling that is bothersome, a trial of ECS is reasonable. Selecting DVT patients for catheter-directed thrombolytic treatment as a means of preventing PTS should be done on a case-by-case basis, with a focus on patients with extensive thrombosis, recent symptoms onset, and low bleeding risk. For patients with established PTS, daily use of

ECS may help to relieve symptoms and edema. Intermittent compression devices can be tried in patients with moderate-to-severe PTS whose symptoms are inadequately controlled with ECS alone. A supervised exercise training program may improve PTS symptoms. Management of post-thrombotic ulcers should ideally involve a multidisciplinary approach. Important areas for future research are summarized.

Hematology Am Soc Hematol Educ Program. 2016 Dec 2;2016(1):413-418.

Epidemiology and Risk Factors for Venous Thrombosis

Mary Cushman

Abstract

Venous thrombosis, including deep vein thrombosis and pulmonary embolism, occurs at an annual incidence of about 1 per 1000 adults. Rates increase sharply after around age 45 years, and are slightly higher in men than women in older age. Major risk factors for thrombosis, other than age, include exogenous factors such as surgery, hospitalization, immobility, trauma, pregnancy and the puerperium and hormone use, and endogenous factors such as cancer, obesity, and inherited and acquired disorders of hypercoagulation. This review focuses on epidemiology of venous thrombosis and the general implications of this in patient management.

Semin Hematol. 2007 Apr; 44(2): 62–69.

DVT

Evaluation of Factor VIII as a Risk Factor in Indian Patients with DVT

Darpanarayan Hazra, Indrani Sen, Edwin Stephen, Sunil Agarwal, Sukesh Chandran Nair, and Joy Mammen

Introduction

Elevated factor VIII population in the Indian population has not been studied as a possible risk factor for deep vein thrombosis (DVT).

High factor VIII level is considered a predisposing factor for DVT and its recurrence.

However, it is known to vary among populations and its exact role in the etiopathogenesis of thrombophilia remains unknown.

Material and Methods

Factor VIII levels of patients with DVT who had undergone a prothrombotic work up as a part of their workup was compared to normal age matched controls in a 1: 3 ratio.

Results

1. There were 75 patients with DVT who had undergone a prothrombotic work up in the course of their treatment for lower limb DVT.

2. In these, 64% had levels of factor VIII more than 150 as compared to 63% of normal controls (p >0.05, not

significant).

Conclusion

1. Elevated factor VIII in the Indians may not be associated with the same thrombotic risk as seen in the West.
2. We find a variation in the levels of factor VIII with a different "normal" than what is reported in other populations.
3. This needs further study to elucidate the role of factor VIII in the evaluation and treatment of thrombophilia.

Surg Res Pract. 2015;2015:307879

Combination of a Normal D-Dimer Concentration and a Non-High Pretest Clinical Probability Score Is a Safe Strategy to Exclude Deep Venous Thrombosis

R.E.G. Schutgens, P. Ackermark, F.J.L.M. Haas, H.K. Nieuwenhuis, H.G. Peltenburg, A.H. Pijlman, M. Pruijm, R. Oltmans, J.C. Kelder, and D.H. Biesma

Abstract

Deep venous thrombosis can be diagnosed or rejected accurately by serial compression ultrasonography. In 2 studies with a follow-up period of, respectively, 3 and 6 months, venous thromboembolic complications were found in only 0.6% and 0.7% of patients with suspected deep venous thrombosis after normal serial ultrasonography.1,2 Serial ultrasonography, however, is inefficient because only 17% to 24% of patients suspected of deep venous thrombosis actually has it,1–6 and only 0.9% develop it after the initial normal ultrasonogram.2 Other noninvasive diagnostic tests, such as the pretest clinical probability score5–7 and the D-dimer measurement,4,7–14 are the subject of studies to reduce the need for ultrasonography. It has been proven safe to withhold anticoagulant treatment in patients with a low pretest clinical probability score and normal initial ultrasonogram6 and in patients with a normal D-dimer and normal ultrasonogram at first presentation.3,11,14 The next step, which is the subject of the present study, is to investigate the safety of the combination of a non-high pretest clinical probability score and a normal D-dimer level to replace ultrasonography as the initial test in the diagnostic management of patients suspected of having deep venous thrombosis.

Background— Serial ultrasonography is reliable for the diagnosis of deep venous thrombosis in symptomatic patients, but the low prevalence of thrombosis in this group renders the approach costly and inconvenient to patients. We studied the clinical validity of the combination of a pretest clinical probability score and a D-dimer test in the initial evaluation of patients suspected of deep venous thrombosis.

Methods and **Results** — Patients with a normal D-dimer concentration (<500 fibrin equivalent units [FEU] μg/L) and a non-high probability score (<3) had no further testing. Patients with a normal D-dimer concentration and a high probability score (≥3) underwent one ultrasonogram. Serial ultrasonography was performed in patients with an abnormal D-dimer concentration. Patients were followed for 3 months. A total of 812 patients were evaluable for efficacy. Only 1 of 176 patients (0.6%; 95% CI, 0.02% to 3.1%) with a normal D-dimer concentration and a non-high probability score developed thrombosis during follow-up. A normal D-dimer concentration and a high probability score were found in 39 patients; 3 of them (7.7%; 95% CI, 1.6% to 20.9%) had thrombosis at presentation, and one (2.8%; 95% CI, 0.07% to 14. 5%) developed pulmonary embolism during follow-up. In 306 of 597 patients (51.3%) with an abnormal D-dimer concentration, thrombosis was detected by serial ultrasonography. Six patients (2.1%; 95% CI, 0.8% to 4. 4%) developed thrombosis during follow-up. No deaths due to thromboembolism occurred during follow-up. The total need for ultrasonography was reduced by 29%.

Conclusion — the combination of a non-high pretest clinical probability score and a normal D-dimer concentration is a safe strategy to rule out deep venous thrombosis and to withhold anticoagulation.

Circulation. 2003 Feb 4;107(4):593-7.

Venous reflux has a limited effect on calf muscle pump dysfunction in post-thrombotic patients

*J*osé H. Haenen; Mirian C. H. Janssen; Alphonsus J. M. Brakkee; Herman Van Langen; Hub Wollersheim; Theo. M. De Boo; Stefan H. Skotnicki; Theo Thien

The purpose of the present study was to evaluate the relationship between calf muscle pump dysfunction (CMD) and the presence and location of valvular incompetence. Deep vein obstruction might influence CMD, and so venous outflow resistance (VOR) was measured. VOR and calf muscle pump function were measured in 81 patients, 7–13 years after venographically confirmed lower-extremity deep venous thrombosis. The supine venous pump function test (SVPT) measures CMD, and the VOR measures the presence of venous outflow obstructions, both with the use of strain-gauge plethysmography. Valvular incompetence was measured using duplex scanning in 16 vein segments of one leg. Venous reflux was measured in proximal veins using the Valsalva manoeuvre, and in the distal veins by distal manual compression with sudden release. Abnormal proximal venous reflux was defined as a reflux time of more than 1 s, and abnormal distal venous reflux as a reflux time of more than 0.5 s. No statistically significant relationship was found between the SVPT and either the location or the number of vein segments with reflux. Of the 81 patients, only nine still had an abnormally high VOR, and this VOR showed no relationship with the SVPT. In conclusion, venous reflux has a limited effect on CMD, as measured by the SVPT. The presence of a venous outflow obstruction did not significantly influence the SVPT. Duplex scanning and the SVPT are independent complementary tests for evaluating chronic venous insufficiency. *Clin Sci (Lond). 2000 Apr;98(4):449-54*

To What Extent Might Deep Venous Thrombosis and Chronic Venous Insufficiency Share a Common Etiology?

P *Colm Malone, P S Agutter*

Abstract

According to the valve cusp hypoxia hypothesis (VCHH), deep venous thrombosis is caused by sustained non-pulsatile (streamline) venous blood flow. This leads to hypoxemia in the valve pockets; hypoxic injury to the inner (parietalis) endothelium of the cusp leaflets activates the elk-1/egr-1 pathway, leading to leukocyte and platelet swarming at the site of injury and, potentially, blood coagulation. Here, we propose an extension of the VCHH to account for chronic venous insufficiency. First, should the foregoing events not proceed to frank thrombogenesis, the valves may nevertheless be chronically injured and become incompetent. Serial incompetence in lower limb valves may then generate "passive" venous hypertension. Second, should ostial valve thrombosis obstruct venous return from muscles via tributaries draining into the femoral vein, as Virchow illustrated, "active" venous hypertension may supervene: muscle contraction would force the blood in the vessels behind the blocked ostial valves to re-route. Passive or active venous hypertension opposes return flow, leading to luminal hypoxemia and vein wall distension, which in turn may impair vasa venarum perfusion; the resulting mural endothelial hypoxia would lead to leukocyte invasion of the wall and remodelling of the media. We propose that varicose veins result if gross active hypertension stretches the valve "rings", rendering attached valves incompetent caudad to obstructed sites, replacing normal centripetal flow in perforating veins with centrifugal flow and over-distending those vessels. We also discuss how hypoxemia-related venous/capillary wall lesions may lead to accumulation of leukocytes, progressive blockage of capillary blood flow, lipodermosclerosis and skin ulceration.

Int Angiol. 2009 Aug;28(4):254-68

Deep Venous Thrombosis Risk Factors

Kevin McLendon; Amandeep Goyal; Maximos Attia.

Definition/Introduction

The pathophysiology of venous thrombosis has been famously described by Rudolf Virchow, known as Virchow's triad, which includes stasis, endothelial injury, and hypercoagulability.[1] Venous thrombosis can be superficial venous thrombosis or deep venous thrombosis (DVT); the latter will be the focus of this article. While the most common origins are in the extremities, where the lower extremity is greater than the upper extremity, venous thrombotic events can occur at other vascular areas such as mesentery, pelvis, cerebral, portal tract, etc. DVTs, on their own, can cause morbidity due to postthrombotic syndrome involving local tissue injury. The most concerning complication with high mortality is associated with pulmonary embolism (PE) secondary to venous thromboembolism (VTE).

Several risk factors, both inherited and acquired, have been specifically studied and associated with venous thrombotic events, and identification of such risk factors can improve diagnostic approaches and, more importantly, the prevention of thrombotic events. Preventive strategies such as using pneumatic devices and prophylactic anticoagulation are a standard of care in hospital medicine, and such strategies are based on identifying the underlying risk factors in an individual patient.

Issues of Concern

Deep Venous Thrombosis Risk Factors

D VTs can either be provoked or unprovoked. Provoked thromboembolisms can be associated with known risk factors, most of which are time-limited, while unprovoked may indicate an increased tendency to clot. Most DVTs diagnosed in the emergency department are unprovoked and carry an increased risk of recurrence versus provoked: 15% versus 5% over the next 12 months. Risk factors for DVTs can be broadly classified as inherited or acquired, and up to 80% of patients experiencing a DVT have at least one and often multiple identifiable risk factors.[2]

Often patients with inherited thrombophilias are unaware of their condition until diagnosed with their first VTE. While their condition increases the risk of occurrence against the general population, their risk of recurrence is the same as those with unprovoked DVTs. The high number of unprovoked cases may be due to undiagnosed thrombophilias.

The incidence of VTEs is 30% to 100% higher in African-Americans than in White race individuals.[3][4] There is no gender predominance of DVTs; however, men are more likely to experience recurrent DVTs.[5] The risk of DVTs increases with advancing age, partially also due to an increase in the prevalence of medical conditions and other risk factors for DVTs in the elderly population. Smoking and obesity both have been associated with a higher risk for DVTs.[6][7]

Acquired

Several risk factors can contribute to the development of DVTs, and more than 50% of patients who suffer from a DVT have more than one acquired risk factor.[2] Further, the presence of an underlying inherited risk, in addition to a major medical illness or acquired risk factor, increases the risk for DVT by an odds ratio up to more than 80, depending on the underlying inherited risk present.[8] Below, we discuss the identified acquired risk factors for developing DVTs.

Surgeries, Trauma, and Immobilization

All surgeries, especially major orthopedic and neurovascular surgeries, are associated with a significantly higher risk of DVTs and PEs, especially in individuals with other risk factors such as advancing age, prior DVTs, and medical illnesses.[9] Prolonged surgical times and post-surgical immobilization times are further associated with increased risk for DVTs. Major, as well as minor trauma, confers significant risk for DVTs due to immobilization as well as anatomic risk.[10]

The 4-year recurrence of surgically provoked DVT is 5 to 11%, depending on the procedure. Immobilization associated with prolonged travel, by air or ground, increases the risk of DVTs by 2 to 4 folds.[11] Immobilization associated with other medical conditions, such as hemiplegia due to stroke, also increases the risk of DVTs.

Prior Thromboembolism

History of a prior thromboembolic event is a significant risk for recurrence, especially in patients with unprovoked DVTs and those with inherited or permanent risk factors.[12] A history of DVT is a risk for recurrent DVT, and a history of PE is a risk for recurrent DVT.

Malignancy

Malignancies are associated with hypercoagulability. In the cancer patient, there are a host of factors that determine the thrombogenic potential. In general, the larger the tumor and the less differentiated the cell line, the higher the risk. Further, using some chemotherapy agents, central venous catheters, and the need for surgery for malignancies also contribute to the risk of thromboembolic events. Venous thrombotic events may be as high as 12% with central venous catheters.[13]

Solid-organ malignancies (lung, pancreas, colorectal, kidney, prostate, etc.), as well as hematological malignancies (myeloproliferative neoplasms such as leukemias and myelomas), are associated with a high risk of VTEs. Metastatic cancers, acute leukemias, and myeloma carry the most significant risk. The following cancers are also known for higher thromboembolic potential: pancreatic, ovarian, stomach, renal, adenocarcinoma, glioblastoma, metastatic melanoma, and lymphoma.

Advanced breast or breast cancer treated with chemotherapy has a 10% rate of clinically significant VTE. Clotting risk in cancers treated with chemotherapy is highest during the induction phase, especially when treated with fluorouracil, tamoxifen, or L-asparaginase. Regardless of tumor stage, chemotherapy adjunctive red blood cell growth factors (EPO) increases risk. The use of thalidomide or lenalidomide for multiple myeloma treatment has also been identified as a risk factor.[14][15][16]

While known malignancies are present in most cases of malignancy-associated VTEs, thromboembolism can precede the diagnosis of malignancy as well.[17] In a Danish study, 78 percent of cancers were diagnosed before the event.[18]

Pregnancy

Pregnancy is a well-known risk factor for DVTs due to the hypercoagulable state and the obstruction of the inferior vena cave by the uterus. The risk is greatest in the post-partum period and in women with multiple pregnancies. The presence of other risk factors such as antiphospholipid antibodies, inherited thrombophilias, obesity, increased maternal age, hypertension, diabetes mellitus, smoking, and obesity further increases the risk. The estimated age-adjusted incidence of VTE is 5 to 50 times higher in pregnant versus non-pregnant women.

Antiphospholipid Antibody Syndrome (APLS)

The presence of antiphospholipid antibodies (APLA) is associated with an increased risk of arterial and venous thrombosis involving any organ system. DVTs are the most common thrombotic complication of APLS and are frequently recurrent.[19] In one study, APLAs were present in 14% of patients with recurrent VTEs.[20]

Chronic Medical Conditions

Several medical conditions have been associated with DVTs, including: Cardiac: Atherosclerosis, heart failure, hypertension, dyslipidemia

Renal: Chronic kidney disease, renal transplant, nephrotic syndrome, microalbuminuria Hematological: Polycythemia vera, paroxysmal nocturnal hemoglobinuria, hyperhomocysteinemia

Rheumatological: Behcet disease, rheumatoid arthritis, systemic lupus erythematosus, Antineutrophil cytoplasmic antibodies-associated vasculitis

Gastrointestinal: Inflammatory bowel disease

Infections: Sepsis, coronavirus disease 2019, tuberculosis Respiratory: Asthma, obstructive sleep apnea

Endocrine: Polycystic ovary syndrome, diabetes mellitus Iatrogenic

Several drugs have been associated with an increased risk of DVTs, contraceptive agents being the most important, especially in young women. Hormone replacement therapy in postmenopausal women is also associated with an increased risk of DVTs. Other drugs implicated as a DVT risk factor include glucocorticoids (especially systemic), tamoxifen, testosterone, heparin (heparin-induced thrombocytopenia), and antidepressants. Intravenous drug use has been associated with DVTs due to local trauma and irritation caused to femoral veins when injected in the lower extremities.

Inherited Risk Factors

While several inherited hypercoagulable disorders leading to a risk of DVT have been identified, the most common are factor V Leiden mutation and prothrombin gene mutation, which account for more than 50% of all inherited thrombophilic disorders. Patients can have more than one inherited thrombophilic disorder, and factor V Leiden mutation has been known to co-exist with protein C

and protein S deficiency. Further, inherited thrombophilic disorders may also co-exist with acquired risk factors in a patient. The presence of more than one inherited thrombophilic disorder or co- existence of inherited and acquired risk factors poses a greater risk for DVT than either one alone.[21] Identified inherited thrombophilic disorders include:

Factor V Leiden mutation Prothrombin gene mutation Protein C deficiency Protein S deficiency Antithrombin deficiency Dysfibrinogenemia

Factor XII deficiency Hyperhomocysteinemia Non-O blood group

Risk Factor Stratification

In clinical practice, the Wells Criteria is often utilized to stratify a patient's risk of DVT.[22] It is pertinent to note that the criteria are intended to use in those patients in whom DVT is clinically suspected and is not a diagnostic criterion but a risk stratification. The scoring provides guidance on the "next best step" for the patient workup, be it D-dimer or ultrasound doppler imaging. This system, however, served as evidenced-based medicine and guided care based on the study of risk factors for DVT. While it is not all-inclusive, it broadly groups the most common risk factors.

The criteria give one point to these components: Active cancer or treated cancer within the past six months, bedridden for more than three days or major surgery within the last four weeks, calf swelling greater than 3 cm more than contralateral leg 10 cm below the tibial tuberosity, collateral superficial veins present, diffuse leg swelling, localized tenderness along with the deep venous system, pitting edema which is greater in the symptomatic leg, paralysis or immobilization of lower extremity, and previous DVT. It gives minus 2 points if an alternate diagnosis is likely.

The sum scores are then classified as low risk (0), medium risk (1 to 2), and high risk (3 or more). Per the originating studies, a low risk is equivalent to a 5% risk, and a negative D-dimer is sufficient to rule out DVT. Medium risk carries a 17% likelihood, and either a high-sensitivity D-dimer can be used or forgone in place of a Doppler study, with a single negative test being sufficient. High risk has a prevalence of 17 to 53%, and US doppler is recommended, although it may not be sufficient. A follow-up 1-week Doppler may be indicated to prevent missed events. If both D-dimer and Doppler are negative, it is considered sufficient to rule out DVT, even in high-risk patients.

Again, it is important to remember that this is a guide and cannot replace clinical judgment. Also, specific criteria such as the Wells criteria for pulmonary embolism (PE) or the Pulmonary Embolism Rule-Out Criteria (PERC) shall be used when there is a concern for PE.

Clinical Significance

The knowledge and identification of these risk factors are important not only in the early recognition and treatment of DVTs but also in the prevention of initial and subsequent DVTs. The presence or absence of these risk factors can guide the use of prophylactic measures such as prophylactic anticoagulation therapy in hospitalized patients. Further, identifying inherited risk factors can be crucial to using appropriate long-term anticoagulation therapy when indicated to prevent future DVTs and complications of DVTs such as PEs.

https://www.ncbi.nlm.nih.gov/books/NBK470215/#[1]

---

1.   https://www.ncbi.nlm.nih.gov/books/NBK470215/

Deep Venous Thrombosis

José A. López, Clive Kearon, Agnes Y.Y. Lee

Abstract

Venous thromboembolism (VTE), manifested as either deep venous thrombosis (DVT) or pulmonary embolism (PE), is an extremely common medical problem, occurring either in isolation or as a complication of other diseases or procedures. Yet, despite its frequency, much remains to be learned regarding the pathogenic mechanisms that initiate VTE, about tailoring its treatment to the individual with her/his specific set of risk factors for recurrence, and about its medical management when associated with specific disease entities, such as cancer. These three topics are addressed in this chapter.

In Section I, Drs. López and Conde discuss the mechanisms by which venous thrombi may be initiated on the vessel wall in the absence of anatomically overt vessel wall injury. The authors propose a model whereby tissue factor (TF)–bearing microvesicles that arise from cells of monocyte/macrophage lineage can fuse with activated endothelial cells in regions of vessel activation or inflammation and initiate blood coagulation. Key components of this model include docking of the microvesicles to the stimulated endothelium through P-selectin glycoprotein ligand– 1 on their surfaces binding to either P-selectin or E-selectin on the endothelium, and the role of hypoxia during blood stasis in initiating local endothelial activation. Elevations in the levels of TF- bearing microvesicles associated with inflammatory conditions would help to explain the increased risk of thrombosis associated with infections and inflammatory states such as inflammatory bowel disease.

In Section II, Dr. Clive Kearon discusses the risk factors for recurrent thrombosis and strategies for determining length of therapy and tailoring specific therapies through risk stratification. Those patients who experience VTE in association with a major reversible risk factor such as surgery are much less likely to experience a recurrence when anticoagulation is discontinued than are patients with a persistent risk factor, such as thrombophilia or cancer unresponsive to therapy. Those with a minor reversible risk factor, such as prolonged air travel, have an intermediate risk of recurrence after discontinuance of anticoagulant therapy. The author provides an algorithm for using risk assessment as a means of determining the length and type of therapy to be used to minimize the rate of recurrence while simultaneously diminishing the risk of bleeding associated with anticoagulation.

In Section III, Dr. Agnes Lee updates the topic of VTE associated with malignancy. Patients with cancer make up approximately 20% of those presenting with first time VTE, and the presence of VTE forebodes a much poorer prognosis for patients with cancer, likely because of the morbidity associated with VTE itself and because VTE may herald a more aggressive cancer. Recent evidence indicates that low-molecular weight heparins (LMWHs) improve survival in patients with advanced cancer through mechanisms beyond their effect as anticoagulants. Because of their improved efficacy and safety and potential anti-neoplastic effect, the LMWHs have become the anticoagulants of choice for treating VTE associated with cancer.

Hematology Am Soc Hematol Educ Program (2004) 2004 (1): 439–456.

D DIMER

D-dimer, P-selectin, and microparticles: novel markers to predict deep venous thrombosis. A pilot study.

Rectenwald JE, Myers DD Jr, Hawley AE, Longo C, Henke PK, Guire KE, Schmaier AH, Wakefield TW.

Abstract

Current plasma markers for diagnosis of deep venous thrombosis (DVT) allow for exclusion of the diagnosis, but lack adequate specificity to establish the diagnosis. Thus, a prospective study was performed to determine the sensitivity and specificity of plasma assays for D-dimer, soluble P-selectin (P-selectin), and total microparticles in patients with documented DVT by duplex ultrasound. Three groups of individuals were examined: 30 normals; 22 positive for DVT on duplex ultrasound (Group 2); and 21 symptomatic, but negative on duplex ultrasound for DVT (Group 3). Group 1 individuals had D- dimer values of 1.53 +/- 0.12 mg/l and P-selectin values of 0.34 +/- 0.05 ng/mg total protein. Group 2 vs. Group 3 individuals had D-dimer values of 7.57 +/- 2.03 vs. 3.19 +/- 0.79 mg/l, p = 0.02; P-selectin values of 0.98 +/- 0.11 vs. 0.55 +/- 0.08 ng/mg total protein, p < 0.01; and micro-particle values of 129 +/- 17% vs. 99 +/- 12% of control, p = ns. Using a logistic regression model with dichotomous variables, we determined a sensitivity of 73%, specificity of 81%, and accuracy of 77% when combining D-dimer, soluble P-selectin, and total microparticles to differentiate Group 2 from Group 3 patients. Logistic regression using continuous variables yielded similar results (p = 0.05). This study demonstrates that plasma markers for DVT can be developed and achieve moderate sensitivity and specificity in diagnosing DVT. However for clinical applicability, the sensitivity/specificity will need to be improved. These studies also suggest the importance of soluble P-selectin in assessing DVT in humans.

Thrombosis and Haemostasis, 2005:Dec 94(6)1312-7

Fibrin fragment D-dimer and the risk of future venous thrombosis

Mary Cushman 1, Aaron R Folsom, Lu Wang, Nena Aleksic, Wayne D Rosamond, Russell P Tracy, Susan R Heckbert

Abstract

Plasma D-dimer concentration rises more than 100-fold during acute deep vein thrombosis, but there are no prospective data concerning D-dimer as a risk factor for incident venous thrombosis in a general population. Incident venous thrombosis was ascertained in 2 prospective observational studies, the Atherosclerosis Risk in Communities Study and the Cardiovascular Health Study. Of 21 690 participants enrolled between 1987 and 1993, after 8 years of follow-up, D-dimer was measured using baseline stored plasma of 307 participants who developed venous thrombosis and 616 who did not. Relative to the first quintile of the distribution of D-dimer, the age-adjusted odds ratios for future venous thrombosis for the second to fifth quintiles of D-dimer were 1.6, 2.3, 2.3, and 4.2, respectively (P for trend <.0001). Following added adjustment for sex, race, body mass index, factor V Leiden, prothrombin 20210A, and elevated factor VIII coagulant activity (factor VIII:c), these odds ratios were 1.5, 2.1, 1.9, and 3.0, respectively (P for trend <.0001). Among those with idiopathic thrombosis or secondary thrombosis unrelated to cancer, the adjusted fifth quintile odds ratios were 3.5 and 4.8, respectively. By contrast, D-dimer in the fifth versus first quintile was not related to occurrence of cancer-associated thrombosis (odds ratio, 1.1). Odds ratios for elevated D-dimer were consistently elevated in subgroups defined by age, sex, race, duration of follow-up, and thrombosis type (deep vein thrombosis or pulmonary embolus). D-dimer is strongly and positively related to the occurrence of future venous thrombosis.

Blood (2003) 101 (4): 1243–1248.

D-dimer as a risk factor for deep vein thrombosis: the Leiden Thrombophilia Study

Astrid C M Andreescu, Mary Cushman, Frits R Rosendaal

Abstract

We studied the association of D-dimer with the risk of deep vein thrombosis (DVT). D-dimer was measured in 474 patients more than 6 months after diagnosis of a first DVT and in 474 age- and sex-matched controls. For D-dimer above the 70th percentile (130.5 ng/ml), the odds ratio (OR) for DVT was 2.2 (95% CI, 1.6-2.9). The association was unchanged with adjustment for other risk factors. Excluding participants with Factor V Leiden, prothrombin 20210A, or factors VIIIc or IX above the 90th percentile, the OR was 1.6 (95% CI, 1.1-2.3). The risks of DVT with the joint presence of high D-dimer and either factor V Leiden or prothrombin 20210A were increased 12.4- fold (95% CI 5.6-27.7) and 7.2-fold (95% CI 2.1-25.1), respectively. Higher D-dimer concentration was associated with the risk of DVT, and was supra-additive to the risks associated with factor V Leiden and the prothrombin 20210A variant. Persistence of this association in the absence of other hemostatic risk factors for DVT suggests that high D-dimer may be related to other, as yet unknown, risk factors for venous thrombosis. Confirmation of these findings is desirable. *Thromb Haemost 2002 Jan;87(1):47-51.*

PREGNANCY

The Treatment of Venous Insufficiency in Pregnancy

B Rodríguez-Nora, E Álvarez-Silvares

Abstract

Chronic venous insufficiency is a long-term pathological condition resulting from anatomical or functional alterations of the venous system. This leads to the appearance of symptoms and physical signs that affect a large part of the population and particularly pregnant women, due to the physiology of pregnancy. The few published studies on the use of pharmacological treatments of venous insufficiency in this group of the population, often makes the management of this condition difficult in routine clinical practice. A review is presented in this article, with all the latest updates in the treatment of this condition during pregnancy. There are numerous general, and some pharmacological, recommendations, that we can safely offer the pregnant patient.

Semergen. 2018 May-Jun;44(4):262-269.

Pregnancy-dependent Blood Flow Velocity Changes in Lower Extremities Veins in Venous Insufficiency

M*ariola Ropacka-Lesiak, Kasperczak Jarosław, Grzegorz Bręborowicz*

Abstract

Introduction: Venous insufficiency in pregnancy is associated witch an increased risk of complications.

Objectives: The aim of the study was to analyse the venous system changes of the lower limbs during pregnancy and puerperium with or without venous insufficiency

Material and methods: The research was carried out on pregnant women divided into two groups according to the presence or lack of venous insufficiency The venous system was examined four times: between 11-14th, 18-22nd, 28-32nd gestational week and at the 6th week of puerperium. The doppler examination included the measurement of the blood flow velocity in selected deep veins of the lower limbs: common femoral vein, the superficial femoral vein and the popliteal vein. Consecutively the changes in the blood flow velocity during pregnancy and puerperium were compared between groups and finally to the results obtained in the 1st trimester

Results: The analysis of the blood flow showed that the blood flow velocity was statistically lower in the group with venous insufficiency Velocity changes in time showed, in majority of cases, a substantial reduction in the blood flow velocity in the third trimester in both groups. This blood flow velocity increases during the puerperium and does not differ from those observed in the first trimester Thus, the tendency of changes in the blood flow velocity were similar in character in both groups.

Conclusions: The pregnancy related changes in venous system of lower extremities showed the reduction of blood flow velocity with advancing gestational age and were more evident in pregnancy complicated by venous insufficiency.

Ginekol Pol. 2015 Sep;86(9):659-65

Risk Factors for the Development of Venous Insufficiency of the Lower Limbs During Pregnancy

Mariola Ropacka-Lesiak , Jarosław Kasperczak, Grzegorz H Breborowicz

Abstract

The venous system alters its function in pregnancy—the changes are both functional and structural. It becomes particularly vulnerable to the development of venous thrombosis and related complications. These adverse factors acting on the veins in pregnancy include: an increase in circulating blood volume, expansion of the uterus, weight gain, reduced physical activity hormonal changes. The changes in the plasma have a significant impact on the venous system. In pregnancy an increased level of fibrinogen and coagulation factors VII, VIII, IX and X, and von Willenbrand factor can be observed. Smooth muscle relaxation and relaxation of collagen fibers are caused by progesterone and estrogen, and it may result in the development of varicose veins, venous thrombosis and venous insufficiency the relationships between the hormones and the muscle pump efficiency has not been proven as yet. Estrogens cause an increase in the synthesis of coagulation proteins and it may result in the high risk of venous thrombosis and its consequences. Progesterone inhibits smooth muscle contraction, while estrogens cause relaxation and loosening of the bonds between the collagen fibers. The increase in the level of progesterone is of particular importance. It has a relaxing effect on the muscle, resulting in disorders of the vein shrinkage, affecting the increase of their capacity and valvular insufficiency, and valvular edges are not in contact with each other due to the vasodilatation. Estrogens have a similar effect, and additionally it may also cause an impairment in the collagen fibers connection and synthesis. This can result in the formation of telanglectasia without venous hypertension. Estrogens may also affect the synthesis of prostaglandins and nitric oxide. Estradiol inhibits vascular smooth muscle cell proliferation and stimulates cell migration and secretion of matrix proteins, as well as regeneration of the damaged vessels. Estrogen inhibits the production of cytokines, adhesion molecules, and reduce platelet response, i.e. the aggregation and adhesion in the presence of monocytes. Estradiol increases the production, activity and bioavailability of nitric oxide, a molecule with a strong vasodilating effect. Additionally adverse affects may appear due to short intervals between pregnancies, genetics, presence of venous thrombosis or venous insufficiency in the superficial and deep system in anamnesis. Caesarean section is also a risk factor for venous thrombosis. Family factors are associated with inheritance of the formation of varicose changes and venous insufficiency in both ways, dominant and recessive, and also sex-related. Among other factors affecting the development of venous insufficiency during pregnancy the following can be distinguished: type of work (standing, sitting, in forced positions and vibration), interval between pregnancies (determining the possibility of regeneration of physiological regeneration of the system). In case of women who were pregnant more than once, the risk of developing varicose veins and other venous insufficiency is doubled.

Ginekol Pol. 2012 Dec;83(12):939-42.

Analysis of Venous Insufficiency Risk Factors and Appearance of Clinical Symptoms During Pregnancy and Puerperium in a Group of Pregnant Women With and Without Symptoms of Venous Insufficiency of the Lower Limbs

Jarosław Kasperczak, Mariola Ropacka-Lesiak, Joanna Musiał-Swider, Grzegorz H Breborowicz

Abstract

Objective: To analyze risk factors for venous insufficiency and the appearance of clinical symptoms during pregnancy and childbirth in the group of pregnant women without (nvi) and with symptoms of venous insufficiency (vi) of the lower limbs that was present during the first visit in the first trimester of pregnancy

Material and methods: The study included 103 pregnant women consulted at the Clinic of Vascular Disease "Calisia" in Kalisz in the years 2006-2008. Venous system was assessed in CEAP clinical classification. Patients were divided into two groups depending on the presence or absence of symptoms of venous insufficiency of the lower limbs during the first examination, which took place in the first trimester of pregnancy. Pregnant women with symptoms of vi qualified for the test group (B), whereas patients without signs of vi constituted the control group (K). The observed changes in each group in the second, third trimester and postpartum were compared to the first trimester

Results: In the control group, clinical symptoms such as telangiectasis, varicose changes, and edema increased with advancing gestational age, with the greatest intensity in the third trimester. Similar intensification of symptoms was observed in the group B. The incidence of some of the observed clinical symptoms decreased at 6 weeks postpartum, whereas some of them remained unchanged. In the group K statistically significant differences were found between the incidence of symptoms in the II and III trimesters compared to the first trimester. There were no statistically significant differences between puerperium and the first trimester. No statistical significance was found in the group B. In the puerperium a gradual reduction of clinical symptoms was observed. In the group K the greatest changes were observed in the prevalence of edema and pain. Similar changes were observed in women with venous insufficiency

Conclusion: Pregnancy predisposes to chronic venous insufficiency. Edema of the lower limbs is not an authoritative exponent of the severity of venous insufficiency during pregnancy due to the emergence of different pathogenesis of these changes during pregnancy. The six-week postpartum period is not sufficient to normalize the functional state of the venous system in terms of changes occurring during pregnancy.

Ginekol Pol. 2012 Mar;83(3):183-8.

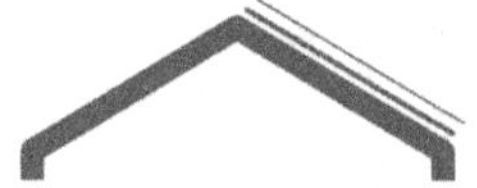

Thrombophilia and unexplained pregnancy loss in Indian patients.

Vora S, Shetty S, Salvi V, Satoskar P, Ghosh K.

Abstract

Background:
The role of acquired and congenital thrombophilias in the aetiology of unexplained pregnancy loss in the Indian population has not been studied in detail.

We studied the association of acquired and inherited markers of thrombophilia in a large group of patients with unexplained pregnancy loss.

Methods:

A total of 602 women with pregnancy loss were referred to us for evaluation of thrombophilia between April 2000 and June 2005.

After investigations to rule out cytogenetic, hormonal, anatomical and microbiological causes, no cause was ascertained in 430 women for the pregnancy loss.

Of these, 49 women, who had a history of only one pregnancy loss, were excluded. The remaining 381 women comprised the study group.

These patients and 100 age-matched women who did not have any obstetric complication and had at least one normal healthy child (controls) underwent detailed investigations for the presence of thrombophilia markers.

These included screening

1. Coagulations tests,
2. Tests for lupus anticoagulant (LA),

1. IgG and IgM antibodies to anticardiolipin antibodies (ACA),
2. Beta2 glycoprotein 1 (beta2GP1) and
3. Annexin V.

The genetic markers studied included

1. Protein C (PC),
2. Protein 5 (PS),
3. Antithrombin III (AT III),
4. Factor V Leiden (FVL),
5. PT gene G20210A,
6. MTHFR C677T,
7. EPCR 23 bp insertion and
8. PAI 4G/5G polymorphisms.

Results:

Of the 381 women with pregnancy loss, 183 had 2 and 198 had > or = 3 pregnancy losses.

Early pregnancy loss occurred in 136 patients, late pregnancy loss in 119, and both early and late pregnancy losses in 126.

The strongest association was observed with

1. ACA (OR 32.5, 95% CI: 8.6-21.8, $p < 0.001$) followed by
2. Annexin V (OR 17.1, 95% CI: 2.9-99.4, $p < 0.001$),
3. LA (OR 8.2, 95% CI: 1.4-47.7, $p = 0.01$) and
4. anti-beta2GP1 (OR 5.8, 95% CI: 1.6-22.1, $p = 0.007$).

No association of antiphospholipid antibodies with the time of pregnancy loss was found except LA

LA which was significantly associated with early pregnancy loss compared with late pregnancy loss (p < 0.05).

The risk of pregnancy loss with PS deficiency (OR 17.8, 95% CI: 3.1-102.9, p < 0.001) was the highest observed for

1. Any heritable thrombophilia followed by

2. PC deficiency (OR 5.8, 95% CI: 1-34, p = 0.06).

There were no statistically significant differences in the frequency of any of the genetic thrombophilias studied between women with early and late pregnancy loss.

A combination of > or = 2 genetic factors was observed in 41 (10.8%) while that of genetic and acquired risk factors were observed in 79 (20.7%) patients.

No more than one risk factor was observed in any of the controls.

In all, 176 (46.2%) patients had at least one acquired thrombophilia while 143 (37.5%) had at least one genetic thrombophilia marker.

Overall, 288 patients (75.6%) had either an acquired, genetic or both markers of thrombophilia.

Conclusion:

Thrombophilia is an important factor in both early and late pregnancy losses.

Natl Med J India. 2008 May-Jun;21(3):116-9.

Pathophysiology of venous insufficiency during pregnancy

J Krajcar, B Radaković, L Stefanić

Abstract

Pregnancy is a risk factor for venous insufficiency. Up to 30 percent of women will develop venous insufficiency during their first pregnancy, and with each next pregnancy its prevalence is higher. Several pathophysiologic mechanisms are involved in the pathophysiology of venous insufficiency during pregnancy. The role of these mechanisms in the pathophysiology of venous insufficiency during pregnancy is still a point of discussion. Mechanical compression of enlarged uterus on pelvic veins was the first considered responsible for the occurrence of venous insufficiency during pregnancy. Soon, it was found that hormonal changes in pregnancy cause reduction in venous tone, and this reduction was postulated to be a major factor in pathophysiology of venous insufficiency. In a large number of subsequent studies both hypotheses were tested, being confirmed or rejected, but no consensus has been reached. This paper reviews current knowledge regarding pathophysiology of venous insufficiency during pregnancy, and discusses the possible role that some as yet uninvestigated mechanisms might have in it.

Acta Med Croatica. 1998;52(1):65-9

The hemodynamic effects of pregnancy on the lower extremity venous system

J Taylor, Caitlin W. Hicks, Jennifer A. Heller

Abstract

Objective

Pregnancy has significant effects on the lower extremity venous system. Increasing venous pressure and blood volume, in combination with reduced flow rates within the deep veins, predisposes pregnant women to both primary and secondary chronic venous insufficiency (CVI). This review article highlights the specific physiologic and hemodynamic changes that occur during pregnancy and examines the nonpharmacologic, pharmacologic, and invasive interventions that are appropriate for both prophylaxis and treatment of CVI and venous thromboembolism (VTE).

Methods

This study is a review article of the key literature related to VTE and CVI in pregnancy. Results

Significant hemodynamic changes occur in the lower extremities during pregnancy. Although well documented and essential to fetal development, these changes can have a negative impact on the maternal lower extremity venous circulation. Consequences of pregnancy can result in venous disease only during pregnancy or, particularly in the multiparous patient, can progress to CVI. An abundance of literature and guidelines exist for the management of VTE during pregnancy; however, the quality and extent of literature based around the management of primary CVI during pregnancy are modest at best.

Conclusions

The physiologic changes throughout the arterial and venous systems during pregnancy are well documented. However, there is a paucity of data available to construct guidelines for care, particularly in the pregnant patient with symptomatic superficial venous insufficiency. Further investigation in the form of prospective randomized trials is required to establish appropriate guidelines for treatment.

https://doi.org/10.1016/j.jvsv.2017.08.001

HYPERLIPEDEMIA

Hyperlipidaemia and venous thromboembolism in patients lacking thrombophilic risk factors

Amparo Vayá, Yolanda Mira, Fernando Ferrando, MaTeresa Contreras, Amparo Estelles, Francisco España, Dolores Corella, Justo Aznar

Abstract

To ascertain the potential contribution of serumlipids to the development of deep vein thrombosis (DVT), acase–control study was conducted in 143 DVT patientslacking thrombophilic risk factors and in 194 age- and sex-matched controls. DVT patients showed significantly higherbody mass indices (BMI), and triglyceride levels than didcontrols (P<0Æ001 andP¼0Æ045 respectively). Usingmultivariate analysis, BMI was the only variable whichremained statistically different, thus the risk of DVT wasassociated with obesity (odds ratio¼2Æ49). These resultswere confirmed when additional control for fibrinogen andplasminogen activator inhibitor type 1 (PAI-1) was carriedout in a subgroup of cases and controls. When idiopathic(n¼39) and secondary (n¼104) patients with DVT werecompared, the former showed a higher mean age, a higherproportion of men, and higher cholesterol levels. Age, sex andtotal cholesterol were statistically different by multivariateanalysis. After age was dichotomized as‡50 years and cho-lesterol‡5Æ69 mmol/l, all three variables constituted inde-pendent risk factors for idiopathic DVT, with odds ratios of2Æ73 for ages‡50 years; 3Æ72 for men and 2Æ67 for choles-terolaemia‡5Æ69 mmol/l. Obesity thus constitutes an inde-pendent risk factor for DVT, possibly in part mediated throughtriglyceride, fibrinogen and PAI- 1 effects on haemostasis. Inaddition, cholesterolaemia levels of‡5Æ69 mmol/l constitutean independent risk factor for idiopathic DVT.

Br J Haematol. 2002 Jul;118(1):255-9.

101

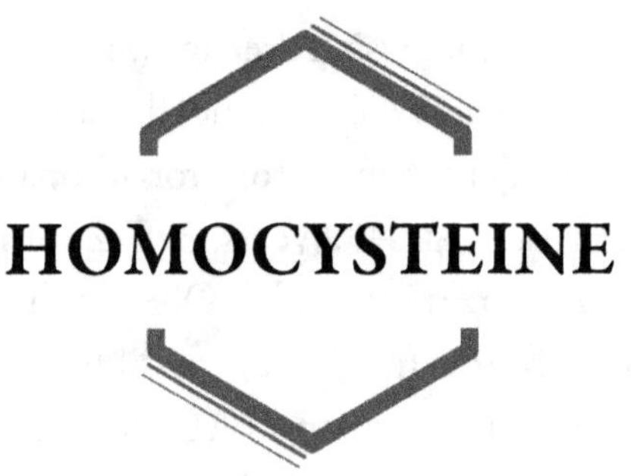

HOMOCYSTEINE

Hyperhomocysteinemia as a Risk Factor for Deep-Vein Thrombosis

M den Heijer, T Koster, H J Blom, G M Bos, E Briet, P H Reitsma, J P Vandenbroucke, F R Rosendaal

Abstract

Background: Previous studies have suggested that hyperhomocysteinemia may be a risk factor for venous thrombosis. To assess the risk of venous thrombosis associated with hyperhomocysteinemia, we studied plasma homocysteine levels in patients with a first episode of deep-vein thrombosis and in normal control subjects.

Methods: We measured plasma homocysteine levels in 269 patients with a first, objectively diagnosed episode of deep-vein thrombosis and in 269 healthy controls matched to the patients according to age and sex. Hyperhomocysteinemia was defined as a plasma homocysteine level above the 95th percentile in the control group (18.5 micromol per liter).

Results: Of the 269 patients, 28 (10 percent) had plasma homocysteine levels above the 95th percentile for the controls, as compared with 13 of the controls (matched odds ratio, 2.5; 95 percent confidence interval, 1.2 to 5.2). The association between elevated homocysteine levels and venous thrombosis was stronger among women than among men and increased with age. The exclusion of subjects with other established risk factors for thrombosis (e.g., a deficiency of protein C, protein S, or antithrombin; resistance to activated protein C; pregnancy or recent childbirth; or oral-contraceptive use) did not materially affect the risk estimates.

Conclusions: High plasma homocysteine levels are a risk factor for deep-vein thrombosis in the general population.

N Engl J Med. 1996 Mar 21;334(12):759-62.

Meta-analysis of Hyperhomocysteinemia as a Risk Factor for Venous Thromboembolic Disease

Joel G. Ray, MD, FRCP

Several mechanisms may lead to hyper-Hcy. Known causes include deficiencies of folate, vitamin B6, and vitamin B125-6; a reduced activity of methylenetetrahydrofolate reductase7; or other enzyme defects within the Hcy metabolic pathway.

METHOD OF STUDY: Studies were identified through MEDLINE (January 1980 to August 1997) using search terms related to both Hcy and VTE. The bibliographies of all review articles and letters were searched for additional relevant articles. English-language studies were selected if they included 10 or more human subjects; a measurement of the plasma, serum, or whole-blood Hcy level; the presence of VTE; and primary data that were not published elsewhere. Seventy-two articles were retrieved, of which 9 met all inclusion criteria. Data were extracted on the study type, subject demographics, methods for matching control subjects with case patients, whether an objective method was used to diagnose VTE, and whether other causes of thrombophilia and elevated Hcy levels were considered. The mean Hcy levels, both in the fasting state and following methionine loading, if done, were recorded, as were the number of patients and control subjects with Hcy levels greater than 2 SDs or greater than the 95th percentile above the mean value of the control group. A total of 856 patients were included in this analysis, with a male-to-female ratio of approximately 1:1.4 and a mean age of 56.7 years (range, 17-91 years). Several studies, but not all, excluded patients with other thrombophilic causes, such as protein C, protein S, or antithrombin III deficiency, as possible confounders. This is probably most important for activated-protein C resistance (factor V Leiden) because 2 studies[18, 21] observed a compounded risk for

VTE in the presence of hyper-Hcy and activated-protein C resistance. A significant positive association was found across all 9 case-control studies for both the fasting and postmethionine-loading states. The magnitude of association was high, with an OR of 2.95, which is statistically and perhaps clinically significant. This finding was even more apparent for patients younger than 60 years.

Arch Intern Med. 1998 Oct 26;158(19):2101-6

LEG ULCERS

Pathophysiology of Chronic Venous Disease and Venous Ulcers

Joseph D Raffetto

Abstract

Chronic venous disease and venous leg ulceration are a common disease affecting millions of individuals. The fundamental problem is venous hypertension with resultant clinical manifestations of venous disease including varicose veins, skin changes, and venous leg ulceration. The pathophysiology leading to venous hypertension is complex and multifactorial, involving genetic predisposition, environmental factors, hormones, endothelial dysfunction, inflammatory cells and molecules and activation on the endothelium and vein wall, and disturbances in the balance of cytokines and matrix metalloproteinases. Understanding the pathophysiology of chronic venous disease and venous leg ulcers identifies cellular pathways, biomarkers, metabolic signatures, and cellular cross-talk for targeted therapy.

Surg Clin North Am. 2018 Apr;98(2):337-347

Venous leg ulcers: Pathophysiology and Classification

B *iju Vasudevan*

Introduction

D **efinition, rationale and scope**
Venous leg ulcers (VLUs) are defined as open lesions between the knee and ankle joint that occur in the presence of venous disease. They are the most common cause of leg ulcers, accounting for 60-80% of them. The prevalence of VLUs is between 0.18% and 1%.Over the age of 65, the prevalence increases to 4%.On an average 33-60% of these ulcers persist for more than 6 weeks and are therefore referred to as chronic VLUs. These ulcers represent the most advanced form of chronic venous disorders like varicose veins and lipodermatosclerosis.

Risk factors for development of VLUs include older age, female sex, obesity, trauma, and immobility, congenital absence of veins, deep vein thrombosis (DVT), phlebitis, and factor V Leiden mutation.

Poor prognostic factors

a. Duration of more than 1 year - recurrence rate in these ulcers is more than 70%

b. Larger wounds

c. Fibrin in >50% of wound surface

d. Ankle-brachial pressure index (ABPI) <0.8

e. History of venous stripping/ligation.

Chronic venous leg ulcer results in reduced mobility, significant financial implications, and poor quality of life. There are no uniform guidelines for assessment and management of this group of conditions, which is reaching epidemic proportions in the prevalence. There is a wide variation in healing and recurrence rates of these ulcers in the Indian population due to differing nutritional status, availability of medical facilities and trained medical staff to diagnose and manage such conditions. These guidelines are devised based on current available evidence to help all concerned in accurately assessing, correctly investigating and also providing appropriate treatment for this condition.

Pathophysiology Venous hypertension

Deep vein thrombosis, perforator insufficiency, superficial and deep vein insufficiencies, arteriovenous fistulas and calf muscle pump insufficiencies lead to increased pressure in the distal veins of the leg and finally venous hypertension.

Fibrin cuff theory

Fibrin gets excessively deposited around capillary beds leading to elevated intravascular pressure. This causes enlargement of endothelial pores resulting in further increased fibrinogen deposition in the interstitium. The "fibrin cuff" which surrounds the capillaries in the dermis decreases oxygen permeability 20-fold. This permeability barrier inhibits diffusion of oxygen and other nutrients, leading to tissue hypoxia causing impaired wound healing.

Inflammatory trap theory

Various growth factors and inflammatory cells, which get trapped in the fibrin cuff promote severe uncontrolled inflammation in surrounding tissue preventing proper regeneration of wounds. Leukocytes get trapped in capillaries, releasing proteolytic enzymes and reactive oxygen metabolites, which cause endothelial damage. These injured capillaries become increasingly permeable to various macromolecules, accentuating fibrin deposition. Occlusion by leukocytes also causes local ischemia thereby increasing tissue hypoxia and reperfusion damage.

Dysregulation of various cytokines

Dysregulation of various pro-inflammatory cytokines and growth factors like tumor necrosis factor- α (TNF-α), TGF-β and matrix metalloproteinases lead to chronicity of the ulcers.

Miscellaneous

Thrombophilic conditions like factor V Leiden mutation, prothrombin mutations, deficiency of antithrombin, presence of antiphospholipid antibodies, protein C and S deficiencies and hyperhomocysteinemia are also implicated.

CLASSIFICATION OF CHRONIC VENOUS INSUFFICIENCY

The classification and staging of chronic venous insufficiency (clinical severity) can be measured by a scoring system called clinical manifestations, etiological factors, anatomical distribution, and pathophysiological conditions (evidence Level D)

Table 1

Classification of venous ulcers

Assessment and stepwise approach to diagnosis of VLU.

CLINICAL ASSESSMENT

1. Rule out arterial disease, which are indicated by:

a. History of intermittent claudication, cardiovascular disease and stroke
b. Absence of pedal pulses
c. Abnormal blood pressure (BP): It gives clues to the

presence of any cardiovascular disease.

It is very important to rule out arterial etiology as application of compression in such cases can cause severe damage (evidence Level D).

1. Obtain clues from history suggesting venous etiology (evidence Level D)

    a. History of previous or current DVT
    b. Family history of leg ulcers
    c. Varicose veins or its treatment

a. History of phlebitis
b. Surgery, trauma or fractures of the affected leg, which can damage the valves
c. Chest pain, hemoptysis or pulmonary embolism
d. Occupations of prolonged standing or sitting
e. Obesity
f. Multiple pregnancies
g. Aching pain in the lower limbs.

1. Clinical examination to confirm the diagnosis of venous ulcer

Examination of ulcer

a. Location: Anterior to medial malleolus, pretibial area, lower third of leg (gaiter region) (evidence Level C)
b. Measurement of size: Serial measurement of surface area of ulcer is a reliable index of prognosis and healing. Measurements of length, width and depth of ulcer with two maximum perpendicular axes are important. Disposable ruler, photography, acetate tracings and computerized calculation (planimetry) following digital photography are the methods which are used in measurement. Measuring the ulcers help in identifying patients not responding to conventional therapy and those requiring alternative therapy (evidence Level C)
c. Characteristics of the ulcer: Shallow depth, irregular shaped edges with well-defined margins
d. Amount and type of exudates: Yellow-white in color
e. Appearance of ulcer bed: Presence of ruddy viable granulation tissue. Thick slough or eschar indicates

arterial insufficiency

f. Signs of infection: Cellulitis, delayed healing despite appropriate compression therapy, increase in local skin temperature, increase in ulcer pain or change in nature of pain, newly formed ulcers within inflamed margins of preexisting ulcers, wound bed extension within inflamed margins, discoloration (esp. dull, dark brick-red), friable granulation tissue that bleeds easily, increase in exudate viscosity, increase in exudate volume, malodor, new-onset dusky wound hue, sudden appearance or increase in an amount of slough, sudden appearance of necrotic black spots and ulcer enlargement (evidence Level D). Take a swab only if these signs are present

g. Ulcer odor

h. Pain associated with ulcer: Pain may be absent, mild or extreme. Pain is more at the end of the day and usually relieved by elevation of the leg.

Periulcer area

Capillary leaking causing edema leading to maceration, pruritus and scaling. Associated warmth and pruritus.

Associated changes in the leg

a. Firm ("brawny") edema

b. Hemosiderin deposit (reddish brown pigmentation)

c. Lipodermatosclerosis

d. Evidence of healed ulcers

e. Dilated and tortuous superficial veins

f. Limb may be warm

g. Atrophie blanche

a. Eczema
b. Altered shape – inverted "champagne bottle"
c. Ankle flare.

1. Regular documentation to compare results before and after treatment and progression with time
2. Assess comorbidities like obesity, malnutrition, intravenous drug use and coexisting medical conditions prior to surgery. Reduced calorie and protein intake hampers ulcer healing (evidence Level D)
3. Rule out complications including severe infections, osteomyelitis and malignant changes (evidence Level D).
4. If no improvement after 12 weeks or in case of recurrence or no response to treatment after 6 weeks: Reassess

a. Risk factors for nonhealing - Increased wound size and duration, history of venous stripping or ligation, history of hip or knee replacement, ankle-brachial index < 0.8, >50% of wound covered in fibrin and undermined wound margin
b. Accuracy of etiology
c. Rule out allergic contact dermatitis to medications and differentiate from venous eczema. Do a patch test in all cases of venous ulcers with eczema. The common sensitizers are lanolin, topical antibiotics (gentamycin, neomycin, and bacitracin), antiseptics, preservatives, emulsifiers, resins and latex. (evidence level C). Positive patch tests in these ulcers range from 40% to 82.5%. (evidence Level B)
d. Any new comorbidities?
e. Think of biopsy (in case of atypical and nonhealing ulcers) - to rule out malignancy, systemic disorders,

collagen vascular disorders and vasculitis (evidence Level D)

f. Take bacterial, mycobacterial and fungal cultures

g. Is the treatment appropriate?

h. Is patient compliant with treatment?

INVESTIGATIONS

Noninvasive

1. ABPI: This is a noninvasive test using the handheld Doppler ultrasound which identifies peripheral arterial disease in the leg. Systolic BP is measured at the brachial artery and at the ankle level.

ABPI = highest systolic foot pressure (dorsalis pedis/posterior tibial artery)/highest systolic brachial BP

a. ABPI: 0.8-1.2: Indicative of good arterial flow. Suggestive of venous etiology if an ulcer is present

b. ABPI: <0.8 with the clinical picture of arterial disease-arterial insufficiency

c. ABPI:>1.2:Suggestive of possible arterial calcification (evidence Level B).

1. Nylon monofilament can be used as a simple screening test to rule out sensory neuropathy (evidence Level C)

2. Duplex ultrasound: It is a noninvasive test which combines ultrasound with Doppler ultrasonography. Blood flow through arteries and veins can be investigated to reveal any obstructions. It allows direct visualization of veins, identifies flow through valves and can map both

superficial and deep veins (evidence Level C)

1. Photoplethysmography: This is a noninvasive test which measures venous refill time. A probe placed on the skin surface just above the ankle is used for the detection. The patient is instructed to perform calf muscle pump exercises for brief periods followed by the rest. The probe actually measures the reduction in skin blood flow following exercise. This determines the efficiency of the calf muscle pump and the presence of any abnormal venous reflux. Patients with problems in superficial or deep veins usually have poor emptying of the veins and abnormally rapid refilling (<25 s) (evidence Level C)

2. Pulse oximetry: This is another noninvasive test which measures the red and infrared light absorption of oxygenated and deoxygenated hemoglobin in a digit. Oxygenated hemoglobin absorbs more infrared light and allows more red light to pass through a digit. Deoxygenated hemoglobin absorbs more red light and allows more infrared light to pass through the digit. However, there is insufficient evidence to recommend this investigation as a primary diagnostic tool (evidence Level C)

3. Toe brachial pressure index (TBPI): Noninvasive test that measures arterial perfusion in toes and feet. A toe cuff is applied to hallux and pressure is divided by the highest brachial systolic pressure, which is the best estimate of central systolic BP. TBPI identifies incompressible calcified arteries in diabetics and renal disease patients

4. Transcutaneous oxygen: Measures amount of oxygen reaching the skin through blood circulation. Presently, insufficient evidence to recommend as primary diagnostic test.

Invasive

1. Biochemical tests
    a. Blood glucose - To rule out diabetes
    b. Hemoglobin - To rule out hematological disorders
    c. Urea and electrolytes
    d. Serum albumin, transferrin - To rule out nutritional deficiencies
    e. Lipids
    f. Rheumatoid factor
    g. Auto antibodies
    h. White blood cell count
    i. Erythrocyte sedimentation rate
    j. C-reactive protein. Liver function tests
        1. Activated protein C: Detected in 25% venous ulcers and 50% of recurrent venous thromboses patients (evidence level D)
        2. Microbiology: Bacterial wound swab when ulcer shows clinical signs of infection like cellulitis, pyrexia, and increased pain, rapid extension of the area of ulceration, malodor and increased exudates (evidence Level C)
        3. Histopathology: Wound biopsy only if malignancy or other etiology is suspected.

SUMMARY [EVIDENCE LEVEL C]

The prevalence of VLUs is on the increase with chronic venous insufficiency being the main culprit. A detailed accurate assessment of leg ulcer in patients is essential to ensure starting of timely and appropriate treatment. It should be an ongoing continuous assessment as signs and symptoms can rapidly change thereby requiring progressive evaluation. Good and accurate quality patient assessment will save time and cost by an enforcement of appropriate treatment regimens.

Indian Dermatol online journal.2014 Jul-Sep; 5(3): 366-370.

Recent Insights Into the Causes of Chronic Leg Ulceration in Venous Diseases and Implications on Other Types of Chronic Wounds

W Y *John Chen, Alan A Rogers*

Abstract

Venous ulceration represents the most prevalent form of difficult-to-heal wounds and these problematic wounds require a significant amount of healthcare resources for their treatment. In order to develop effective treatment regimens a clearer understanding of the underlying pathological processes that lead to skin breakdown is required. However, to date, most of these studies have tended to focus on describing the pathology of already-established ulcers. By bringing together relevant aspects of diverse disciplines such as inflammation, cardiovascular, and connective tissue biology, we aim to provide an insight into how circulatory abnormalities that are caused by the underlying disease etiology can induce local tissue inflammation resulting in tissue breakdown. Initially this results in internal tissue damage but if the underlying disease is not treated, the internal tissue damage can worsen and lead to open ulceration. This article discusses the cause-and-effect relationships between chronic venous insufficiency and venous ulceration, focusing particularly on the biological processes that lead from the underlying disease condition to overt ulceration. Available evidence also suggests that formation of pressure, diabetic foot and arterial ulcers, and ulcers as results of blood disorders, is also likely to share some of the same biological processes as venous ulcers.

Wound Repair Regen. Jul-Aug 2007;15(4):434-49.

The Causes of Skin Damage and Leg Ulceration in Chronic Venous Disease

P*hilip Coleridge Smith*

Abstract

Chronic venous disease with skin changes of the leg is a common condition affecting up to 1 in 20 people in westernized countries. The causes of this problem are not fully understood, although research in recent years has revealed a number of important mechanisms that contribute to the disease process. Patients with chronic venous disease suffer persistently raised pressures in their deep and superficial veins in the lower limb. Leucocytes become "trapped" in the circulation of the leg during periods of venous hyper-tension produced by sitting or standing. Studies of the plasma levels of neutrophil granule enzymes shows that these are increased during periods of venous hypertension, suggesting that this causes activation of the neutrophils. Investigation of the leucocyte surface ligands CD11b and CD62L shows that the more activated neutrophils and monocytes are sequestered during venous hypertension. Measurement of plasma levels of the soluble parts of the endothelial adhesion molecules VCAM, ICAM, and ELAM show that these are all elevated in patients with chronic venous disease compared to controls. Following 30 minutes of venous hypertension produced by standing, these levels are further increased. These data suggest that venous hypertension causes neutrophil and monocyte activation, which in turn causes injury to the endothelium. Chronic injury to the endothelium leads to a chronic inflammatory condition of the skin that we know clinically as lipodermatosclerosis. This is mediated by perivascular inflammatory cells, principally macrophages, in the skin microcirculation. These stimulate fibroblasts in the skin leading to tissue remodeling and laying down of fibrous tissue. Vascular endothelial growth factor stimulates proliferation of capillaries within the skin. Skin in this state has the potential to ulcerate in response to minor injury.

Int J Low Extrem Wounds. 2006 Sep;5(3):160-8.

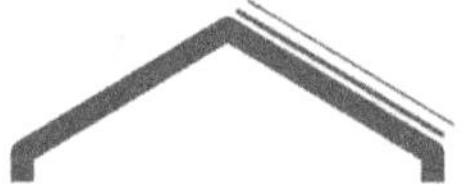

Pathomechanism of chronic venous insufficiency and leg ulcer.

T *Sándor*

Abstract:

Uniform view of chronic venous diseases has been formed in the last 3 decades.

Chronic venous insufficiency (CVI) is a functional disorder of the venous system of the lower limb.

The basis of the pathology is always the venous hypertension caused by valvular insufficiency and reflux with or without venous outflow obstruction.

Epifascial, subfascial and transfascial forms of CVI can be distinguished. In the practice these forms are almost always combined.

The consistent venous hypertension is the initiating factor in alterations in the microcirculation which leads to skin changes and venous ulceration.

The precise mechanism of the development of venous leg ulcer is still uncertain.

A recent hypothesis suggests that leukocytes are trapped in the capillaries and attaching to the endothel they become activated and release proteolytic enzymes, free radicals which have destructive effects on lipid membranes, proteins as well as on many connective tissue compounds.

The endothelium plays active role in the complex mechanism.

Increased expression of tissue metalloproteinases has been observed in the periulcer skin.

The presence of perivascular leukocyte infiltration and fibrin cuff is a reflexion of an inflammatory process.

The clinical stages of CVI are likely to be the results of a systemic inflammatory response to a period of venous hypertension.

Acta Physiol Hung:. 2004;91(2):131-45.

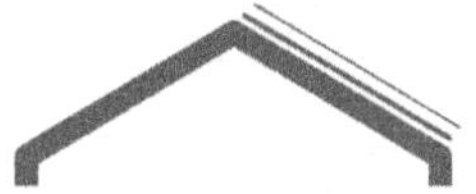

Leg ulcer etiology-a cross sectional population study

N*elzén O, Bergqvist D, Lindhagen A.*

Abstract

Method:

Three hundred eighty-two (382) patients with active leg ulcers were clinically examined after random selection out of a population of 827 patients identified within a previous cross-sectional population survey.

Bidirectional Doppler ultrasonography was used for objective assessment of arterial and venous circulation.

Aim:

The purpose was to register causative factors and the etiologic spectrum.

Results:

Venous insufficiency was present in 332 (72%) of 463 legs with active ulceration; deep insufficiency occurred in 176 (38%), and purely superficial insufficiency was present in 156 (34%).

Ankle/brachial index was 0.9 or less in 185 (40%) of ulcerated legs.

Venous insufficiency was the dominating causative factor in 250 legs (54%), of which 60% was the result of deep venous insufficiency.

Arterial insufficiency was judged to be the possible dominating factor in 12%, and 6% showed clearly ischemic ulcers.

Mixed ulcers with combined arterial and venous insufficiency were found to be common as were patients with diabetes and arterial impairment.

In 10% of the legs a multifactorial origin was present, and in 10% no venous or arterial impairment was detectable.

Thus after classification of causes 40% of all ulcerated legs showed potentially surgically curable circulatory disturbances.

Conclusion:

It is necessary to objectively assess all patients with chronic leg ulcers to be able to detect patients with potentially surgically curable disease.

Journal of Vascular Surgery, Oct:1991; 14(4), 557–564.

The venous ulcer continues to be a clinical challenge

Ting Xie, Junna Ye, Kittipan Rerkasem, and Rajgopal Manicorresponding

Abstract

Venous ulcers are a common chronic problem in many countries especially in Northern Europe and USA. The overall prevalence of this condition is 1% rising to 3% in the over 65 years of age. Over the last 25 years, there have been many developments applicable to its diagnosis and treatment. These advances, notwithstanding healing response and recurrence, are variable, and the venous ulcer continues to be a clinical challenge.

The pathogenesis of venous ulcers is unrelieved or ambulatory venous hypertension resulting mostly from deep venous thrombosis leading to venous incompetence, lipodermatosclerosis, leucocyte plugging of the capillaries, tissue hypoxia and microvascular dysfunction. It is not known what initiates venous ulcers. Triggers vary from trauma of the lower extremity to scratching to relieve itchy skin over the ankle region. Venous ulcers can be painful, and this condition presents an increasing burden of care. A systematic analysis of the role of technology used for diagnosis and management strongly supports the use of compression as a mainstay of standardised care. It further shows good evidence for the potential of some treatment procedures to accelerate healing. This article reviews the pathogenetic mechanisms, current diagnostic methods and standard care and its limitations.

Burns & Trauma (2018) 6:18

Varicose Veins. Chronic Venous Insufficiency. Lower Limbs Venous Ulcers. Point of View

F ^{Becker}

Abstract

Purpose: Lower limbs chronic venous disorders are still considered as a minor disease from a university hospital point of view, yet it is a very common problem, affecting the quality of life, generating disability, and expensive for healthcare resources. Its teaching is neither satisfactory nor easy to do. Apart from the fact that it rarely causes death, the complexity of venous anatomy and physiopathology, the lack of animal model, common practices lumping together visible varicose veins and chronic venous insufficiency, and moreover a certain carelessness in the vocabulary probably largely explain these difficulties. Our purpose is to discuss chronic venous disorders (varicose veins, chronic venous insufficiency, venous ulcers) on the basis of semantic, of anatomical, haemodynamic and clinical forms and finally of nosology.

Rev Med Interne. 2004 Jan;25(1):65-73.

Chronic Venous Insufficiency and Venous Ulceration

P C Alguire, B M Mathes

Abstract

Objective: To review and summarize the literature on the normal venous circulation of the leg, and the epidemiology, pathophysiology, and treatment of chronic venous insufficiency (CVI).

Data sources: English-language articles identified through a MEDLINE search (1966-1996) using the terms venous insufficiency or varicose ulcer and epidemiology, pathophysiology, diagnosis, and clinical trial (pt), and selected cross-references.

Study selection: Articles on epidemiology, pathophysiology, and treatment of CVI. Randomized, controlled studies were specifically sought for treatment efficacy.

Data extraction: Data were manually extracted from selected studies and reviews: emphasis was placed on information relevant to the general internist.

Data synthesis: Chronic venous insufficiency is a common primary care problem associated with significant morbidity and health care costs. The clinical spectrum of disease ranges from minor cosmetic concerns to severe fibrosing panniculitis and ulceration. Duplex Doppler ultrasonography may be the single best test to rule out deep venous thrombosis and other entities that can mimic CVI. Leg elevation and compression stockings are effective treatments for CVI; recalcitrant cases may require intermittent pneumatic compression. Topical antiseptics, antibiotics, enzymes, or growth factors offer no clear advantages in ulcer healing. Ulcer dressings remain a matter of convenience, cost, and physician judgment. The role of surgery in CVI appears to be limited.

Conclusions: Chronic venous insufficiency is a recalcitrant, recurrent medical problem. This condition can be managed by primary care physicians with relatively inexpensive treatment modalities in association with lifestyle modification.

J Gen Intern Med. 1997 Jun;12(6):374-83.

Venous ulcers of the lower limb: Where do we stand?

Sasanka S. Chatterjee

Abstract

In the course of a lifetime, almost 10% of the population will develop a chronic wound, with a wound-related mortality rate of 2.5%. Of these, underlying venous pathology is the most common aetiology of lower extremity ulceration. Even in the 21st century, studies revealed the following effects of ulceration: pain, itching, altered appearance, loss of sleep, functional limitations, social isolation, depression and disappointment with treatment. In 2011, an integrative review of previous studies on quality of life in patients with venous ulcers was published, which confirmed the negative impact of the disease on health-related quality of life.

Venous ulcers are the result of breakdown of skin due to failure of preventing the consequence of chronic venous insufficiency. The disease has been known for more than 3.5 millennia, with wound care centers established as early as 1500 BC. Unfortunately, still today, it is a very poorly managed clinical condition by most physicians despite acquiring a great deal of knowledge about the pathogenesis and treatment for venous ulcerations.

There is no available statistics related to the incidence of venous ulcers in India. But, an epidemiologic study on railway workers in 1972 found the incidence of varicose veins to be significantly higher in South Indians than in their northern counterparts.

The morbidity of the disease, inadequate management, necessary logistic support and prolonged continuous care makes this disease a financial burden both at a personal and at the Government level. In the US, 80% of the lower extremity ulcers are venous ulcers, and the financial burden is $2 billion per year. Venous leg ulceration alone has been estimated to cost the NHS £400 m a year in the United Kingdom. Studies in Germany calculated the mean total cost of a venous ulcer per patient per year to be €9569.

Anatomy and Pathophysiology

Venous return of the leg is dependent on two systems: deep and superficial, connected by perforator veins. Nomenclature of "deep" and "superficial" signifies their anatomic situations, either deep or superficial to the muscular fascia. There are unidirectional valves guiding the venous flow towards the heart. The deep system also includes the venous sinuses within, mainly, the soleus and, to a lesser extent, the gastrocnemeii muscles. There are innumerable perforators between ankle and groin. They may be direct, draining to the axial deep veins (e.g., tibial, peroneal, popliteal, femoral) or indirect, draining to the venous sinuses in muscles. Powerful muscular contraction drives the blood within the venous sinuses as well as the deep system of the veins towards the heart. The superficial venous system empties into the deep systems via the perforators both at the junction of the deep and superficial systems and throughout the lower limb. However, in the feet, the flow is from the deep to the superficial system. Therefore, any derangement in the unidirectional venous flow towards the heart will affect the ankle region the most. Communicating veins are those connecting the veins within the same system, i.e. deep to deep, e.g. between the vena comitantes around the arteries, or superficial to superficial. The universal structure in venous system is venous valve - a thin fold of endothelium supported by connective tissue. They remain open during supine position. As soon as a person stands up, there is a temporary retrograde flow for about 0.5 s, which is normal. Thereafter, the valves close, converting the entire venous system into segments of blood columns. The deep venous systems empty due to muscular actions in feet, calf and thigh, and the blood from the superficial system passes on to them guided by perforators and the intact valves. Approximately 90% of the venous drainage in lower limbs is through the deep system.

There are usually two main saphenous tributaries in the leg, an anterior branch and the posterior arch vein, which begins behind the medial malleolus and joins the great saphenous vein just distal to the knee. The posterior arch vein drains a network of medial ankle veins and is important in that the posterior tibial perforators join this vein rather than the main trunk of the great saphenous vein. There are two main tributaries in the thigh with an important perforator in the adductor canal. The small saphenous vein usually drains in the popliteal vein but communications exist with the great saphenous system, and its terminations are variable. In addition, there is a system that becomes important only under pathological conditions. Included in these are lateral superficial veins of the leg, which are remnants of the embryonic vena marginalis lateralis, the sciatic drainage system from the posterior thigh to the internal iliac system, the lateral subdermic system draining toward the femoral and inferior gluteal veins, the obturator veins and alternative venous pathways along the round ligament.

The aetiological factors resulting in disturbance in venous return from the lower limb are: Primary venous disease

The aetiology of the functional, biochemical and structural changes associated with varicose veins remains unclear. Proposed mechanisms have included hypoxia-mediated endothelial changes cell cycle dysfunction with inhibition of programmed cell death, changes in enzyme activity and underlying defects in venous tone. These ultimately result in loss of venous contractility and tone of veins, leading to dilatation and stretch. Valvular incompetence is a secondary phenomenon.

Secondary venous disease

Obstruction in the deep system is either due to thrombosis or destruction due injury. Post-thrombotic recanalisation process does not always destroy the valves, which, in majority of the patients, are protected by fibrinolytic activity in their vicinity. Yet, in about 10% of the patients, this mechanism fails and valves are destroyed. In secondary venous disease, both obstruction and reflux involving all the systems of veins ultimately play their roles in development of ulcers.

Failure of the valves

This may occur both in deep and superficial systems as well as perforators. There may be paucity in numbers, inherent weakness of valves, failure secondary to degenerative process or destruction of the valves by thrombotic process.

Others

Old age, obesity, asthenia, calf muscle dysfunction and prolonged dependent posture are contributory factors in poor circulation and excess load on the valves.

Any of the above will ultimately lead to chronic venous hypertension. The severity of chronic venous disease is related to the magnitude of venous hypertension, with 100% ulceration at pressures greater than 90 mmHg. As long as compensation can occur, the circulation will be normal although at the cost of increased load in the perforating and the superficial systems, which will ultimately fail, resulting in superficial varicosities, oedema, diapedesis and presence of various macromolecules in the interstitium leading to inflammatory reactions. Ulceration results from inflammation and theories that have been proposed are:

1. Leukocytes repeatedly trapped in microcirculation as a result of venous dilatation and pooling start releasing proteolytic enzymes that destroys tissues. Investigations proved about 24% less clearance of leukocytes in patients with ulceration in comparison with the normal or even in patients with varicose veins without ulceration. The clearance improves with response to treatment. Endothelial damage, platelet aggregation and intracellular oedema follow as a consequence and contribute to impaired wound healing.

2. Interepithelial pore widening, deposition of fibrin and other macromolecules in dermis trap growth factors thus rendering them unavailable for wound repair. There is also an abnormality in the fibrinolytic system. Immunohistochemical examinations have shown the presence of S-100 positive cells with dendritic cell morphology in the intima and media of veins with varicosity and thrombophlebitis. These dendritic cells are postulated to stimulate T lymphocytes in various immune responses and their co-localization indicate the role of inflammation in the aetiopathogenesis of venous ulcers.

Clinical Etiological Anatomical Pathological Classification

Developed under the auspices of the American venous forum, the clinical etiological anatomical pathological (CEAP) classification encompasses clinical (based on objective signs), aetiological (congenital, primary and secondary), anatomical (distribution of reflux and obstruction) and pathophysiological (related to reflux or obstruction) mechanisms of venous disease. The clinical portion includes seven categories from non-existent venous disease to ulceration.

1. No visible or palpable evidence of venous disease

2. Telangiectasia and/or reticular veins
3. Varicose veins
4. Oedema

1. Changes ascribed to venous disease: pigmentation, venous eczema, lipodermatosclerosis
2. Skin changes as defined above with healedulceration
3. Skin changes as defined above with active ulceration. Clinical features

History should include events of deep venous thrombosis thrombophlebitis, trauma and different medications. Many of these patients are old and arterial disease, diabetes mellitus, neurotrophic ulceration should be excluded. Syndromic and non-syndromic vascular malformation, if any, should be looked for. Venous ulcers are shallow, usually around the ankle, with unhealthy granulation tissue and fibrinous exudate in the floor .The base is schirrhous. Varicose veins are visible if not obscured by hyperpigmented, dermatosclerotic skin around the ulcers, which can be quite large. Sometimes, small cystic areas are seen, which are sites of impending rupture of skin. Tenderness over the course of superficial veins indicate thrombophlebitis. Clinical examination to visualize perforator incompetence can be done by use of a rubber tourniquet at different levels in the lower limb. Important ones are junctional perforators like saphenofomoral and saphenopopliteal. Another important one in the thigh is at the adductor canal and in the calf. In addition, there are perforators connecting the posterior arch vein to the tibial system and ankle perforators and the small saphenous vein and tributaries to the pernoeal system. However, judgment of their incompetence can be difficult in lipodermatosclerosis. The use of tourniquet can also identify deep venous obstruction. The patient has a bursting sensation on walking due to obstruction in the superficial system by the tourniquet if the deep system is not patent.

Investigations

Duplex scan with colour flow is the investigation of choice in venous pathology. It is non-invasive, gives valuable information regarding venous flow, thrombotic obstruction, patency and reflux, the effect of muscle contraction, proximal and distal compression and the Valsalva maneuver on each segment of the veins.

Plethysmography and venous pressure data are important in determining the need for surgical bypass or valve replacement. Quantitative data on venous obstruction, calf muscle pump ejection fraction and reflux are provided by air plethysmography, whereas venous pressure studies assess the physiological importance of anatomic obstruction because the collaterals may or may not provide adequate compensation for an obstructed pathway.

Ascending and descending venography are important only in candidates who are being considered for deep vein reconstruction.

For long-standing ulcers, chronic osteomyelitis and malignant transformation should be kept in mind and, if necessary, appropriate investigations undertaken.

Treatment

Treatment of venous ulceration should take into consideration treatment of underlying venous hypertension that of the ulcer and pharmacotherapy directed against inflammatory reactions.

Conservative Management Leg elevation

Any venous ulcer will heal if the patient takes rest with the lower limb elevated. Elevation above the heart level reduces oedema, improves venous drainage and microcirculation, reduces stress on the valves and hastens ulcer healing. It has been shown to be beneficial if used for 30-min sessions, three or four times a day, which may not be practical in the present day settings. It is more effective when combined with compression therapy. In addition, life style changes in the form of weight reduction, exercise and avoiding prolonged standing help improve quality of life.

Compression therapy

(Inelastic, elastic, intermittent pneumatic) is the standard of care and is associated with a decreased rate of ulcer recurrence. Although compression therapy is of proven benefit, the effect of intermittent pneumatic therapy is less evident. It reduces oedema and pain, improves venous circulation and enhances ulcer healing. Lifelong maintenance of compression therapy after ulcer healing reduces the rate of recurrence. However, in the presence of eczematous dermatitis, obesity, pain and discharging ulcer, strict adherence to the regime of compression therapy becomes cumbersome. Clinically significant arterial insufficiency and heart failure are contraindications to compression therapy.

Inelastic compression, although effective during ambulation and muscle contraction, provides no resting pressure. It fails to conform to the changes in size of the limb. Exemplified by Unna boot of yesteryears, it has practical difficulties of use due to foul-smelling discharge and need for frequent reapplications.

Elastic compression sustains pressure during both ambulation and rest. In ulcerations, a pressure of around 35–40 mmHg is necessary. In the absence of ulcer, a pressure between 25 and 30 mmHg may suffice. Elastic bandages or stockings may be used. The latter is more useful as it provides a graded pressure from below upwards, highest being at the ankle. It should be taken off at night and changed usually after 6 months as pressure is reduced by regular washing.

Multilayered elastic bandages have proved to be more effective than single layered ones, but require skilled application and frequent change in the presence of discharge.

Medications

Pentoxifylline (400 mg three-times daily) has been shown to be of additive beneficial effect to compression by dint of action on leucocyte metabolism, inhibition of platelet aggregation, reduction in viscosity of blood and consequent improvement in microcirculation. But, its effect as monotherapy has not been shown to be cost effective.

Aspirin (300 mg daily) is effective when used with compression therapy. It acts by reducing platelet adhesion.

Intravenously administered iloprost may be beneficial through vasodilatation and its effect on platelet aggregation, but supporting data are limited and it is expensive.

Oral zinc, despite having an anti-inflammatory effect, has not been shown to be useful.

Micronised purified flavanoid fraction-Daflon 500 mg and prostaglandin E1 analogue-are used due to their action on leucocyte metabolism. These drugs are most effective when used in conjunction with compression. Antibiotics are used in case of suspected cellulitis, and its routine use is not recommended.

Mechanical

Negative pressure wound therapy has been shown to reduce the size of ulcers of various aetiologies. But, available data are insufficient to support its use in venous ulcers. Moreover, it interferes with compression therapy and thus limits its use in venous ulcers.

Hyperbaric oxygen therapy

It has potential antibacterial and anti-inflammatory effects that have been found to be useful in diabetic foot ulcers, but proof of its benefits in venous ulcers is lacking.

Dressings

A wide variety of dressings are in use, including hydrocolloids, foams, hydrogels, pastes and simple non-adherent dressings. There is no evidence to prove superiority of one above the other and, therefore, the choice is based on available resources, personnel and individual preferences.

Surgical management

Surgical management is indicated for ulcers that are large, of prolonged duration or not responsive to conservative measures, including pharmacotherapy. Although more research is needed regarding the comparative efficacy of various surgical approaches, options include debridement, human skin grafting and surgery for venous insufficiency, which is associated with a reduced rate of ulcer recurrence and may be helpful for severe or refractory cases. Artificial skin grafting with human skin equivalent may be effective when used with compression therapy, but concerns regarding infection transmission still remain.

Debridement

Debridement is the first step in the treatment of any wound or ulcer. This may be sharp and surgical, mechanical, autolytic, enzymatic or biological (larvae). Many a times, morbidity and logistics come in the way of surgical debridement. In such situations, autolysis and subsequent mechanical debridement takes place due to regular lavage and change of dressings. Enzymatic preparations help in removal of necrotic tissue, but the process is slow and not practical for large ulcers. Usually, venous ulcers cause very little necrotic tissue and, in its presence, other causes like arterial insufficiency should be looked for.

Ulcer

Treatment for ulcer is not different from any other ulcer. Split-thickness skin grafts, full-thickness skin grafts, local flaps [usually perforator based and microvascular flaps all are suitable as cover provided the underlying pathology is dealt with. Sufficient evidence for efficacy of skin grafting alone for treatment of venous ulcers is lacking in the literature.

Underlying venous pathology

Surgical treatment aimed at correction of venous reflux should logically attack the sites of leakage, i.e. junctions of superficial and deep veins-the saphenofemoral and saphenopopliteal junctions as well as the incompetent perforator veins, particularly in the leg and sometimes also in the thigh. The tributaries of the great saphenous veins in the groin must also be ligated in order to prevent varicosity in them and in others through their connections in the future. Incompetent varicose veins have attenuated walls and act as venous lakes, creating peripheral blood pool. Their ablation helps improve venous circulation.

When the deep venous system is involved, there are three categories: (1) when there is a primary venous disease with valvular incompetence, (2) when there is a post-thrombotic destruction of valves or segments of deep veins, i.e. secondary venous disease and (3) a combination of both. In order to correct the failure of venous valves, direct surgery on them to prevent reflux was performed in cases of primary valvular disease. When there was total destruction of the valves in a small segment, either a bypass with grafts containing competent valves or transposition of an adjacent competent venous segment was carried out.

Any of the above, but usually in combination, is aimed at correction of underlying venous reflux, and this is more effective than compression therapy alone.

Techniques Conventional surgery

Conventional surgery consists of saphenofemoral/saphenopopliteal flush ligation, disconnection of major tributaries, stripping/avulsion of varicose veins and perforator ligation through long incisions. This surgery aims at only the superficial venous system.

Subfascial endoscopic perforator ligation

Standard laparoscopic equipment with two 10-mm ports are used to ligate the incompetent perforator veins. Carbon dioxide at a pressure of 30 mmHg is used to insufflate the subfascial space

to facilitate dissection and a pneumatic tourniquet is used in the thigh to obtain a bloodless field. This reduces morbidity and avoids the technical difficulties of working in lipodermatosclertotic tissue.

Sclerotherapy

Sodium tetradecylsulphate, polydocanol and 20% hypertonic saline are used to intentionally induce chemical phlebitis at the site of reflux and varicosities. Compression is to be ensured immediately after the injection, and this is an essential part for obliteration of the pathological vein. Mixing of sclerosant with air or carbon dioxide in various ratios to form a foam increases the efficacy of sclerotherapy. The use of ultrasound probe to track the needle and guide to the appropriate site of injection, and even track the dispersion of foam, is a further development in sclerotherapy. Sclerotherapy, although popular as an outpatient department procedure, is effective for only small varicosities and localized form of the disease.

Radiofrequency ablation

Basically, this consists of delivery of infrared energy to the vein walls by directly heating the catheter tip with radiofrequency energy. Currently available equipment can monitor the core temperature of the catheter tip to about 120°C. Heat delivered to the vein wall causes shrinkage, and the catheter is withdrawn gradually until the entire vein is treated. This is performed in 7-cm segments. Advanced technology has ensured destruction, specifically of the vein wall, without carbonization or destruction of the surrounding tissue.

Endovenous laser surgery

Under perivascular infiltration of dilute local anesthesia, laser fibre is inserted in the great or small saphenous veins through a small puncture and under ultrasonic guidance advanced to the groin or knee crease. The laser is activated while it is withdrawn, resulting in obliteration of the vein.

In a randomized trial comparing four modalities of treatments of great saphenous venous reflux viz. endovenous laser ablation, radiofrequency ablation, ultrasound-guided foam sclerotherapy and surgical stripping, technical failure was highest after sclerotherapy. The end point in this study however was ablation of great saphenous vein. Short-term recovery was best in the radiofrequency and foam sclerotherapy groups, but 1-year results were similar in each group.

Surgery for deep venous reflux

Surgery for deep venous insufficiency is a more difficult proposition. Here, there are two categories each with two subcategories of surgical procedure: (1) primary valve failure and (2) Secondary valve failure as a result of post-thrombotic destruction.

For primary valve failure, the attempted procedures are either intraluminal repair of valves or extraluminal support of the valve. Intraluminal repair consisted of tightening by sutures at the commissural level and, thereby, re-establishment of competence of the failed valve. Extraluminal support was provided by tightening of the vein wall externally at the site of the valve cusps without entering its lumen. The results however were better in the former.

For destroyed valves, either a segment of vein with normal valves is transplanted for the diseased segment or an adjacent normal vein is transposed in the diseased segment. Long-term results reported in the literature in respect of ulcer recurrence after this procedure have been equivocal.

Conclusion

Venous ulcers are the most common of all leg ulcers, with high morbidity and strain on economic resources, and have a negative impact on quality of life. It is unfortunate that many a times it is not properly diagnosed and, unnecessarily, expensive treatment is undertaken. Conservative management with leg elevation and compression therapy is effective and is the mainstay of therapy, particularly in the elderly and infirms not suitable for surgery. Dressings are dictated by economic and logistic factors and also preference of the treating physicians. No particular dressing material has been found to be superior to the others. Ulcers of prolonged duration not responding to conservative measures or patients who, for life style reasons, are unable to undertake it, will require surgery. The surgical procedures are directed at prevention of venous reflux at various levels and ablation of varicose veins followed by cover of the ulcers. However, compression therapy needs to be continued.

Indian J Plast Surg. 2012 May;45(2):266-74.

Leg Ulcers

T J Phillips, J S Dover

Abstract

The treatment of leg ulcers is a common and sometimes difficult problem. They can be costly to treat and are associated with loss of working capacity and sometimes significant morbidity. In the western world, leg ulcers are most frequently caused by venous insufficiency, arterial insufficiency, neuropathy (usually diabetic), or a combination of these factors. The pathogenesis, clinical features, and management of these types of leg ulcers are emphasized in this review.

J Am Acad Dermatol. 1991 Dec;25(6 Pt 1):965-87.

Chronic venous insufficiency and venous leg ulceration

Isabel C. Valencia, Anna Falabella, Robert S. Kirsner, William H. Eaglstein

Abstract

Venous ulcers are the most common form of leg ulcers. Venous disease has a significant impact on quality of life and work productivity. In addition, the costs associated with the long-term care of these chronic wounds are substantial. Although the exact pathogenic steps leading from venous hypertension to venous ulceration remain unclear, several hypotheses have been developed to explain the development of venous ulceration. A better understanding of the current pathophysiology of venous ulceration has led to the development of new approaches in its management. New types of wound dressings, topical and systemic therapeutic agents, surgical modalities, bioengineered tissue, matrix materials, and growth factors are all novel therapeutic options that may be used in addition to the "gold standard," compression therapy, for venous ulcers. This review discusses current aspects of the epidemiology, pathophysiology, clinical presentation, diagnostic assessment, and current therapeutic options for chronic venous insufficiency and venous ulceration. (J Am Acad Dermatol 2001;44:401-21.)

Learning objective: At the conclusion of this learning activity, participants should be familiar with the 3 main types of lower extremity ulcers and should improve their understanding of the epidemiology, pathogenesis, risk factors, clinical presentation, diagnostic assessment, and current therapies for chronic venous insufficiency and venous ulcers.

J Am Acad Dermatol. 2001 Mar;44(3):401

Long-term prognosis for patients with chronic leg ulcers: a prospective cohort study.

Nelzén O, Bergqvist D, Lindhagen A.

Abstract

Objectives:

To assess the long-term prognosis of leg ulcers.

Design:

A 5 year prospective cohort study.

Materials:

A random sample of 382 patients with open leg ulcers (foot ulcers included) treated in the community.

Methods:

Interim analyses were made at 15 months (arterial ulcers) and at 20 months (varicose ulcers). Long- term healing was assessed at 54 months by a postal questionnaire. Five year survival was assessed by official population registries.

Results:

At 54 months 212 patients (55%) were still alive, of whom 124 (58%) had healed their ulcers, 80 (38%) had open ulcers and eight (4%) were amputated. The healing was worst for patients with venous ulcers, only 44% had healed their original ulcers without recurrence. The 5 year survival was 52%, significantly lower than for age- and sex-matched controls (68%) (p = 0.0002). Patients with venous ulcers had a survival not significantly different from controls and patients with arterial or other aetiologies had a doubled risk of death. Diabetic patients had a lower survival than non- diabetics (p < 0.05) and controls (p < 0.0001), but the healing prognosis was not significantly different.

Conclusion:

Only patients with non-venous ulcers have a higher mortality than expected. The long-term healing prognosis for leg ulcer patients is poor and worst for patients with venous ulcers.

Eur J Vasc Endovasc Surg. 1997 May;13(5):500-8

Pathomorphological Peculiarities of Trophic Ulcer Developed During Chronic Venous Insufficiency of the Lower Limbs

G Arabidze, H Chkhaidze

Abstract

Trophic ulcers caused by chronic venous insufficiency are regarded as severe pathology. Despite numerous investigations, lots of issues need further classification. Special emphasis must be put on studying the morphologic changes, developing in tissues during the venous insufficiency. The aim of our research was to study the morphologic changes, taking place in the soft tissues of the lower third part of the calf, caused by chronic venous insufficiency. The study material was represented by the trophic ulcer, adjacent coetaneous layer and soft tissues removed from the lower third part of the calf. The investigation showed that three zones can be distinguished in case of the inflammation around the trophic ulcer. The first inner zone is located adjacent to the ulcer in multi-layer corneal epithelium. This zone is represented by acute purulent inflammation. Then there comes the middle zone, which is represented by granulative-proliferative inflammation; is the early stage of the purulent exudates organization. The outer zone is created after the granulative tissue becomes mature and is represented by fibrous hyaline connective tissue with inflammatory cellular infiltration residues in it. It is recommended to cut fibrous connective tissue scar and the adjacent soft tissues during surgery treatment. Therefore, during surgery treatment it is necessary to cut out not only fibrous connective tissue scar but the adjacent soft tissues as well.

Georgian Med News. 2008 Oct;(163):58-61.

Pathomechanism of Chronic Venous Insufficiency and Leg Ulcer

T Sándor

Abstract

Uniform view of chronic venous diseases has been formed in the last 3 decades. Chronic venous insufficiency (CVI) is a functional disorder of the venous system of the lower limb. The basis of the pathology is always the venous hypertension caused by valvular insufficiency and reflux with or without venous outflow obstruction. Epifascial, subfascial and transfascial forms of CVI can be distinguished. In the practice these forms are almost always combined. The consistent venous hypertension is the initiating factor in alterations in the microcirculation which leads to skin changes and venous ulceration. The precise mechanism of the development of venous leg ulcer is still uncertain. A recent hypothesis suggests that leukocytes are trapped in the capillaries and attaching to the endothel they become activated and release proteolytic enzymes, free radicals which have destructive effects on lipid membranes, proteins as well as on many connective tissue compounds. The endothelium plays active role in the complex mechanism. Increased expression of tissue metalloproteinases has been observed in the periulcer skin. The presence of perivascular leukocyte infiltration and fibrin cuff is a reflexion of an inflammatory process. The clinical stages of CVI are likely to be the results of a systemic inflammatory response to a period of venous hypertension.

Acta Physiol Hung. 2004;91(2):131-45

Evaluation and Treatment of Leg Ulcers Associated With Chronic Venous Insufficiency

William Marston

Abstract

The successful management of patients who have leg ulcers related to chronic venous disease requires optimal management of the wound bed, elimination of edema with compression, and correction of venous hypertension whenever possible. Healing of the wound itself requires compression, debridement, bacterial control, and stimulation of the wound bed. Prevention of ulcer recurrence is most effective if the patient is amenable to correction of the venous insufficiency. This is most successful when the superficial or perforator veins are the primary source. Quality diagnostic studies are critical in determining the anatomy and hemodynamic importance of various venous abnormalities and can guide appropriate interventional treatment. Venous corrective procedures usually can be performed using minimally invasive endovenous methods, which are associated with fewer complications and more rapid recovery than are major surgical techniques.

Clinics in Plastic Surgery. Volume 34, Issue 4, October 2007, Pages 717-730.

The role of primary varicose veins in venous ulceration

Hoare MC, Nicolaides AN, Miles CR, Shull K, Jury RP, Needham T, Dudley HA.

Abstract

"Venous" ulceration is usually ascribed to deep venous insufficiency.

Method:

We record the cases of 20 patients with 23 ulcers without a history suggestive of deep vein disease who were found to have a normal deep venous system when evaluated by

    a. Doppler ultrasound,

    b. ambulatory venous pressures, and

a. photoplethysmography.

Results:

All had gross varicose veins present for many years (mean 24 years; range 10 to 35 years), and only 14 limbs had incompetent calf perforating veins.

Conclusion:

Effective treatment is facilitated by recognition of the relationship of varicose ulcer to superficial venous disease, usually incompetence of the saphenofemoral junction, with or without the presence of incompetent calf perforating veins.

Surgery, 1982, Sept:92(3).

LIPODERMATOSCLEROSIS

Lipodermatosclerosis: A Commonly Misdiagnosed Complication of Chronic Venous Insufficiency

Mohammad Kazem Fallahzadeh, Mohammad Khalesi, and Mohammad Reza Namazi

Abstract

Lipodermatosclerosis is a complication of severe chronic venous insufficiency that results from high venous pressure and resulting increased capillary permeability, perivascular fibrin cuffing, and tissue hypoxia. These events culminate in fibrosis and membranous fat necrosis.

Lipodermatosclerosis can present as painful, red, indurated plaques that may be easily misdiagnosed as cellulitis, thrombophlebitis, and morphea. It initially develops on the medial aspect of the ankle and then spreads to involve the entire leg circumferentially. In its advanced states, lipodermatosclerosis, along with a lymphedematous upper portion of the leg and an edematous foot, can look like an inverted champagne bottle.

Compression therapy, drugs such as stanozolol, and surgical procedures are the current therapeutic options available for this recalcitrant conundrum.

Scientific World Journal. 2010 Apr 1;10:576-7

The Clinical Spectrum of Lipodermatosclerosis

R S Kirsner, J B Pardes, W H Eaglstein, V Falanga

Abstract

Lipodermatosclerosis refers to the skin induration and hyperpigmentation of the legs that often occurs in patients who have venous insufficiency. Lipodermatosclerosis has also been termed hypodermitis sclerodermiformis and appears to be similar if not-identical to the recently described sclerosing panniculitis of the leg. There has been much confusion about the nature, clinical course, and treatment of lipodermatosclerosis. We believe that lipodermatosclerosis has an acute, inflammatory phase and a chronic, fibrotic stage, although a spectrum exists. Direct immunofluorescence studies of early and late lesions are helpful in that they show dermal pericapillary fibrin deposits without other immunoreactants. Treatment of lipodermatosclerosis consists of compression therapy with either graded stockings or elastic bandages. We and others have found that the anabolic steroid stanozolol improves this condition rapidly and consistently.

J Am Acad Dermatol. 1993 Apr;28(4):623-7.

Skin damage in chronic venous insufficiency: does an oxygen diffusion barrier really exist?

T R Cheatle, G M McMullin, J Farrah, P D Smith, and J H Scurr

Abstract

Eleven patients with lipodermatosclerosis (LDS) and 14 patients without venous or arterial disease underwent measurement of xenon-133 (133Xe) half-clearance times from the gaiter region of the leg. Xenon has similar diffusion characteristics to oxygen, and the investigation reflects the ability of the isotope to diffuse from the skin surface into capillary blood. Median skin half-clearance time for skin in the LDS group was 2.2 min and in the control group 2.1 min. From the subcutaneous tissues, the respective times were 14.1 and 17.4 minutes. These differences are not statistically significant. The study fails to yield evidence suggesting that an oxygen diffusion barrier exists in lipodermatosclerosis.

J R Soc Med. 1990 Aug;83(8):493-4.

MEDICAL TREATMENT

Treatment of chronic venous insufficiency

S uman W. Rathbun MD, MS & Angelia C. Kirkpatrick MD, MPH

Abstract

Chronic venous insufficiency (CVI) results from venous hypertension secondary to superficial or deep venous valvular reflux. Treatment modalities are aimed at reducing venous valvular reflux, thereby inhibiting the ensuing pathologic inflammatory process. Compression therapy using pumps, bandaging, and/or graded compression stockings is the mainstay of treatment for CVI. Compression therapy has been shown to be effective in reducing venous hypertension retarding the development of inflammation and pathologic skin changes. Pharmacologic agents such as diuretics and topical steroid creams reduce swelling and pain short term but offer no long-term treatment advantage. Herbal supplements may reduce the inflammatory response to venous hypertension, but are not licensed by the US Food and Drug Administration, and vary in their efficacy, quality, and safety. However, several randomized controlled trials using the herbal horse chestnut seed extract containing aescin have shown short-term improvement in signs and symptoms of CVI. Endovascular and surgical techniques aimed at treatment of primary and secondary venous valvular reflux have been shown to improve venous hemodynamics promoting healing of venous ulcers and improving quality of life. The newer endovascular treatments of varicose veins using laser, radiofrequency ablation, and chemical foam sclerotherapy show some promise.

Curr Treat Options Cardiovasc Med. 2007 Apr;9(2):115-26

Medical Management of Venous Ulcers

L uigi Pascarella, Cynthia K Shortell

Abstract

Venous disease is the most common cause of chronic leg ulceration and represents an advanced clinical manifestation of venous insufficiency. Due to their frequency and chronicity, venous ulcers have a high socioeconomic impact, with treatment costs accounting for 1% of the health care budget in Western countries. The evaluation of patients with venous ulcers should include a thorough medical history for prior deep venous thrombosis, assessment for an hypercoagulable state, and a physical examination. Use of the CEAP (clinical, etiology, anatomy, pathophysiology) Classification System and the revised Venous Clinical Severity Scoring System is strongly recommended to characterize disease severity and assess response to treatment. This venous condition requires lifestyle modification, with affected individuals performing daily intervals of leg elevation to control edema; use of elastic compression garments; and moderate physical activity, such as walking wearing below-knee elastic stockings. Meticulous skin care, treatment of dermatitis, and prompt treatment of cellulitis are important aspects of medical management. The pharmacology of chronic venous insufficiency and venous ulcers include essentially two medications:

pentoxifylline and phlebotropic agents. The micronized purified flavonoid fraction is an effective adjunct to compression therapy in patients with large, chronic ulceration.

Semin Vasc Surg. 2015 Mar;28(1):21-8

The treatment of varicose veins: an investigation of patient preferences and expectations.

Shepherd AC, Gohel MS, Lim CS, Hamish M, Davies AH

Abstract

Objectives: A number of modalities are now available for the treatment of varicose veins. The aim of the study was to investigate the factors considered important by patients when contemplating treatment of their varicose veins.

Methods: Consecutive new patients referred to a vascular surgery service were invited to complete a short anonymous questionnaire prior to their consultation. The questionnaire consisted of 13 multiple choice questions relating to symptoms, potential varicose vein treatments and patient knowledge of existing therapies.

Results: Of 111 patients, there were 83 complete responses (75%). Symptoms of pain or aching were reported as moderate or severe by 77/103 (75%) of patients and significantly limited the activities of 47/101 (47%). Although the majority (89/103 [86%]) of patients were aware of surgery, only 52/103 (51%) knew of the existence of endothermal ablation (either laser or radiofrequency) and only 23/103 (22%) were aware of foam sclerotherapy. Some

58/92 (63%) were in favour of local anaesthetic treatment. Most patients (74/103, 72%) felt inadequately informed to express a preference regarding treatment type prior to their consultation, although 24/103 (23%) expressed a preference for endovenous treatment. Interestingly, 74/92 (80%) stated that the opinion of their vascular surgeon would be likely to or definitely influence their treatment decision and the majority of patients stated that what they had read in magazines (54/80, 64%) or on the Internet (51/85, 60%) would have no influence on their decision regarding treatment, respectively.

Conclusion: Only a minority of patients referred with varicose veins were aware of endovenous treatments or felt adequately informed to express a treatment preference prior to consultation. Over half of patients expressed a preference for local anaesthetic therapy and a preference for a single visit treatment, although most would be strongly influenced by the opinion of their vascular surgeon and not influenced by media advertising.

Phlebology. 2010 Apr;25(2):54-65

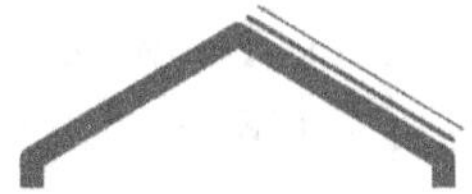

Varicose Veins Pain Relief, Symptoms, Causes, Pain Relief, Treatments, Surgery, and Prevention

Shabir Bhimji, Amy Smookler, Mara Aloi
Varicose Veins Overview

Veins are blood vessels that return deoxygenated blood from the outer parts of the body back to the heart and lungs. When veins become abnormally thick, full of twists and turns, or enlarged, they are called varicose veins. Generally, the veins in the legs and thighs have a tendency to become varicosed. The thickened, twisting or dilated parts of the vein are called varicosities. Varicose veins can form anywhere in the body, but they are most often located in the legs. In the United States alone, about 19% of men and 36% of women have varicose veins.

Varicose veins tend to be inherited and become more prominent as the person ages. Veins in the leg are either superficial or deep.

The superficial veins and their branches are close to the skin. These veins typically become varicosed. Also included in this category are the communicator or perforator veins, which connect the superficial veins with the deep veins.

The deep veins are encased by muscle and connective tissue, which help to pump the blood in the veins and back to the heart. The veins have one-way valves to prevent them from developing varicosities.

Generally, blood travels from the superficial veins to the deep veins. From there, the blood travels through a network of larger veins back to the heart.

Varicose Vein Causes

Many theories exist for why varicosities occur in veins, but the consensus is that defective/damaged valves within the veins are to blame.

Valves prevent backward flow of blood within the vein. They keep blood in the vein moving toward the heart. Why the valves stop working is up for debate.

Some experts think inherited problems cause some people to have too few valves or valves that do not function properly.

Some people may be born with abnormalities of the vein wall. The resulting weakness may predispose the valves to separate and become leaky.

The result is that when a person with poorly functioning valves stands up, the blood flow actually reverses and flows down the superficial veins, when it should be flowing up, toward the heart.

When the muscles surrounding the deep veins contract, emptying the deeper veins, a build-up of pressure occurs.

This causes even more blood to go the wrong way from the deep to the superficial veins through faulty valves in the perforator veins.

This increases pressure in the superficial veins and causes varicosities. Many factors can aggravate the situation.

• Pregnancy is associated with an increase in blood volume. Also, added pressure on the veins in the legs by the weight of the growing uterus and the relaxation effects of the hormones estrogen and progesterone on the vein walls contribute to the development of varicose veins during pregnancy

- Prolonged standing
- Obesity or distended belly

- Straining: Chronic constipation, urinary retention from an enlarged prostate, chronic cough, or any other conditions that cause you to strain for prolonged periods of time causes an increase in the forces transmitted to the leg veins and may result in varicose veins. These mechanisms also contribute to the formation of hemorrhoids, which are varicosities located in the rectal and anal area.
- Prior surgery or trauma to the leg: These conditions interrupt the normal blood flow channels.
- Age: Generally, most elderly individuals show some degree of varicose vein occurrence. Varicose Vein Symptoms

Varicose veins are relatively easy to identify and can be a cosmetic nuisance for many people.

- They protrude or bulge from under the skin and feel ropey.
- The legs often ache and feel heavy and itchy.
- Symptoms can intensify after a long day of standing on one's feet.

One may have severe pain upon standing or even have cramps in the legs at night.

Varicose veins can be more prominent or first appear during menstruation or pregnancy, and they may be more bothersome during these times.

Some people may have no symptoms at all. For most people, varicose veins are mainly a cosmetic problem.

Varicose veins are prone to developing superficial thrombophlebitis, which is a blood clot along with inflammation of a segment of vein.

Blood clots in the superficial veins are easy to detect and troublesome but are usually harmless. You may feel an area of tenderness and pain in the varicose vein, along with redness and swelling. The area may also feel hard or firm.

Sometimes such areas can represent infection within the vein, so it is a good idea to visit your health care provider if you should develop any of these symptoms.

This condition is not to be confused with a deep vein thrombophlebitis, which is a blood clot in a deep vein. Deep vein thrombophlebitis is more serious because of the clot's potential to travel toward the heart and lodge in the lung. This condition requires emergent admission to the hospital for treatment with blood thinning medication

Exams and Tests

Making the diagnosis of varicose veins is a relatively easy task. They are easy to identify just by their characteristic appearance on physical examination.

Your health care provider most likely will take a thorough medical history and examination looking not only for the extent of your varicose veins, but also for potential risk factors.

He or she may do any of several simple tourniquet tests to identify points of reverse blood flow. The simplest test uses only a blood pressure cuff.

Another useful device aiding in localizing the extent of the problem is a Doppler ultrasound. This handheld device is skimmed over the surface of the leg to map out the veins and faulty valves. This device is similar to those used in pregnancy to identify the developing fetus.

Duplex scanning, a similar but more detailed test, can also be done to rule out the presence of clots in the deeper veins.

Magnetic resonance venography is another test performed when the Duplex scan test is unclear. This test can even look for blood clots in the deep veins

Medical Treatment

Sclerotherapy involves injecting a chemical inside the vein that obliterates it. The treatment is only helpful for the spider veins and very small veins. It has no use in the treatment of large varicose veins.

Even for the smaller veins, many treatments are usually necessary.

The therapy is not totally successful in helping symptoms and preventing formation of more varicose veins.

Complications associated with this technique include allergic reactions to the chemical used, stinging or burning at the various injection sites, inflammation, skin ulcerations, and permanent discoloration of the skin.

Bandages often remain in place for as long as 3 weeks.

Wearing compression stockings is usually recommended after treatment.

Lasers have received attention recently as a treatment for varicose veins but are frequently used in the treatment of smaller spider veins, medically referred to as telangiectasias.

These veins are small, measuring only up to 1 millimeter in diameter, and represent dilated capillaries.

Using lasers to treat these smaller vessels can cause changes in the color or texture of the skin. Multiple treatments are often required.

Since this mode of therapy is relatively new, only time and experience will tell if it is as effective as older techniques.

If you have superficial thrombophlebitis, your health care provider will usually recommend warm compresses and pain medication. Additional treatment depends on whether your physician thinks you may have an infection

Surgery

Several surgical procedures are available to relieve varicose veins, but not everyone with varicose veins is a candidate for surgery.

If you are pregnant or recently pregnant, it is advisable to wait at least 6 weeks after delivery before considering this option, because many of the varicose veins you have during pregnancy will fade.

If your veins bother you only because of the way they look, and you are not bothered by pain or inflammation, then surgery may not be your best option.

Surgery is usually reserved for people who either do not get relief from the home care techniques or lifestyle changes, or who for cosmetic reasons want to try methods other than sclerotherapy or laser treatment to make their veins less prominent.

Most of the surgical procedures are performed on an outpatient basis.

The surgery involves either vein ligation (tying) or stripping or avulsion (pulling away) of the smaller branches.

With any surgery, risks and benefits exist. These should be discussed with the health care provider and with the specialist involved.

Recurrence of varicose veins does occur and may be due to incompetent perforator veins or failure to ligate the vein more proximally in the groin.

Ligation

This usually involves an incision at the groin. The incision measures about 2-4 cm, and the saphenous vein is identified where it enters the femoral vein. It is tied just at the entrance. The procedure can be performed under local anesthesia.

When the varicosities occur behind the lower leg, the incision is made behind the knee joint to access the lesser saphenous vein.

Ligation alone carries a low rate of recurrence of varicose veins, as long as the valves of the perforator veins are competent. Stripping of the veins is usually performed for the very large, thick, and tortuous veins that are unsightly. Vein stripping is being performed less often now, so that the veins can be preserved if the patient requires coronary artery bypass surgery in the future.

Avulsion: This requires many tiny incisions and removal of the varicose veins that have been outlined on the skin.

Stripping

This involves at least 2 incisions, 1 at the groin and 1 at the knee.

A tunneling device is placed under the skin between the 2 points, and the saphenous vein is dragged or pulled out of the tunnel.

This technique will leave not only scars from the incisions but also a significant amount of bruising and possibly bleeding. The bleeding is easily controlled by pressure dressings and stops immediately. The bruising is usually noticeable for a few weeks.

For vein stripping, a recovery period of 5-10 days is needed before returning to a regular routine. For just vein ligation, a few days off is more than adequate.

A possibility of persistent numbness from damage to the nerves in the skin exists (for this reason, usually only the vein to the knee is stripped, not the vein below the knee). The numbness is only mild in nature and does not cause any future problems.

Endovascular laser therapy

Endovenous laser therapy is a new technique that uses a laser to destroy the vein. The procedure is usually performed in a doctor's office and takes about 30-45 minutes. The small laser is passed into the vein with guidance from the ultrasound machine. The laser is then fired up and the entire vein is fibrosed. The laser is fired at multiple locations and the entire procedure is performed with some local anesthesia.

Recovery is rapid and involves minimal pain. The procedure is relatively new and except for some mild bruising and a numbing sensation, no other effects have been seen in the short term.

Radiofrequency ablation

Radiofrequency ablation is a similar technique to endovascular laser, but it uses heat to destroy the vein. The probe is placed in the vein under ultrasound and once in position, the vein is heated along the entire length. The procedure is performed under local anesthesia and takes about 30 minutes. It is a relatively new procedure and short-term results are excellent

Prevention

You cannot change your genes, but you can keep your weight under control, exercise, eat a healthy diet high in fiber, and try to stick to loose comfortable clothing when possible. If you are genetically destined to develop varicose veins, they may appear despite all your best efforts.

Ted stockings are the best nonsurgical treatment of varicose veins. They prevent skin breakdown and worsening of the varicosities. Most people have decreased swelling in their feet and less tiredness at the end of the day when using Ted stockings

Outlook

Varicose veins that you have now will not go away unless you have treatment, such as sclerotherapy or ligation and stripping. At times the veins may seem more prominent, such as in warm weather. However, once they appear, they will not go away on their own.

Prevention is the key. The earlier you start the lifestyle modifications outlined in Self-Care at Home, the better your chances of preventing new varicose veins from forming. In some cases, varicose veins may be one stage in the continuum of chronic poor vein functioning.

Some people may progress from having no symptoms, to the development of varicose veins, and then on to problems with leg swelling, and finally to ulcers caused by stagnant blood flow.

A small number of these people will have deep vein clots as a cause for their signs and symptoms, but most will not.

The more severe problems, such as skin ulcers, tend to be very difficult to prevent completely. Once these ulcers occur, they are very difficult to cure.

Even when they are eliminated, these ulcers tend to recur.

A deep vein blood clot has the potential to travel through the bloodstream and lodge in the lung. This is called a pulmonary embolism. Pulmonary embolism does not occur from varicose veins.

Pulmonary embolism can be life threatening, because the blood clot can interrupt the circulation of blood.

Common symptoms of pulmonary embolism are chest pain and shortness of breath. Varicose Veins

These are enlarged, tortuous veins that usually appear on the legs. Varicose veins are a common condition and it affects up to 25-40% of all females and 10-15% of males. It estimated to affect nearly 15-20% of all adults.

What Are the Causes of Varicose Veins?

Risk factors are age, family history and pregnancy whereas obesity, prolonged standing and trauma, infection have all been known to make varicose veins worse.

The main problem is that these veins have "faulty or damaged" valves. These one-way valves are located throughout the length of the inside of these veins. "Faulty or damaged" valves are also known as incompetent valves.

Veins should return blood from the legs to the heart and usually there are one-way valves that prevent the blood from flowing backwards (reflux). These one-way valves are located throughout the length of the inside of these veins. When these valves become "faulty or damaged", they are called incompetent valves and the blood now flows in both directions thereby causing pooling. This pooling of blood in the leg veins over a period of time causes the veins to bulge and protrude from the skin surface

What Are the Symptoms?

- Some patients have no symptoms whilst others may experience:
- Bleeding
- Calf aches
- Calf heaviness
- Discolouration of the skin

- Ezcema
- Hardening of the skin
- Itching
- Nocturnal calf cramps
- Swelling of the legs
- Thrombophebitis
- Ulcer formation
- Prevention

Whilst it is difficult to prevent the onset of varicose veins, certain actions can be taken to reduce the severity of these varicose veins.

- Avoid prolonged standing
- Avoid wearing high heels
- Do not cross your legs
- Elevate legs when possible
- Regular exercise especially brisk walking, jogging
- Support stockings
- Weight management

Duplex Ultrasound

Before treatment can be instituted, a duplex ultrasound should be performed. The ultrasound will be performed by our surgeon. It is performed to determine the exact pattern of abnormal blood flow (reflux) and the location of the abnormal or "faulty" valves.

Treatment for varicose veins is targeted at the superficial leg veins or the long saphenous vein. It is important that the deep leg veins are assessed before treatment to ensure they are normal.

The duplex ultrasound is performed in the clinic with conduction gel, there is no downtime, no pain or needles.

The results of the scan are immediate and with this result, the best treatment plan can be tailored for each individual patient.

Treatment

- Endovenous Laser Therapy (EVLT®)
- Conventional Vein Surgery
- Ultrasound Guided Sclerofoam Therapy (UGFT®)
- Ambulatory Phlebectomy

https://w[1]ww.emedicinehealth.com/varicose_veins/ article_em.htm[2]

---

1. *http://www.emedicinehealth.com/varicose_veins/article_em.htm*

2. *http://www.emedicinehealth.com/varicose_veins/article_em.htm*

Therapeutic Guidelines in Chronic Venous Insufficiency

D *von Uslar*

Abstract

Chronic venous insufficiency is characterized by decreased efficiency of the veno-muscular pump function. Resulting symptoms are polymorphous and eyecatching and therefore often distract attention from the treatment of the basic functional disorder. This is avoided by using quantifying and localizing diagnostic methods routinely. Best accepted by the patients are noninvasive methods that are supplied with photoplethysmography and Doppler-ultrasound. Synopsis of the findings gained by both mutually completing methods makes it possible to plan the most suitable therapy for the patient. Whereas a predominantly extrafascial localization of the defect can be repaired by a definitive therapy like operation or sclerotherapy according to TOUR-NAY, the prevalence of intrafascial damage inevitably leads to lifelong compression-therapy.

Zeitschrift für Hautkrankheiten: 1988:63 Suppl 4:87-91..

Evaluation and Management of Chronic Venous Disease Using the Foundation of CEAP

Teresa L Carman, Ali Al-Omari

Abstract

Purpose of the review: Venous disease is common. Depending on the population studied, the prevalence may be as high as 80%. Significant chronic venous disease with venous ulcers or trophic skin changes is reported to affect 1-10% of the population. A systematic assessment of the clinical findings associated with chronic venous disease will facilitate appropriate imaging. Based on imaging and assessment, patients with reflux or obstruction can be recommended proper medical and endovascular or surgical management.

Recent findings: Many types of endovascular management are available to treat reflux and eliminate varicose veins and tributaries. More recently adopted non-thermal non-tumescent techniques have been shown to be comparable with more widely performed laser or radiofrequency ablation techniques. A thorough clinical assessment, appropriate duplex ultrasound imaging, and use of advanced imaging when needed will allow clinicians to optimize therapy for patients with chronic venous disease based on the etiology, anatomy involved, and the pathophysiology.

Curr Cardiol Rep. 2019 Aug 30;21(10):114.

Pharmacological Treatment and Prevention of Chronic Venous Ulcers

A M Cerbone, A Tufano, A Coppola, E Cimino, M N Di Minno,
G Di Minno

Abstract

Chronic venous insufficiency and chronic venous ulcers represent an important medical problem, because of the high incidence and prevalence in the general population, and need to be considered as a lifelong degenerative condition, with socioeconomic consequences. Ulceration is a severe complication of the post-thrombotic syndrome, often precipitated by minor trauma. The rate of post- thrombotic syndrome varies between 20% and 100% of patients with deep vein thrombosis, mostly occurring within two years of an initial thrombotic event. This syndrome is difficult to treat, causes significant disability and reduces the quality of life. To date, there are no effective therapies of chronic venous ulcers and no definite strategies for identifying patients at risk for the development of ulceration. The role of adequate compression with elastic stockings is well recognized. Several systemic drugs have been tested for a possible effect on chronic venous ulcer healing, but none has been widely accepted as standard therapy in this setting. It has been suggested that extended oral anticoagulation should be investigated as a possible preventative measure. Waiting for the results in this field, an adequate management of anticoagulation in terms of anticoagulant intensity and duration should be recommended for the prevention of recurrent deep vein thrombosis, post- thrombotic syndrome and chronic venous ulcers.

Minerva Cardioangiol. 2015 Jun;63(3):231-8.

Possibilities of Pharmacotherapy for Chronic Venous Insufficiency With Diosmin Preparations From the Position of the Endothelial Functional State

R E Kalinin, I A Suchkov, A S Pshennikov, N D Mzhavanadze

Abstract

Despite a high level of the development of modern angiology and vascular surgery, the problem of chronic venous insufficiency (CVI) complicating the course of various venous diseases seems to have no tendency towards being solved, thus calling forth permanent search for optimization of methods of treatment and rehabilitation of patients presenting with the above-mentioned syndrome. The article presents a review of contemporary studies dedicated to the problem of correcting CVI. Special attention is paid to the endothelial state in CVI and possibilities of correcting endothelial dysfunction with the use of bioflavonoids, in particular, diosmin. Also presented herein are the results of an original experimental study dedicated to peculiarities of the endothelial functional state, endothelial dysfunction, and correction thereof on the background of the existing CVI.

Angiol Sosud Khir. 2015;21(3):91-4, 96-7.

Chronic Venous Insufficiency and the Therapeutic Effects of Daflon 500 Mg

J*ohn J Bergan*

Abstract

Chronic venous insufficiency is linked to venous hypertension and forces of shear stress on the endothelium. Venous hypertension depends upon two forces: the weight of a column of blood from the right atrium transmitted through the valveless vena cava and iliac veins to the femoral vein, and pressure generated by contracting skeletal muscles of the leg transmitted through failed perforating veins. When valve failure occurs in superficial axial veins and perforating veins, the venous pressure in the veins and venules of the skin and subcutaneous tissue is raised. The skin changes in chronic venous insufficiency are directly related to the severity of the venous hypertension. Also, pathologic changes in the valves are linked to venous hypertension and leukocyte infiltration and activation. It is hypothesized that acute venous pressure elevations cause a shift in the venous hemodynamics with changes in wall shear stress. This initiates the inflammatory cascade. Daflon 500 mg ameliorates the effects of chronic inflammation. In randomized trials, 60 days of therapy with Daflon at a dosage of 500 mg 2 tablets daily was effective, in addition to elastic compression, in accelerating venous ulcer healing. Because venous insufficiency is linked to venous hypertension and an inflammatory reaction, it appears that Daflon 500 mg 2 tablets daily shows a great potential for accomplishing blockade of the inflammatory cascade.

Angiology. 2005 Sep-Oct;56 Suppl 1:S21-4

Balneohydrotherapy in the Treatment of Chronic Venous Insufficiency

Romain J Forestier, Gisèle Briancon, Alain Francon, Fatma B Erol, Jean M Mollard

Abstract

Background: Physical therapy has not been evaluated much for the treatment of chronic venous insufficiency before. The question is whether balneohydrotherapy and usual care combined is superior to usual care alone.

Patients and methods: In a randomized trial comparing spa therapy versus waiting list patients were treated on an out-patient basis in a private spa center. Patients had to be between 18 and 80 years old, with chronic venous insufficiency (stage 3 or 4 according to the CEAP classification). The balneohydrotherapy group received 18 days of treatment in Aix-Les-Bains spa center continuing their usual care. The control group continued their usual care as well during the study. The balneohydrotherapy program consisted of Kneipp therapy (10 minutes), walking 10 minutes in a special mineral water pool with underwater jets at 23 °C, massage and bathing in a mineral water tub at 34 °C. The main outcome criterion was the number of patients with 20 % self assessed improvement on the Chronic Venous Insufficiency Questionnaire at three months after therapy.

Results: 192 patients were assessed for eligibility, 99 were randomized 5 retired drew back their consent and were not included in the intention to treat analysis. None were lost to follow up. After three months 32 (66 %) patients improved in the balneohydrotherapy group and 13 (28 %) in the control group. The difference between groups was significant (odd ratio 5.08 [1.94 - 13.55], relative risk reduction 2.33 [1.42 - 3.84]).There were no serious side effects.

Conclusions: Balneohydrotherapy seems to improve quality of life of patients with chronic venous insufficiency.

Vasa. 2014 Sep;43(5):365-71

Experience of Severe Chronic Venous Insufficiency Of The Lower Extremities Treatment

A *V Ponomarenko*

Abstract

The results of treatment of 246 patients on different forms of chronic venous insufficiency of the lower extremities were presented. The leading diagnostic criterion when choosing tactics consider patients ultrasound duplex scanning with color mapping. Patients in the presence of large ulcers basic treatment is autodermoplasty. The complex treatment include pharmacotherapy, the use of elastic compression hosiery.

Klin Khir. 2015 Jun;(6):41-3.

Treatment of Chronic Venous Diseases in Children and Adolescents

I N Nurmeev, L M Mirolubov, A L Mirolubov, N Nurmeev, A Yu Osipov, A R Nurmeeva, L F Rashitov

Abstract

Presented herein is experience in diagnosis and treatment of chronic diseases of lower-limb veins in a total of 242 children and adolescents. The authors used CEAP classification; C1 class was more often encountered in children. Treatment included surgical interventions, sclerotherapy, laser coagulation of pathological veins of lower extremities. Therapeutic outcomes were satisfactory in all patients, with no complications observed. It was determined that in paediatric phlebological practice prevailing are class C1 chronic venous diseases; characteristic is high concern of both the patient and parents. A timely commenced conservative program of treatment for children makes it possible to improve quality of life in class C1 and C2 chronic venous diseases. Laser coagulation of varicose saphenous veins of lower limbs in children makes it possible to remove pathological vessels, significantly improving quality of life of patients and shortening the terms of hospitalization twofold. Application of transcutaneous laser coagulation (Nd:YAG, 1064 nm) and microfoam sclerotherapy in children makes it possible to completely remove class C1 varicose veins, improving quality of life.

Angiol Sosud Khir. 2016;22(1):105-9.

Chronic Venous Insufficiency: Prevention and Drugless Therapy

J M Mollard

Abstract

The superficial and deep venous network of patients with chronic venous insufficiency is constantly undergoing change requiring careful follow-up and adapted therapy. Prevention, whether physical or medical, is recommended at all stages of the disease. The veins must be protected from factors which worsen venous abnormalities and drugs improving venous return should be prescribed. It is essential to avoid further aggravation of chronic venous insufficiency. The treatment has two objectives. First, and most important, to diminish or alleviate global or local venous hyperpressure which can be attained by surgery or sclerotherapy of venous leaking, via the crosses or perforating veins, into the superficial network. Venous hyperpressure can also be reduced by re-establishing normal venous haemodynamics with conservative techniques included elastic support or surgical techniques including CHI-VA. Finally, the second objective is to diminish or alleviate inaesthetic varicose veins and telangiectases.

Presse Med. 1994 Feb 10;23(5):251-8.

Clinical Benefits of Daflon 500 Mg in the Most Severe Stages of Chronic Venous Insufficiency

A Ramelet

Abstract

Chronic venous insufficiency (CVI) affects a large number of people in Western countries, and is responsible for considerable inconvenience, discomfort, suffering, and costs. Micronized purified flavonoid fraction (MPFF, 450 mg diosmin plus 50 mg hesperidin-Daflon 500 mg) is a potent venotropic drug used in the treatment of venous insufficiency. Pharmacological and clinical studies demonstrated the comprehensive mode of action of Daflon 500 mg: it increases venous tone, it improves lymph drainage, and it protects the microcirculation. Clinical international, prospective, multicenter, randomized, controlled studies versus placebo studies documenting the effects of Daflon 500 mg in CVI at advanced stages with edema, skin changes, and venous leg ulcer are reviewed. In edema, one of the most frequent complaints of patients, Daflon 500 mg brings about a significant reduction in leg circumference, thanks to its capacity to inhibit inflammatory reactions and to decrease capillary hyperpermeability. The rationale for the use of Daflon 500 mg for treatment of skin disorders and venous leg ulcer is its action on the microcirculation-damaging processes. Regarding skin changes, Daflon 500 mg has been shown to improve venous trophic disorders, like gravitational (stasis) dermatitis, and dermatofibrosclerosis. In venous leg ulcer, Daflon 500 mg's clinical efficacy has been demonstrated in addition to standard treatment or versus standard treatment alone. Daflon 500 mg, thanks to its comprehensive mode of action on the veins, lymphatics, and microcirculation, is the method of choice not only in the early stages of CVI treatment, but also in the severe stages of this condition, in combination with compression treatment, sclerotherapy, and surgery if appropriate.

Angiology. 2001 Aug;52 Suppl 1:S49-56

Pathophysiological Mechanisms of Lower Limb Chronic Venous Insufficiency and Possibility of Its Correction With Antistax

Iu M Stoĭko, V G Gudymovich

Abstract

Symptoms of lower limb chronic venous insufficiency (CVI) are related to hypertension in vena cava inferior system. All changes that take place in macrocirculatory segment of hemodynamics are reflected at microcirculatory level, including metabolic and trophic processes—the most important function of microcirculation, which is named "transcapillary exchange". Endothelial dysfunction and blood-venous wall interface changes play a crucial role in the development of pathology. Drug therapy remains the main and integral part of CVI treatment. One of its aims is to protect venous wall, normalize permeability and alleviate CVI symptoms at microcirculatory level. Antistax efficiency in patients with CVI was demonstrated in several trials and warranted the inclusion of this drug into complex treatment of lower limb CVI.

Angiol Sosud Khir. 2006;12(3):77-82

The Effectiveness of the Method CHIVA in Patients with Chronic Venous Insufficiency and Comorbid Lesions: own Experience

Y*arka A.*

Introduction.

Chronic venous insufficiency (CVI) of the lower extremities is one of the most popular topics both in vascular surgery and the entire practice of medicine. A particular problem arises when it comes to the choice of treatment of CVI in patients with comorbid lesions. Some authors consider it expedient to apply a compression technique for the treatment of patients with comorbid lesions, but life-long use of it has certain disadvantages. This is also indicated by the latest consensus on the treatment of CVI, where the CHIVA method is distinguished as quite effective, but not widely used.

The aim of the study was to examine the effectiveness of the method CHIVA in patients with comorbidities.

Materials and methods. In the period from 2011 to 2015 were treated 37 patients with CVI, the selected treatment was CHIVA. The average age of patients was 78 years. Operations were carried out under the local anesthesia.

Results and discussion. In all the patients there was observed a regression of signs of CVI. 23 (62.1 %) patients achieved a stable cosmetic effect when observed for 3 years. In the postoperative period the recurrent bleeding from varicose nodes was not observed in any of the patients. Paresthesia in the cut places was observed in 14 (37.8 %) patients, subcutaneous hematomas were observed in 3 (8.1 %) patients. The thrombosis of saphenous veins without signs of inflammation were found by the control ultrasound examination in 11 (29.7 %) patients. Thrombosis of the deep venous system were not observed. In patients with concomitant diseases the systemic complications and exacerbations of the main chronic diseases in the early postoperative period were not observed.

By applying the CHIVA surgery procedure, we did not try to achieve a quick cosmetic effect, as is the case with the use of classical methods of surgery and other non-invasive interventions. The goal of CHIVA's low-invasive operations is to achieve a reduction in pressure in the superficial venous system, which is the main pathogenetic mechanism of occurrence of CVI and causes undesirable consequences of this disease. Transversal venous outflow from the source of pathological reflux allows you to achieve the goal.

According to our study, the overwhelming majority of patients treated with CHIVA were elderly and had severe comorbid lesions, which posed a risk for the use of a classic surgical intervention in the presence of CVI. In some patients, deformation of the trunk of the large subcutaneous vein and its mouth, as well as pronounced dilation, did not allow for endovascular laser or radiofrequency ablation. Operative treatment was needed because of the presence of severe forms of CWI and its complications. The use of local anesthesia also had a positive effect, since it minimized the medication effect on the body, made it possible to maximally reduce the length of stay of the patient in the hospital. The average length of stay of a patient in a hospital of 1,2 days minimized the occurrence of such a phenomenon as a hospital pneumonia

Conclusions. Using the method CHIVA therapy in the treatment of chronic venous insufficiency is a safe and effective method and can be used in patients with comorbidities

Lviv clinical bulletin 2015, 4(12): 39-41

Drugs in Chronic Venous Insufficiency—The Challenge of Demonstrating Clinical Efficacy

A*nke Esperester, Tanja Schütt, Bertram Ottillinger*

Abstract

Approximately 90% of German adults show alterations of their lower limb veins; about every fifth suffers from symptoms of chronic venous insufficiency (CVI). With compression therapy showing low compliance, CVI oedemas and accompanying subjective symptoms are frequently treated with anti-oedematous drugs of herbal origin. A guideline outlines the requirements for clinical studies with CVI drugs. Water displacement plethysmometry (volumetry) is the gold standard for determining the reduction ofoedemas. Besides reducing oedemas, drugs should also demonstrate effects on accompanying symptoms influencing quality of life. Despite assistance provided by the guideline, clinical studies in CVI are complex and subject to multiple error sources in planning and execution. The corroboration of successful studies in further confirmatory studies is good practice and demanded by regulatory authorities. This practice reduces the risk of drugs being accepted as effective just based on the play of chance. As an example, placebo controlled studies with an extract from red vine leaves show that a careful definition of patients as well as meticulous study planning and execution can reproducibly verify significant and clinically relevant treatment effects. When evaluating clinical studies it is recommended to refer to the CONSORT statement. Publications missing certain minimum information make interpretation difficult and may result in a biased judgment of the effects of therapy.

Med Monatsschr Pharm. 2013 Feb;36(2):44-51.

Drug Treatments of Chronic Venous Insufficiency: Pharmaco-Clinical Evaluation

M. Chauveau

Abstract

There are many methods for the assessment of venotropic drugs. Clinical trials based on randomized comparison with placebo are essential. The different methodes used for the evaluation of the functional effects are chosen on the basis of their performance and pertinence for the study objectives. These include three aims which we feel are essential: increased venous tone, decreased capillary permeability and reversal of microcirculatory impairment. Calf plethysmography is highly adapted for the evaluation of venous tone. The mercury gauge works well, but the future will tell if air plethysmography is more adapted here. For capillary permeability, fluoresceine angioscopy is without a doubt the most sensitive and specific method. Unfortunately many laboratories do not have this equipment. If it is not available, the suction cup test or the Landis isotope test may be used although these tests have their limits. For impaired microcirculation, the most interesting test is the laser-Doppler; the results are well correlated with the severity of the chronic venous insufficiency and return to normal after treatment. TcPO2 and capillaroscopic measurements are less sensitive, but are useful in severe cases. Other investigations may be important in individual cases depending on the impact of the medication under study. Drug-induced serum fibrinolytic activity can be measured by the euglobulin lysis time. A haemorheologic effect can be assessed with routine assays (Haematocrit, serum fibrinogen) and measured with tests of red cell deformability and erythrocyte agreggation capacity.

Presse Med. 1994 Feb 10;23(5):243-9.

Clinical and Hemodynamic Outcomes in Patients With Chronic Venous Insufficiency After Oral Micronized Flavonoid Therapy

C Ting, S W Cheng, L L Wu, G C Cheung

A

Abstract

The aim of this study was to prospectively investigate the clinical efficacy of Daflon therapy in patients with mild to moderate chronic venous insufficiency (CVI) (clinical class 1-4) and to assess the changes in venous hemodynamics by using air plethysmography (APG). Fifty-six limbs in 28 patients were studied. They all had primary venous insufficiency with no venous obstruction, and mixed deep and superficial venous incompetence was found in 64% of the limbs. There was a significant decrease in symptom score for swelling and heaviness after 6 months of Daflon therapy. The symptom score for cramps also showed improvement though it did not reach statistical significance. Pain was significantly reduced with a mean pain score of 21.8 +/- 19.3% before comparing to 10.4 +/- 20.2% after 6 months of Daflon therapy (p < 0.01). This was also associated with a decrease in mean calf circumference from 37.0 +/- 4.3 to 36.4 +/- 4.3 cm (p < 0.001). There was no significant change in the venous filling index

(VFI), ejection fraction (EF), and residual volume fraction (RVF) before and after 6 months of Daflon therapy (VFI: 3.7 +/- 3.5 vs 3.4 +/- 2.5 mL/s, EF: 54.5 +/- 15.9% vs 57.7 +/- 19.7%, RVF: 41.4 +/- 19.2% vs 39.4 +/- 24.2%). The clinical

improvement without associated changes in venous hemodynamics as measured by APG suggests that Daflon mainly works by modifying the microcirculatory environment not detected by APG and this microcirculatory change is associated with clinical improvement. In this regard, Daflon would be especially useful for symptomatic relief in patients with functional venous insufficiency who do not have clinical evidence of varicose veins but suffer from symptoms of venous insufficiency.

Vascular and Endovascular Surgery, 2001 Nov-Dec;35(6):443-7.

Diagnosis and Treatment in the Management of Chronic Venous Insufficiency

H$^{S\ Yuwono}$

Abstract

Chronic venous insufficiency (CVI) is caused mainly by an alteration in the elasticity of venous walls and the dysfunction of venous valves. The diagnosis and treatment for CVI management are discussed in this paper.

Clinical Hemorheology and Microcirculation, 2000 vol. 23, pp. 233-237,

COMPRESSION BANDAGES

Medical Compression Stockings Reduce Hypertension of Nailfold Capillaries at the Toe of Patients With Chronic Venous insufficiency

A*nja Oelert, Manuela Kittel, Martin Hahn, Hermann Haase, Michael Jünger*

Abstract

In five patients who suffered from chronic venous insufficiency clinical stage C4 (n = 3) and C6 (n = 2) the capillary blood pressure was measured twice by means of invasive direct cannulation of nailfold capillaries of the toe. During one measurement course the patients wore below knee medical compression stockings (40 mmHg) during the other they did not have compression therapy. With the patient in supine position, the CP was investigated by the servo-nulling technique under resting conditions and under dynamic conditions: the calf-muscle/ankle joint venous pump was simulated by means of inflating a blood pressure cuff, which surrounded the mid lower leg, to 60 mmHg for 60s.

Results: The simulated calf-muscle contraction induced a steep increase of CP with 5.65 mmHg/s (Q1 5.27 mmHg/s, Q3 5.92 mmHg/s), which was significantly (p = 0.013) reduced by MCS to

2.47 mmHg/s (Q1 1.65 mmHg/s, Q3 3.0 mmHg/s). Time needed to reach the max. CP was 11.35 s, which was lengthened by MCS to 23.4 s (p = 0.134).

Conclusion: Compression therapy prevents capillary hypertension, the major hemodynamic reason for the development of advanced stages of chronic venous insufficiency which are defined by skin disease like hyperpigmentation, lipodermatosclerosis and ulcer.

Clin Hemorheol Microcirc. 2018;69(1-2):115-121.

Compression for venous leg ulcers

N*icky A Cullum, E Andrea Nelson, Alison Fletcher, Trevor Sheldon*

Abstract

Background Around one percent of people in industrialised countries will suffer from a leg ulcer at some time.

The majority of these leg ulcers are due to problems in the veins, resulting in an accumulation of blood in the legs.

Leg ulcers arising from venous problems are called venous (varicose or stasis) ulcers.

Surgical repair of the veins is not commonly undertaken and the main treatment, used for thousands of years, has been to apply a firm compression garment (bandage or stocking) to the lower leg in order to help the blood return back up the leg.

There is a large number of compression garments available and it is unclear whether they are effective in treating venous ulcers and which compression garment is the most effective.

Objectives To assess the effectiveness and cost-effectiveness of compression bandaging and stockings in the treatment of venous leg ulcers.

Search strategy

1. Searches of 19 databases, hand searching of journals,

conference proceedings and bibliographies.

2. Manufacturers of compression bandages and stockings and an Advisory Panel were contacted for unpublished studies.

Selection criteria

1. Trials that evaluated compression bandaging or stockings, as a treatment for venous leg ulcers.
2. There was no restriction on date or language.
3. Ulcer healing was the primary endpoint.
4. Data collection and analysis
5. Details of eligible studies were extracted and summarised using a data extraction sheet.
6. Data extraction was verified by two reviewers independently. Main results

Twenty two trials reporting 24 comparisons were identified.

1. Compression was more effective than no compression (4/6 trials).
2. When multi-layered systems were compared, elastic compression was more effective than non- elastic compression (5 trials).
3. There was no statistically significant difference in healing rates between 4-layer bandaging and other high compression multi-layered systems (3 trials).
4. There was no statistically significant difference in healing rates between elastomeric multi- layered systems (4 trials).
5. Multi-layered high compression was more effective than single layer compression (4 trials).
6. Compression stockings were evaluated in two trials.

a. One found a high compression stocking plus a thrombo stocking to be more effective than a short stretch bandage.
b. The second small trial reported no difference between the

compression stockings and Unna's boot.

1. There were insufficient data to draw conclusions about
    the relative cost-effectiveness of different regimens.

Conclusions

Compression increases ulcer healing rates compared with no compression.

Multi-layered systems are more effective than single-layered systems. High compression is more effective than low compression but there are no clear differences in the effectiveness of different types of high compression.

doi.org/10.1002/14651858.CD000265

Chronic Venous Insufficiency: prevalence and effect of compression stockings Owayed Al Shammeri, Nourah AlHamdan, Bushra Al-hothaly, Farid Midhet, Mahboob Hussain, and Abdulrahman Al-Mohaimeed

Abstract

Introduction

Chronic venous insufficiency (CVI) is a common disease affecting mainly lower limbs and significantly influencing the quality of life. This study aims to estimate the prevalence of CVI in the Qassim Region and test the effectiveness of compression stockings as an intervention option.

Methods

A cross sectional study was conducted to assess the prevalence of CVI among patients visiting primary health care (PHC) centers in the Qassim Region. CVI patients were diagnosed and classified using the clinical, etiologic, anatomical, and pathophysiological (CEAP) scale. They were randomly divided into two groups, one using compression stockings and the other standard medical therapy. A clinical follow up was done using multiple scale system including CEAP scale. Data analysis was performed using SPSS.

Results

Among the 226 screened patients, 138 (61.1%) were diagnosed as having CVI (69% female and 45% male, $p<0.001$). Compared to the baseline, both the clinical and venous scores for CVI at the follow-up were significantly lower among patients using compression stockings, $p=0.002$ and $p=0.003$, respectively. Regression analysis suggested that, after controlling for age, sex and body mass index, compliance was the main factor responsible for a significant reduction in the clinical score among CVI patients.

Conclusions

Chronic venous insufficiency is very common in the Qassim Region. Compression stockings are highly effective in improving clinical symptoms and signs of CVI.

Int J Health Sci (Qassim). 2014 Jul;8(3):231-6

Effects of Preventive Use of Compression Stockings for Elderly With Chronic Venous Insufficiency and Swollen Legs: A Systematic Review and Meta-Analysis

Kristin Thuve Dahm, Hilde Tinderholt Myrhaug, Hilde Strømme, Brynjar Fure, Kjetil Gundro Brurberg

Abstract

Background: Many home-dwelling elderly use medical compression stockings to prevent venous insufficiency, deep venous thrombosis, painful legs and leg ulcers. Assisting users with applying and removing compression stockings demands resources from the home based health services, but the effects are uncertain. This systematic review aims to summarize the effects of preventive use of medical compression stockings for patients with chronic venous insufficiency and swollen legs.

Methods: We conducted a search in six databases (Epistemonikos, Cochrane Database of Systematic Reviews, MEDLINE, Embase, CENTRAL and CINAHL) in March 2018. Randomized controlled trials evaluating the preventive effects of European standard compression stockings class 3 or 2 for elderly with chronic venous insufficiency and swollen legs were included.

Primary outcomes were thrombosis, leg ulcers and mobility. Secondary outcomes were other health related outcomes, e.g. pain, compliance. We assessed risk of bias in the included studies and used the Grading of Recommendations Assessment, Development and Evaluation (GRADE) tool for evaluating the overall quality of evidence.

Results: Five randomized controlled trials met the inclusion criteria. Comparing compression stockings class 2 to class 1, meta-analysis showed a reduction in leg ulcer recurrence at 12 months (RR 0.52; 95% CI 0.30 to 0.88). The quality of evidence was assessed as moderate by GRADE. One study (100 participants) did not detect a difference between compression stockings class 3 versus class 2 on ulcer recurrence after six months (RR 0.64; 95% CI 0.20 to 2.03). In another study, patients wearing class 3 compression stockings had lower recurrence risk compared with patients without stockings (RR 0.46; 95% CI 0.27 to 0.76) at six months and (RR 0.43; 95% CI 0.27 to 0.69) at 12 months. We found no difference between class 2 and class 1 stockings on subjective symptoms of chronic venous insufficiency or outcomes of vein thrombosis or mobility.

Conclusion: Compression stockings class 2 probably reduce the risk of leg ulcer recurrence compared to compression stockings class 1. It is uncertain whether the use of stockings with higher compression grades is associated with a further risk reduction. More randomized controlled trials on vein thrombosis and mobility are needed.

BMC Geriatr 19, 76 (2019).

A Summation Analysis of Compliance and Complications of Compression Hosiery for Patients With Chronic Venous Disease or Post-thrombotic Syndrome

Hadyn K N Kankam, Chung S Lim, Francesca Fiorentino, Alun H Davies, Manj S Gohel

Abstract

Objectives: Compression stockings are commonly prescribed for patients with a range of venous disorders, but are difficult to don and uncomfortable to wear. This study aimed to investigate compliance and complications of compression stockings in patients with chronic venous disease (CVD) and post-thrombotic syndrome (PTS).

Methods: A literature search of the following databases was carried out: MEDLINE (via PubMed), EMBASE (via OvidSP, 1974 to present), and CINAHL (via EBSCOhost). Studies evaluating the use of compression stockings in patients with CVD (CEAP C2-C5) or for the prevention or treatment of PTS were included. After scrutinising full text articles, compliance with compression and associated complications were assessed. Compliance rates were compared based on study type and degree of compression. Good compliance was defined as patients wearing compression stockings for >50% of the time.

Results: From an initial search result of 4303 articles, 58 clinical studies (37 randomised trials and 21 prospective studies) were selected. A total of 10,245 limbs were included, with compression ranging from 15 to 40 mmHg (not stated in 12 studies) and a median follow-up of 12 months (range 1-60 months). In 19 cohorts, compliance was not assessed and in a further nine, compliance was poorly specified. Overall, good compliance with compression was reported for 5371 out of 8104 (66.2%) patients. The mean compliance, weighted by study size, appeared to be greater for compression ≤25 mmHg (77%) versus > 25 mmHg (65%) and greater in the randomised studies (74%) than in prospective observational studies (64%). Complications of stockings were not mentioned in 43 out of 62 cohorts reviewed. Where complications were considered, skin irritation was a common event.

Conclusions: In published trials, good compliance with compression is reported in around two thirds of patients, with inferior compliance in those given higher degrees of compression. Further studies are required to identify predictors of non-compliance, to help inform the clinical management of these patients. Complications of compression are not documented in many studies and should be given more consideration in the future.

Eur J Vasc Endovasc Surg. 2018 Mar;55(3):406-416.

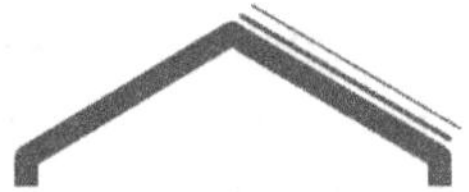

The 4 Rights of Compression Therapy for Patients With Chronic Venous Insufficiency and Venous Ulceration

N *A Bauer*

Abstract

Compression therapy has become an ever increasing component in the care of patients with Chronic Venous Insufficiency (CVI) and venous ulcerations. Although compression therapy is of great benefit to many of these patients, this treatment option does not come without risks. The increased use of compression therapy has coincided with an increase in its improper application. This article simplifies the principles of compression and highlights the common pitfalls of its use, with an emphasis on the home healthcare setting.

Home healthcare nurse 1998 Jul;16(7):443-8

Effectiveness of Compressive Hosiery for Therapy of Chronic Venous Insufficiency

A V Karalkin, S G Gavrilov, A I Kirienko

Abstract

Total 40 patients with III grade chronic venous insufficiency underwent conservative treatment with compressive hosiery <<VENOTEKS THERAPY>>. Patients were divided into 2 groups: the first group used compressive stockings, the second—tights. To objectivize the assessment, all patients underwent volumetry, radionuclide phlebography and regional blood volume measurements. It was shown that in the first group pain syndrome was coped in 73% of patients, edematous—in 60%. According to volumetry data, mean calf volume has reduced by 183+/-41 ml, phlebography has revealed an improvement of muscular-venous pump capacity in 11 patients; in 9 patients it remained unchanged. Blood filling in the affected limb decreased in 16 patients from 10.7% to 8.2% and from 7.5% to 5.3% for thigh and calf, respectively. In the second group an improvement of venous return parameters was more pronounced. Compressive tights relieved pain in lower extremities in 95%, decreased led edema—in 90% of patients. There was significant reduction in calf volume—by 259+/-

31 ml to the end of treatment course. Radionuclide phlebography has shown significant improvement of muscular-venous pump evacuatory function and reduction of blood filling in all patients of the second group. In conclusion, results of the study evidenced the effectiveness of compressive hosiery for treatment of chronic venous insufficiency.

Angiol Sosud Khir. 2006;12(2):65-71.

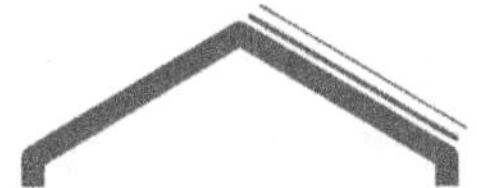

A Short Review of Diagnosis and Compression Therapy of Chronic Venous Insufficiency

Nada Kecelj Leskovec, Milos D Pavlović, Tomaz Lunder

Abstract

Introduction: Chronic venous insufficiency (CVI) is a venous disorder in the lower extremities associated with changes in the skin and subcutaneous tissue. Treatment with short-stretch compression bandages is highly recommended for advanced stages of CVI.

Methods: The compression systems Rosidal Sys, Porelast, Coban, and Proguide were evaluated in 4 groups of mobile and active patients (n = 18) with CVI stage II or III. Sub-bandage pressures at point B1 were measured in the upright and supine positions 30 min and 12 h after the bandage was applied. Average pressures and values of the static stiffness index (SSI) were calculated for each group.

Results: The Porelast, Rosidal Sys and Coban systems had SSI values in excess of 10 mmHg, 30 min and 12 h after application. The corresponding values for Proguide were below 10 mmHg.

Conclusion: Porelast, Rosidal Sys and Coban are very stiff systems, whereas Proguide is more similar to long-stretch compression bandages with a lower degree of stiffness.

Acta Dermatovenerologica Alpina, Pannonica Adriatica, 2008 Mar;17(1):17-21.

Pathogenesis of Chronic Venous Insufficiency and Possible Effects of Compression and Pentoxifylline

P *D Coleridge Smith*

Abstract

It has been recognized for over 2000 years that ulceration of the leg may be associated with visible varices of the lower limb. More recent physiological investigation has shown that the pressure in the veins of the lower limb remains raised in patients with venous ulceration during ambulation, whereas in normal subjects the pressure in superficial veins falls to a low level. This elevated pressure appears to cause damage to the superficial capillaries in the skin culminating in the production of venous ulceration. Events in the dermal capillaries which result in skin destruction have yet to be fully defined. Pericapillary fibrin cuffs have been demonstrated histologically and suggested as a cause of diminished nutrition to the skin. White blood cells have been shown to accumulate in the lower limb of patients with venous disease and these accumulations are particularly located around the dermal capillaries. Activated white blood cells releasing free radicals and destructive enzymes may precipitate skin destruction. An understanding of these mechanisms may help to explain the efficacy of compression hosiery and bandaging as well as some of the new pharmacological agents which have been shown to influence venous ulcer healing.0

Angiology. 2000 Mar;51(3):231-9

SCLEROTHERAPY

Sclerotherapy in the management of varicose veins and its dermatological complications.

Subbarao NT, Aradhya SS, Veerabhadrappa NH.

Abstract

Background: Varicose veins and its dermatological complications like stasis dermatitis, ulcers, spontaneous bleeding are commonly seen in the dermatology clinics. Surgery has been the most often used treatment for varicose veins. Sclerotherapy refers to introduction of sclerosing solution into the varicose veins, which causes endothelial damage and subsequent fibrosis. Sclerotherapy is being practised extensively by dermatosurgeons in the west. However, there are no Indian studies which specifically evaluate the role of sclerotherapy in the management of varicose veins and its skin complications. Hence, this study aims to evaluate the efficacy of sclerotherapy in managing varicose veins and its complications.

Aims: To study the safety and efficacy of sclerotherapy in the treatment of varicose veins and its dermatological complications.

Methods: This is a prospective study involving 50 patients with varicose veins and its dermatological complications attending the dermatology out-patient department. The study was conducted over a period of 18 months. After thorough clinical, laboratory, and radiological evaluation, the patients were treated with sclerotherapy using Sodium Tetradecyl Sulphate of various concentrations depending on the vessel size. The patients were then followed up to look for disappearance of veins, healing of ulcers and eczema, and any complications.

Results: Patients showed a good response to treatment with sclerotherapy. 70-80% of patients showed symptomatic improvement along with disappearance of veins and healing of eczema and ulcers. Most of the complications were minor, which resolved over a period of few weeks.

Conclusion: Sclerotherapy is a simple, safe and effective procedure for the treatment of varicose veins and its dermatological complications. The procedure is particularly effective for smaller, early varicosities and also for residual veins after surgery. Hence we recommend more and more of our fellow dermatologists to take up this procedure, which can be an efficient tool to manage patients with varicose veins and its related complications.

Indian J Dermatol Venereol Leprol. May-Jun 2013;79(3):383-8.

Standard guidelines for care: Sclerotherapy in dermatology

N iti Khunger, S Sacchidanand

Abstract

Definition: Sclerotherapy is defined as the targeted elimination of small vessels, varicose veins and vascular anomalies by the injection of a sclerosant. The aim of sclerotherapy is to damage the vessel wall and transform it into a fibrous cord that cannot be recanalized. It is a simple, cost-effective, efficacious and esthetically acceptable modality for both therapeutic and esthetic purposes. Indications: Therapeutic indications include varicose veins and vascular malformations. Esthetic indications include telangiectasias and reticular veins. In the management of varicose veins, it may need to be combined with other surgical methods of treatment, such as ligation of the saphenofemoral junction, stab ligation of perforators and stripping. A surgical opinion may be necessary. Methodology: A thorough knowledge of the anatomy and physiology of the venous system of the legs, basic principles of venous insufficiency, methods of diagnosis and, in addition, uses, mechanisms of action and complications of sclerosing agents and proper compression techniques are important pre-requisites to successful sclerotherapy. Although various sclerosing agents are available, polidoconal and sodium tetradecyl sulfate are most commonly used. More recently, these sclerosants have been used in microfoam form for increased efficacy. The basic principle of a successful sclerotherapy technique is the use of an optimal volume and concentration of the sclerosant according to the size of the vessel. The sclerosant is injected carefully into the vessel and compression is applied. Contraindications: Contraindications include superficial and deep venous thrombosis, sapheno-femoral junction incompetence, pregnancy, myocardial decompensation, migraine, hypercoagulable state, serious systemic illness, dependency edema, immobility, arterial disease, diabetes mellitus and allergic reactions to sclerosants. Complications: While sclerotherapy is usually a safe procedure, complications may occur due to inappropriate patient selection or improper injection techniques. The complications may be acute or delayed. Complications include hyperpigmentation, matting, local urticaria, cutaneous necrosis, microthrombi, accidental intra-arterial injection, phlebitis, deep vein thrombosis, thromboembolism, scintillating scotomas, nerve damage and allergic reactions. Physician Qualification: Sclerotherapy may be administered by a surgeon or dermatologist who has acquired adequate training during post-graduation or through recognized fellowships and workshops dedicated to sclerotherapy. He should have an adequate knowledge of the anatomy of the venous system, be able to diagnose and manage venous disease and its associated consequences as well as possess the necessary skills to perform the procedures, understand the appropriate indications and limitations, technique modifications and management of the potential adverse sequelae associated with sclerotherapy and also understand the pharmacology of the sclerosing solutions. Facility: The procedure may be performed in the physician's procedure room.

Indian J Dermatol Venereol Leprol. Mar-Apr 2011;77(2):222-31

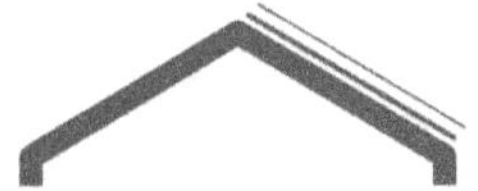

Ultrasound-guided Foam Sclerotherapy for Severe Chronic Venous Insufficiency Guilherme Camargo Gonçalves de-Abreu, Otacílio de Camargo Júnior, Márcia Fayad Marcondes de- Abreu, José Luís Braga de-Aquino

Abstract

Chronic venous insufficiency is characterized by cutaneous alterations caused by venous hypertension; in severe forms, it progresses to lower limb ulcers. Lower limb varicose veins are the main cause of chronic venous insufficiency, and the classic treatment includes surgery and compressive therapy. Minimally invasive alternative treatments for varicose veins include new techniques such as venous thermal ablation using laser or radiofrequency. The use of different methods depends on clinical and anatomical factors. Ultrasound-guided foam sclerotherapy is the venous injection of sclerosing foam controlled by Doppler ultrasound. Sclerotherapy is very useful to treat varicose veins, and probably, is cheaper than other methods. However, until the present, it is the less studied method.

Rev Col Bras Cir. Sep-Oct 2017;44(5):511-520.

Severe Chronic Venous Insufficiency: Primary Treatment with Sclerofoam

John J Bergan, Luigi Pascarella

Abstract

Venous insufficiency, for practical purposes, can be divided into primary venous insufficiency and chronic venous insufficiency. The latter is characterized by advanced skin changes of hyperpigmentation, edema, ulceration, scarring from healed ulcers or open ulcerations. These are summarized in the CEAP classification as Classes 4, 5 and 6. Pretreatment evaluation is done with a standing ultrasound reflux examination. Thorough mapping of the extremity reflux is desirable. Physiologic tests of venous function, such as plethysmography, are unnecessary. Treatment is directed at closing refluxing axial veins as well as controlling those perforating veins with outward flow. Varicose veins contribute to axial reflux and must be obliterated. Arterial occlusive disease may complicate venous ulceration in as many as 15% of cases. Initial treatment of severe chronic venous insufficiency is usually carried out by controlling the edema with elastic bandaging or nonelastic support, such as the Unna boot or the CircAid dressing. Surgical intervention has been successful but the advent of foam sclerotherapy has proven to be an attractive alternative to surgery and has added a new tool for the treatment of severe chronic venous insufficiency. In this preliminary experience, the results are quite satisfactory and the technique has been shown to be effective, pain-free, inexpensive, with very little morbidity. Guidelines for obtaining sclerosants for use in foam sclerotherapy legally are provided.

Semin Vasc Surg. 2005 Mar;18(1):49-56

SURGICAL TREATMENT

Autologous Platelet-Rich Plasma in Treatment of Chronic Venous Leg Ulcers: A Prospective Case Series

Seyhan Yilmaz, Eray Aksoy, Suat Doganci, Adnan Yalcinkaya Adem I Diken, Kerim Cagli

Abstract

Study: We report our results on a case series of 19 patients receiving platelet-rich plasma application in treatment of patients with chronic unhealing venous leg ulcers.

Material and methods: There were 16 males and three females with a mean age of 38.55 ± 16.46 years. Planimetric size measurements were performed and pain was tested throughout the treatment period. Follow-up was made in seven-day periods. Patients received 5 ml of platelet-rich plasma for each 5 cm(2) of the wound surface with half of the amount being injected 1-2 mm deep into the wound and the wound surface was covered with the remaining half.

Results: Complete wound healing occurred in 18 of 19 patients (94.7%) within a mean of 4.82 ±

2.16 week. There were significant reductions in wound area among all consecutive measurements except for first week. A significant reduction in wound volume was apparent even in first week and sustained among consecutive measurements.

Conclusion: Platelet-rich plasma seems effective in terms of promoting healing of venous leg ulcers. Improvement in wound depth was slightly more prominent than that in wound area, indicating a potential role of platelet-rich plasma especially in deep venous ulcers.

Vascular. 2015 Dec;23(6):580-5.

Thermal and Nonthermal Endovenous Ablation Options for Treatment of Superficial Venous Insufficiency

Misaki M Kiguchi, Ellen D Dillavou

Abstract

Open saphenous removal, phlebectomy, and venous ligation were historic mainstays of surgical treatment of venous disease. Duplex ultrasound has become standard to diagnose venous insufficiency. Percutaneous modalities have allowed treatments to include thermal and nonthermal endovenous ablation. These treatments vary in preoperative planning, procedural steps, and postprocedural care, but all are safe and effective. An individualized approach should be taken in determining which modality is offered to each patient. Endovenous options, which often are minimally invasive and safely performed in an outpatient setting, allow access to effective treatments with low risk and discomfort.

Surg Clin North Am. 2018 Apr;98(2):385-400.

Popliteal venous aneurysm: a report on three cases presenting with chronic venous insufficiency without embolic events

J T Christenson

Abstract

Objectives: Popliteal venous aneurysms (PVA) are rare, but represent a significant potential source of thromboembolus. Most often the patients present with pulmonary embolism, which can also be detected in patients presenting with chronic venous insufficiency.

Methods: Three patients without any clinical evidence of pulmonary emboli were diagnosed by venous duplex scanning during workup for superficial venous insufficiency. None of the PVAs contained thrombus. The mean diameter of the aneurysm was 30 mm. Surgery included tangential aneurysmectomy and lateral venorrhaphy.

Results: None of the patients had evidence of pulmonary embolism, and there were no postoperative deep venous thromboses diagnosed. All patients received anticoagulation therapy for three months postoperatively, and patency was confirmed by duplex scanning during follow-up four, nine and 12 months after surgery.

Conclusions: It is recommended that PVAs should be ruled out in patients undergoing workup for chronic venous insufficiency, even in the absence of embolic events. A good quality venous duplex scanning is sufficient for diagnosis and treatment. Surgical treatment of PVAs is advocated. Tangential aneurysmectomy with lateral venorrhaphy is the surgical technique of choice. It is a safe procedure with a low complication rate.

Phlebology. 2007;22(2):56-9.

Surgical Management of Chronic Venous Insufficiency

K *A Löfgren*

Abstract

C hronic venous insufficiency is a pathologic condition of the skin and subcutaneous tissues in the lower extremity caused by stasis of the blood flow. Incompetency or failure of the venous valves results in reflux and ambulatory venous hypertension, which is more severe with deep than with superficial venous incompetency. Superficial chronic venous insufficiency (varicose veins) is effectively managed with ligation and stripping of incompetent perforator and superficial veins to restore normal venous physiology. Deep chronic venous insufficiency (postphlebitic leg) presents a widespread pathologic disorder that is refractory to surgical correction. Adjunctive surgical measures such as removal of incompetent perforators or superficial veins to lessen local stasis or skin grafting of ulcers are often indicated in selected cases. The underlying chronic venous insufficiency requires management with elastic compression, elevation of the legs, and exercise for best results.

Acta Chir Scand Suppl. 1988;544:62-8.

Medical and Surgical Therapy for Advanced Chronic Venous Insufficiency

R onnie Word

Abstract

Venous ulceration is the most serious consequence of chronic venous insufficiency. The disease has been known for more than 3.5 millennia with wound care centers established as early as 1500 BC. Unfortunately, still today it is a very poorly managed medical condition by most physicians despite that a great deal has been learned about the pathogenesis and treatment for venous ulcerations. We find that many wound care clinics treat the wound and not the cause of the problem. In this article, we review the basic pathophysiology of advanced chronic venous insufficiency and review the most up-to-date information with regard to medical therapy and different options of surgical therapy to address the underlying venous pathology responsible for chronic ulcers.

Surg Clin North Am. 2010 Dec;90(6):1195-214

In Vivo Assessment of Two Endothelialization Approaches on Bioprosthetic Valves for the Treatment of Chronic Deep Venous Insufficiency

Jeremy J Glynn, Casey M Jones, Deirdre E J Anderson, Dusan Pavcnik, Monica T Hinds

Abstract

Chronic deep venous insufficiency is a debilitating disease with limited therapeutic interventions. A bioprosthetic venous valve could not only replace a diseased valve, but has the potential to fully integrate into the patient with a minimally invasive procedure. Previous work with valves constructed from small intestinal submucosa (SIS) showed improvements in patients' symptoms in clinical studies; however, substantial thickening of the implanted valve leaflets also occurred. As endothelial cells are key regulators of vascular homeostasis, their presence on the SIS valves may reduce the observed thickening. This work tested an off-the-shelf approach to capture circulating endothelial cells in vivo using biotinylated antikinase insert domain receptor antibodies in a suspended leaflet ovine model. The antibodies on SIS were oriented to promote cell capture and showed positive binding to endothelial cells in vitro; however, no differences were observed in leaflet thickness in vivo between antibody-modified and unmodified SIS. In an alternative approach, valves were pre-seeded with autologous endothelial cells and tested in vivo. Nearly all the implanted pre-seeded valves were patent and functioning; however, no statistical difference was observed in valve thickness with cell pre-seeding. Additional cell capture schemes or surface modifications should be examined to find an optimal method for encouraging SIS valve endothelialization to improve long-term valve function in vivo.

J Biomed Mater Res Part B: Appl Biomater, 104B: 1610-1621, 2016.

Venous Valve Reconstruction in Patients With Secondary Chronic Venous Insufficiency

A Rosales, J J Jørgensen, C E Slagsvold, E Stranden, Ø Risum, A J Kroese

Abstract

Objectives: To evaluate the durability of venous valve reconstruction (VVR) and its benefits in terms of symptom improvement, ulcer healing and symptom/ulcer recurrence among patients with secondary chronic venous insufficiency (SCVI) in whom superficial venous surgery and compression treatment had failed.

Methods: During a ten year period (1993-2004) 1800 patients with chronic venous insufficiency (CVI) were evaluated by colour duplex ultrasound (CDU) and ambulatory venous pressure measurement (AVP). Approximately two thirds of patients had SCVI. Initial treatment consisted of compression therapy for a 6 month period. In addition, superficial vein and perforator surgery was performed in those presenting with reflux in these venous systems. 121 patients who did not improve with this treatment were investigated by ascending venography, descending video venography, air plethysmography and measurement of post-ischaemic venous pressure gradient. Thirty two cases having venous reflux without obstruction were selected for VVR.

Results: The ulcer healing rate within three months was 68% (13/19 patients). VVR resulted in valvular competence and a clinical success rate of 47% and 40% after 3 and 7 years respectively. In 8/13 (54%) of patients with a healed leg ulcer, a median post-operative AVP reduction of 33 mm Hg (range 20-38) was recorded. The durability of clinical success was numerically longer in patients with haemodynamic improvement (n=10) median 24 months (12-108), when compared with that in those without haemodynamic improvement (n=22) median 18 months (6-108). Popliteal vein reconstruction was part of the VVR procedure in all patients with haemodynamic improvement (post-op. AVP reduction >or=20 mm Hg). VVR at the popliteal level alone or combined with inguinal reconstruction seemed to be the one significant factor associated with haemodynamic improvement (P=0.014, Chi squared).

Conclusion: VVR may lead to ulcer healing, but when performed at the popliteal level, haemodynamic improvement can be obtained along with a longer recurrence-free period (durability). VVR should be considered in the treatment of patients with SCVI who do not respond to superficial venous surgery and compression treatment.

Eur J Vasc Endovasc Surg. 2008 Oct;36(4):466-72.

Postthrombotic or Non-Postthrombotic Severe Venous Insufficiency: Impact of Removal of Superficial Venous Reflux With or Without Subcutaneous Fasciotomy Jan T Christenson

Abstract

Background: Severe chronic venous insufficiency is often associated with therapy-resistant or recurrent venous leg ulcers, either as a result of deep vein thrombosis (DVT) - (postthrombotic syndrome [PTS]) or superficial venous insufficiency (SVI). Frequently present dermatoliposclerosis affects the skin as well as the subcutaneous and subfascial structures, which may impact tissue pressures and compromise skin perfusion. This study was undertaken to measure tissue pressures in PTS and SVI limbs and to evaluate the impact of removal of superficial venous reflux with or without concomitant subcutaneous fasciotomy.

Material: In eight patients with recurrent, therapy-resistant venous leg ulcers, due to PTS (11 limbs, 12 ulcers) and 14 patients with severe SVI (14 limbs, 14 ulcers), subcutaneous fasciotomy was performed in addition to removal of superficial reflux. They were compared with eight patients with PTS (11 limbs, 11 ulcers) and 10 patients with SVI (13 limbs, 13 ulcers) who did not have fasciotomy in addition to removal of their superficial venous reflux. Intramuscular (i.m.) and subcutaneous (s.c.) tissue pressures and transcutaneous oxygen tension (TcPO(2)) were measured prior to, immediately after, and 3 months following the surgical intervention. Healing of ulcer (spontaneous or by skin grafting) at 3 months was also observed.

Results: There were no statistical differences between the groups regarding gender and age distribution or ulcer age at the time of surgery. All patients had in addition to surgery compression stockings class II (30 mm Hg). The i.m. tissue pressure was higher in patients with PTS compared with SVI patients, while s.c. tissue pressure and TcPO(2) did not differ between the groups. When fasciotomy was performed, i.m. and s.c. tissue pressures decreased and TcPO(2) increased significantly. Without fasciotomy, only s.c. tissue pressure decreased first at 3 months postoperatively. In the SVI-group, i.m tissue pressure was significantly decreased at 3 months in the group without fasciotomy.

Conclusions: Patients with severe chronic venous insufficiency with therapy-resistant or recurrent ulcer disease due to deep and superficial insufficiency have higher i.m. tissue pressures than patients with only superficial venous reflux, even though both groups have higher i.m. and s.c. tissue pressures compared with normal values. Eradication of all superficial reflux lowers s.c. tissue pressure, while additional fasciotomy lowers both i.m. and s.c. tissue pressures and increases TcPO(2), which seems to promote ulcer healing.

J Vasc Surg. 2007 Aug;46(2):316-21.

Surgical Treatment of Chronic Venous Insufficiency in Own Material

Mariusz Kózka, Jan Kulawik, Anna Zub

Abstract

Nowadays most issues regarding venous disorders are described as chronic venous insufficiency (CVI)-which is defined as all symptoms that manifestate as impaired blood outflow from the lower limbs or in general the result of blood stasis in the deep and superficial venous system. Due to the fact that the symptomatology of venous diseases is wide, the treatment should be multioriented and often as well multi-specialized. The treatment of CVI needs a good understanding of the etiology of the primary insufficiency of the superficial and the deep venous systems. The main purpose of the surgical therapy is to remove the reflux in the great saphenous vein and the perforating veins. Additionally, during the surgical treatment the various veins should be removed in a way that gives the best cosmetic effect. In this article we presented the analysis of different surgical treatments in patients diagnosed with CVI 2-4 grade according to CEAP scale. The patients were hospitalized in our Clinic between April 1998 and April 2003. This group consisted of 311 patients, among them were 257 patients with primary varices, 25 patients with recurrent varices and 29 with postthrombotic syndrome. The choice of surgery was based on clinical examination and the result of venous USG. The most frequent (62%) surgical therapy was removal of the great saphenous vein with miniphlebectomy. To make the treatment more efficient we used the endoscopic method of obliteration of the insufficient perforating veins in lower limbs, called subfascial endoscopic perforating surgery (SEPS).

Przegl Lek. 2003;60 Suppl 7:48-52.

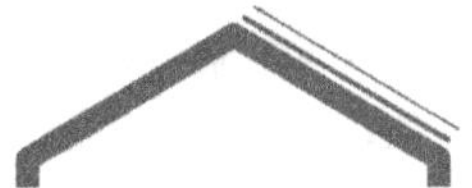

Treatment of Superficial and Perforator Venous Incompetence Without Deep Venous Insufficiency: Is Routine Perforator Ligation Necessary?

Robert R Mendes, William A Marston, Mark A Farber, Blair A Keagy

Abstract

Purpose: We investigated whether routine ligation of incompetent perforator veins is necessary in treatment of symptomatic chronic venous insufficiency (CVI) due to combined superficial and perforator vein incompetence, without deep venous insufficiency.

Methods: This was a retrospective review of prospectively collected data. Twenty-four limbs with both superficial and perforator venous incompetence but no deep venous insufficiency were identified at venous duplex scanning. Air plethysmography (APG) was performed preoperatively, to obtain venous volume (VV), venous filling index (VFI), ejection fraction (EF), and residual volume fraction (RVF) of the affected limb. Saphenous vein stripping from the groin to knee and powered transilluminated phlebectomy for varicosity ablation were performed in all patients. Postoperatively, all patients underwent duplex scanning and APG to determine the status of the perforator veins and hemodynamic improvement from surgery.

Results: Average patient age was 55.8 years; 62% of patients were women. CVI was class 3 in 4 limbs, class 4 in 12 limbs, and class 5 and class 6 in 4 limbs each. Postoperative duplex scans demonstrated that 71% of previously incompetent perforator vessels were now competent or absent. Significant improvement in all APG values was documented after superficial surgery. VFI improved from 6.0 +/- 2.9 preoperatively to 2.2 +/- 1.3 after surgery (P <.001); EF improved from 56.3 +/- 18

to 62 +/- 21 (P =.02); and RVF improved from 40.1 +/- 19 to 28.3 +/- 18 (P =.009). Mean preoperative symptom score (5.3 +/- 1.9) was significantly improved at mean follow-up of 18.3 months (1.4 +/- 1.2; P <.001).

Conclusion: Patients with superficial and perforator vein incompetence and a normal deep venous system experienced significant improvement in APG-measured hemodynamic parameters and clinical symptom score after superficial ablative surgery alone. This suggests that ligation of the perforator veins can be reserved for patients with persistent incompetent perforator vessels, with abnormal hemodynamic parameters or continued symptoms after superficial ablative surgery.

J Vasc Surg. 2003 Nov;38(5):891-5.

Correlation of Clinical Findings With Venous Hemodynamics in 386 Patients With Chronic Venous Insufficiency

S McEnroe, T F O'Donnell Jr, W C Mackey

Abstract

Deep venous insufficiency secondary to deep valvular incompetence predominated over superficial venous insufficiency in an unselected patient population with advanced chronic venous insufficiency. Venous obstruction was uncommon (5 percent), suggesting that venous bypass surgery may have limited applicability in the management of chronic venous insufficiency. Although the majority of patients (72 percent) with stage III venous disease (ulcer) had deep venous insufficiency alone and would be potential candidates for deep valvular reconstruction, 13 percent were found to have superficial venous insufficiency alone, and the remaining 15 percent, deep venous insufficiency with a hemodynamically significant component of superficial venous insufficiency. These findings suggest that not all patients with stage III disease have altered hemodynamics on the basis of deep venous valvular incompetency. Although most stage III chronic venous insufficiency is secondary to altered deep venous hemodynamics, as demonstrated by shortened venous refill time, there is a significant group of patients with severe chronic venous insufficiency having superficial venous insufficiency alone or in combination with deep venous insufficiency (28 percent). Thus, it is imperative that those patients with superficial venous insufficiency be identified by a widely available and reproducible method, such as light reflection rheography, since they may respond to surgery of the superficial venous system alone.

Am J Surg. 1988 Aug;156(2):148-52.

Long-term results of venous valve reconstruction: a four- to twenty-one-year follow- up

Masuda EM, Kistner RL

Abstract

Purpose: The purpose of this study is to describe the very long-term clinical, hemodynamic, and imaging results of venous valve reconstruction for reflux disease in patients with chronic venous insufficiency. Methods: There were 51 extremities (48 patients) with follow-up of 4 to 21 years with a mean of 10.6 years. Clinical severity was graded as asymptomatic (class 0), mildly symptomatic (class 1), moderately symptomatic but without ulceration (class 2), or severely symptomatic with or without ulceration (class 3). Preoperative and postoperative evaluation consisted of history and physical examination, ascending venography (preoperative only), ambulatory venous pressures or photoplethysmography, and descending venography or duplex scanning.

Results: Before surgery, 49 (96%) of 51 limbs demonstrated severe, class 3 disease, and two limbs were classified as class 2 disease. After venous valve reconstruction by either direct femoral vein valve repair, transposition, or transplantation, long-term clinical success of achieving a class 0 or 1 result (by life-table analysis) was 60% at 10 years. Thirty-three percent demonstrated a class 0 result in which the limbs were free from symptoms and had no need for long-term elastic support. After 6 years clinical results were stable and did not deteriorate. Incompetent perforators were identified in 31 cases and were treated selectively. Three disease patterns of chronic venous insufficiency were identified: primary valve insufficiency 43%, postthrombotic syndrome 31%, and a group consisting of both primary valve insufficiency of the superficial femoral vein and postthrombotic syndrome of the calf veins (primary valve insufficiency-postthrombotic syndrome) 26%. Ten-year cumulative clinical success was clearly superior in limbs with primary valve insufficiency corrected by valve repair (73%) as opposed to those with postthrombotic syndrome treated by either valve transposition or transplantation (43%) (p = 0.029). Clinical outcome correlated strongly with postoperative imaging results, and durability of valve repair was confirmed by demonstrating competence up to 16 years after the operation. Significant improvement in ambulatory venous pressure (mean percentage of pressure fall and refill time) was found in limbs with class 0 or 1 outcome; however, values did not reach "normal" levels in all cases. Recurrent ulcerations after the operation were attributed to failed reconstructions (10), incompetent profunda femoris veins (three), incompetent perforators (three), and concomitant lymphedema (one).

Conclusions: This report highlights a difference found in very long-term prognosis of surgical treatment of primary valve insufficiency as opposed to postthrombotic syndrome. Long-term elimination of symptoms of chronic venous insufficiency is achieved by valve repair for primary valve insufficiency beyond 10 years, whereas late results of treatment of postthrombotic syndrome in this study was accompanied by high recurrence rates and warrants further investigation.

J Vasc Surg. 1994 Mar;19(3):391-403.

STENTS

Venous Stents: Current Status and Future Directions

Susan M Shamimi-Noori, Timothy W I Clark

Abstract

Venous outflow obstruction is a dominant contributor to chronic venous disease. Treatment of venous disease has historically been limited by available vascular stent technology not specifically designed for the venous system. The ideal venous stent must provide requisite flexibility, strength, and accurate deployment for the anatomical and pathophysiological conditions of chronic venous disease. Venous stent technology is advancing with multiple dedicated venous stents currently available in Europe and with investigational device exemption studies ongoing in the United States. These technological advancements are promising for patients suffering from chronic venous disease. This article discusses the current status and future directions of venous stents.

Tech Vasc Interv Radiol. 2018 Jun;21(2):113-116.

Iliac Vein Stenting for Chronic Venous Insufficiency

Firas F Mussa, Eric K Peden, Wei Zhou, Peter H Lin, Alan B Lumsden, Ruth L Bush

Abstract

Chronic venous insufficiency has devastating sequelae in terms of patients' lifestyles and negative economic impact on society. Traditional surgical procedures have yielded variable patency results, and follow-up has not always been reported. This review summarizes the current applications, patency rates, stent selection, and complications of balloon angioplasty and stenting in the treatment of chronic venous outflow obstruction in the lower extremity. We conclude that endovenous stenting is the current method of choice in the treatment of chronic venous obstruction.

A) An antegrade common femoral vein approach was used, and an ascending venogram showed narrowing of the left common iliac vein (arrow), along with venous collateral vessels consistent with May-Thurner syndrome. B) Two 20- × 55-mm self-expanding stents were placed. C) A completion venogram showed the position of the stent in the inferior vena cava and satisfactory venographic resolution of the left common iliac lesion.

Texas Heart Institute Journal (Vol. 34, Issue 1)

Long-term Outcomes of Stent Placement for Symptomatic Nonthrombotic Iliac Vein Compression Lesions in Chronic Venous Disease

Kaichuang Ye, Xinwu Lu, Weimin Li, Ying Huang, Xintian Huang, Min Lu, Mi'er Jiang

Abstract

Purpose: To assess the clinical and patency results of stent placement for the management of symptomatic nonthrombotic iliac vein compression lesions (NIVCLs) in chronic venous disease (CVD).

Materials and methods: A retrospective analysis of patients with CVD was conducted at a single institution from January 2000 to May 2010. In 2,093 patients with CVD, venous computed tomography (CT) angiography or transfemoral venography was selectively performed in patients with severe symptoms and in patients with symptom recurrence after endovenous laser ablation (EVLA) for superficial venous insufficiency in the left lower extremity. NIVCLs were found in 297 patients (41 NIVCLs were found in 74 patients whose symptoms recurred after EVLA for superficial

venous insufficiency). In 205 patients, NIVCLs were successfully treated with stent placement. Among these 205 patients, 117 patients (132 limbs) with associated superficial reflux were treated by EVLA for superficial venous insufficiency. Quality of life and the severity of venous disorders were evaluated by questionnaire and clinical examination before and after treatment. Patency was evaluated by duplex Doppler ultrasound.

Results: A total of 227 stents were placed in 205 patients (224 limbs; median age, 50.53 years). The rate of technical success was 100%. Three limbs were treated with two stents because of proximal migration of the incipient stent. Follow-up periods ranged from 1-117 months (mean 50 months ± 36). The primary and assisted-primary cumulative patency rates at a mean of 4 years were 98.7% and 100%. The cumulative edema relief rate was 89.1% (156 of 175), and the healing rate for active ulcers was 82.3% (51 of 62). The pain level (using a visual analogue scale from 0-10) declined from a median level of 4.3 before the procedure to 0.4 after the procedure. Quality of life improved significantly after intervention. Complications were minor and improved quickly.

Conclusions: Venous stent placement is an effective and durable treatment for NIVCL, with long- term high patency and results in significant relief of the major symptoms of CVD. NIVCL is an important reason for symptom recurrence after left lower extremity varicose vein surgery.

J Vasc Interv Radiol. 2012 Apr;23(4):497-502.

ENDOVASCULAR LASER

Study on the Long-Term Results of Endovenous Laser Ablation for Treating Varicose Veins

Seung Je Go, Byung Sun Cho, Yun Su Mun, Yoon Jung Kang, Hye Young Ahn

Abstract

Background Endovenous laser ablation (EVLA) is widely performed since the early 2000s, but there are few long-term results.

Objectives The aim of this study was to evaluate the long-term results of EVLA employed for treating varicose veins of the lower limbs by duplex ultrasonographic study.

Methods A total of 24 limbs of 17 patients who underwent EVLA between 2004 and 2007 were examined with duplex ultrasonographic scans. The mean follow-up period was 66.1 months.

Results There were five recurrences of saphenofemoral junction reflux. The occlusion rate was 79.2% at a mean follow-up of 66.1 months. There were 14 recanalizations and 5 recurrences of the great saphenous vein. Five partial and nine total recanalizations were observed.

Conclusions EVLA is an effective and minimally invasive treatment for varicose veins. Our long-term result was acceptable, but the result was not outstanding.

Int J Angiol. 2016 Jun; 25(2): 117–120.

Case Report: Successful results of direct varicose vein ablation with EVLA in chronic venous insufficiency patient in Indonesia

Taofan T , Utoh J , Dakota I , Indriani S , Abdillah C , Kartamihardja AHA , Adiarto S , Sukmawan R

ABSTRACT

Background: Varicose veins are considered a chronic venous disease. Delaying treatment might cause several late complications that contribute to a high burden on healthcare systems. It may be treated with endovenous laser ablation (EVLA) and stab avulsion as additional procedures.

Varicose direct ablation has been promoted to replace stab avulsion in certain conditions. Here we report the case of a 71-year-old female who presented with chronic venous insufficiency managed by an endovascular therapeutic approach using direct varix ablation for the first time in National Cardiovascular Center – Harapan Kita, Jakarta, Indonesia.

Case report: A 71-year-old female came to the outpatient clinic with a large bulging vein in her leg. Duplex ultrasound showed that the great saphenous vein (GSV) was incompetent with a varicose vein in the medial part of proximal GSV below the knee. The patient underwent EVLA with direct varicose ablation using Utoh's technique. Duplex sonography evaluation showed the right GSV was utterly obliterated, including the varicose vein. The patient was discharged two days after the procedure without significant complaints nor pain medication.

Conclusions: Direct varicose ablation was proposed as a better alternative than stab avulsion. The varicose vein can be managed with EVLA without a scalpel, incision, avulsion, or phlebectomy. In this case presentation, the endovascular therapeutical approach with Utoh's ablation technique showed promising results, and no complication was found in the patient.

DOI: 10.12688/f1000research.133161.2.

Mid-Term Report on the Safety and Effectiveness of Endovenous Radiofrequency Ablation for Varicose Veins

K*iyoshi Tamura, Toshiyuki Maruyama*

Abstract

Objective: Endovenous radiofrequency ablation (RFA), a relatively new technique for treating great saphenous varicose veins, is less invasive compared with stripping surgery. This study examined the mid-term safety and effectiveness of RFA for varicose veins.

Materials and **Methods**: We enrolled 104 patients (147 limbs) who underwent RFA for varicose veins of the lower extremities (females, 67; 64.4%). The mean age was 68.9±9.2 years (39–85 years). In 121 limbs (82.3%), there were great saphenous veins. All patients were observed as outpatients for 12 months after the procedure. RFA was performed using ClosureFast™ catheters with tumescent local anesthesia.

Results: There was 99.4% occlusion of the treated veins, and partial recanalization was observed in one limb. Endovenous heat-induced thrombosis (EHIT) was identified in five limbs (3.4%). All EHITs were class 1 according to the Kabnick classification, and they disappeared within 1 month of the intervention without antithrombotic therapy. No other major complications were observed. Mean venous clinical severity scores improved from 5.31 at the baseline to 1.10, 0.39, 0.14, and

0.06 at 1, 3, 6, and 12 months, respectively.

Conclusion: RFA is a safe and effective strategy for varicose veins of the lower extremities.

Ann Vasc Dis. 2017 Dec 25;10(4):398-401

PREVENTION

Can Early Detection Prevent Venous Leg Ulceration?

Michelle Porter

Abstract

Venous leg ulceration is the most common form of leg ulceration, affecting 1.5% of the UK adult population. This was reviewed within the latest best practice statement (2016) which set out to create clear guidance on the assessment, management and preventing the reoccurrence of venous leg ulceration. With a growing elderly population at risk of venous insufficiency, early identification of those at risk is vital in the fight to reduce the number of people suffering with chronic venous ulceration. This article looks at the need for early assessment and commencement of appropriate treatment in order to reduce the occurrence of venous ulceration and improve clinical processes across the UK.

Br J Community Nurs, 2018 Dec 1;23(Sup12):S14-S17.

Prophylaxis of Recurrent Venous Leg Ulcer

K *Kroeger, M Storck, P Kujath, E Rabe, J Dissemond*

Abstract

Venous leg ulcer (VLU) counts among the most common chronic wounds in Europe. Treatment is lengthy, cumbersome and costly, and there is a high rate of recurrence. This review shows the measures that should be offered to every patient with healed VLU to permanently prevent recurrence. To prevent VLU in case of varicose veins, the progression of chronic venous insufficiency (CVI) has to be stopped. There is convincing evidence that the effective treatment of varicose veins reduces the recurrence rate in patients with VLU. In patients with post-thrombotic syndrome (PTS), further thrombosis should be prevented through targeted prophylaxis of new thromboembolic events. The benefit of endovascular revascularization on the VLU recurrence rate in patients with post-thrombotic damage in the pelvic veins has not been proven in clinical studies. On the other hand, it has been clearly demonstrated in several studies that compression therapy is the basic procedure for the prevention of recurrent VLU in patients with varicose veins or PTS, regardless of whether other measures have been implemented or not. Good adherence in patients with compression therapy is more important than choosing the highest possible compression class. Future efforts for patients with VLU must aim to provide therapists with tools and treatment strategies to guide their patients and to increase patients' acceptance and understanding of the importance of self-management, in particular regarding compression therapy for the prevention of recurrent VLU

Zentralbl Chir. 2017 Jun;142(3):306-311.

NATURAL COURSE and RELAPSES

Sequelae of Untreated Venous Insufficiency

S tephen C. Nicholls

Abstract

Untreated venous insufficiency results not only in a gradual loss of cosmesis but also in variety of complications including persistent pain and discomfort, hemorrhage, superficial thrombophlebitis, and progressive skin changes that may ultimately lead to ulceration. In rare instances, chronic soft tissue changes may lead to stiffness of the ankle joint, fixed plantar flexion, and periostitis. This article reviews the variety of complications caused by venous insufficiency.

Semin Intervent Radiol. 2005 Sep;22(3):162-8

Natural History of Venous Thromboembolism

C*live Kearon*

Abstract

Most deep vein thromboses (DVTs) start in the calf, and most probably resolve spontaneously. Thrombi that remain confined to the calf rarely cause leg symptoms or symptomatic pulmonary embolism (PE). The probability that calf DVT will extend to involve the proximal veins and subsequently cause PE increases with the severity of the initiating prothrombotic stimulus. Although acute venous thromboembolism (VTE) usually presents with either leg or pulmonary symptoms, most patients have thrombosis at both sites at the time of diagnosis. Proximal DVTs resolve slowly during treatment with anticoagulants, and thrombi remain detectable in half of the patients after a year. Resolution of DVT is less likely in patients with a large initial thrombus or cancer. About 10% of patients with symptomatic DVTs develop severe post-thrombotic syndrome within 5 years, and recurrent ipsilateral DVT increases this risk. About 10% of PEs are rapidly fatal, and an additional 5% cause death later, despite diagnosis and treatment. About 50% of diagnosed PEs are associated with right ventricular dysfunction, which is associated with a approximately 5-fold greater in- hospital mortality. There is approximately 50% resolution of PE after 1 month of treatment, and perfusion eventually returns to normal in two thirds of patients. About 5% of treated patients with PE develop pulmonary hypertension as a result of poor resolution. After a course of treatment, the risk of recurrent thrombosis is higher (ie, approximately 10% per patient-year) in patients without reversible risk factors, in those with cancer, and in those with prothrombotic biochemical abnormalities such as antiphospholipid antibodies and homozygous factor V Leiden.

Circulation. 2003;107:I-22–I-30

How Does Chronic Venous Disease Progress From the First Symptoms to the Advanced Stages?

Nicos Labropoulos

Abstract

Risk factors for the development of progression chronic venous disease (CVD) and varicose veins are widespread and include advanced age, excess body weight, sedentary lifestyles and occupations, family history, and pregnancy. Varicose veins and CVD are associated with venous hypertension, venous reflux, dysfunctional venous valves, and vein wall inflammation, though the precise etiologies are unclear. Once venous pathology develops, it can progress through a vicious cycle of inflammation and leukocyte recruitment that leads to further deterioration of vein walls and valves, increased hypertension, and release of additional proinflammatory mediators. Early treatment of symptomatic varicose veins and CVD as well as lifestyle changes can help break the inflammatory cycle and alleviate symptoms. Physicians and patients should be aware of the risk factors for CVD, the treatments and measures available to slow disease progression, and the serious consequences of allowing the disease to progress unchecked.

Advances in Therapy (2019), 10.1007/s12325-019-0885-3

COMPLICATIONS

Latent Dystrophic Subcutaneous Calcification in Patients With Chronic Venous Insufficiency

Shown Tokoro, Takahiro Satoh, Yoshiko Okubo, Ken Igawa, Hiroo Yokozeki

Abstract

Dystrophic calcification in the skin occurs in association with a variety of disorders. To determine the association between subcutaneous calcification and chronic venous insufficiency, X-ray examinations were performed in 20 patients with chronic venous insufficiency and in 20 control subjects to detect latent calcification in their lower legs. Of the 20 patients, 13 (65%) had subcutaneous calcification, and the prevalence appeared to increase with disease duration, while only 4 control subjects (20%) had minimal calcification. Two types of calcification were identified based on their radiographic features: punctate and trabecular/reticular types. Patients with trabecular/reticular calcification had longer disease duration and more severe clinical scores than patients with punctate calcification. None of the control subjects had trabecular/reticular types of calcification. The identification of the presence and progression of latent calcification in the lower legs is useful, and may be necessary for the long-term management of chronic venous insufficiency, since calcification of skin tissues impedes wound healing and can be a risk factor for refractory ulcers.

Acta Derm Venereol. 2009;89(5):505-8.

HOLISTIC

Varicoceles, Pelvic Varices and Pelvic Congestion Syndrome: Interventional Radiology in Diagnosis and Treatment

Francine Paisant-Thouveny, Vincent Le Pennec, Romaric Loffroy

Abstract

Genital venous insufficiency in men is usually of constitutional origin due to valvular incontinence. Genital venous insufficiency in female is more often generated by major, lasting, and possibly repeated pregnancy-related hyperpressure phenomena. Genital venous insufficiency in men is usually expressed by visible and recognizable peritesticular varicocele. Of simple anatomic structure, it is easily accessible to endovascular treatment by embolization, which is the first-line therapy nowadays. Genital venous insufficiency in women results in a pelvic predominant varicosis, which should be evoked in case of chronic pelvic pain or atypical venous afferents to the lower limbs. Precise and guided interrogation and clinical examination allow the attending physician to be the first actor in the detection of symptomatic pelvis venous insufficiency in men and women. A chronic pelvic pain in female should evoke a pelvic congestion syndrome, symptomatic translation of pelvic varicosis, especially if it increases at the end of the day, at the effort, in pre-menstrual period. Treatment with endovascular embolization is the only therapeutic option for female pelvic venous insufficiency, of complex architecture and deep anatomical situation. The interventional radiologist offers a complete, minimally invasive and efficient treatment with limited hospital costs and perioperative constraints.

Presse Med. 2019 Apr;48(4):419-434.

Central Venous Pathologies: Treatments and Economic Impact

Kenneth Ouriel

Abstract

Chronic venous insufficiency (CVI) is responsible for significant costs to society in the form of medical and surgical treatment and, importantly, unmeasurable lost work productivity due to pain and disability. Symptomatic chronic central vein obstruction, a cause of CVI, is potentially treatable using open surgical and endovascular techniques to restore vessel patency. Although upper extremity central vein obstruction often requires an open surgical procedure for durable relief, endovascular stents have proven remarkably useful for iliofemoral disease. Containment of healthcare resources requires accurate diagnosis, durable treatment modalities, and appropriate patient selection so that therapy is targeted to those individuals most likely to benefit. In this regard, identification of appropriate lesions should be based on intravascular ultrasound and 3-dimensional imaging studies. Treatment with dedicated venous stents offers the potential for long-term symptomatic improvement and increased work productivity when used in a well-defined, anatomically appropriate population with significant, symptomatic CVI.

Methodist Debakey Cardiovasc J. Jul-Sep 2018;14(3):166-172.

Chronic Venous Insufficiency: Worldwide Results of the RELIEF Study

G *Jantet*

Abstract

Chronic venous insufficiency (CVI) results in considerable morbidity and may seriously affect patients' quality of life. The RELIEF (Reflux assessment and quality of life improvement with micronized Flavonoids) Study was a prospective controlled study designed to assess differences in the severity and in the evolution of symptoms and signs of CVI according to presence or not of venous reflux. Patients were thus separated into 2 comparative groups: those presenting venous reflux and those without venous reflux. The design of the study was multicentric and international, carried out in 23 countries over 2 years, in which 5,052 symptomatic patients assigned to classes C0 to C4 (on the basis of CEAP clinical classification) were enrolled. Patients were treated with micronized purified flavonoid fraction (MPFF), consisting of 450 mg of micronized diosmin and 50 mg of flavonoids expressed in hesperidin over 6 months. In order to document changes in the quality of life of these patients during MPFF treatment, a new validated Quality of Life Questionnaire specific to CVI (CIVIQ) was used. The study also set out to gather epidemiologic data including the prevalence of venous reflux in symptomatic patients. The RELIEF study provided important information about the epidemiology and clinical manifestations of CVI. Of particular interest was the observation that venous reflux was found to be absent in 57% of patients diagnosed as suffering from CVI belonging to CEAP classes C0 to C4. A positive relationship between symptoms of CVI (pain, leg heaviness, sensation of swelling, and cramps) and presence of venous reflux was found in the RELIEF study: symptoms were more frequent and more severe at presentation in patients with venous reflux. Moreover, during MPFF treatment, all symptoms showed a greater decrease in the group without venous reflux compared with the other group. This difference in the evolution of symptoms between the 2 groups was significant for pain, sensation of swelling, and cramps. Regarding leg heaviness and signs such as edema (assessed by leg circumference), patients improved equally independently of the presence or not of venous reflux. The significant and progressive improvement in the signs of CVI was reflected in significant changes in the clinical class of the CEAP classification, ie, from more severe to less severe stages. Continuous clinical improvement was found throughout the study and after treatment with MPFF for 6 months, the clinical scores of all symptoms and signs had significantly decreased (p=0.0001 versus DO) in both groups. This improvement was also associated with a significant and continuous progression in the quality of life scores of all patients. Age of patients, average time since diagnosis, and presence of venous reflux increased with the severity of the disease. The relationship shown in this study between these parameters and clinical CEAP classification reflects the progressive nature of CVI. Despite obvious symptoms of CVI, a very low percentage (21.8%) of the "intention-to-treat" (ITT) population had previously been treated. This was the case whether venous reflux was present or not.

Angiology. May-Jun 2002;53(3):245-56.

Association Between Testosterone Replacement Therapy and the Incidence of DVT and Pulmonary Embolism: A Retrospective Cohort Study of the Veterans Administration Database.

Rishi Sharma, Olurinde A Oni, Guoqing Chen, Mukut Sharma, Buddhadeb Dawn, Ram Sharma, Deepak Parashara, Virginia J Savin, Rajat S Barua, Kamal Gupta

Background Testosterone replacement therapy (TRT) prescriptions have increased several-fold in the last decade. There have been concerns regarding a possible increased incidence of DVT and pulmonary embolism (PE) with TRT. Few data support the association between TRT and DVT/PE. We evaluated the incidence of DVT and PE in men who were prescribed TRT for low serum total testosterone (sTT) levels. METHODS This is a retrospective cohort study, conducted using data obtained from the Veterans Affairs Informatics and Computing Infrastructure. We compared the incidence of DVT/PE between those who received TRT and subsequently had normal on-treatment sTT levels (Gp1), those who received TRT but continued to have low on-treatment sTT (Gp2), and those who did not receive TRT (Gp3). Those with prior history of DVT/PE, cancer, hypercoagulable state, and chronic anticoagulation were excluded. RESULTS The final cohort consisted of 71,407 subjects with low baseline sTT. Of these, 10,854 did not receive TRT (Gp3) and 60,553 received TRT. Of those who received TRT, 38,362 achieved normal sTT (Gp1) while 22,191 continued to have low sTT (Gp2). The incidence of DVT/PE was 0.5%, 0.4%, and 0.4% in Gp1, Gp2, and Gp3, respectively. Univariate, multivariate, and stabilized inverse probability of treatment weights analyses showed no statistically significant difference in DVT/PE-free survival between the various groups. CONCLUSIONS This study did not detect a significant association between testosterone replacement therapy and risk of DVT/PE in adult men with low sTT who were at low to moderate baseline risk of DVT/PE.

Chest. 2016 Sep;150(3):563-71

Association Between Testosterone Replacement Therapy and the Incidence of DVT and

Enhanced functional stability of plasminogen activator inhibitor-1 in patients with livedoid vasculopathy.

Agirbasli M, Eren M, Eren F, Murphy SB, Serdar ZA, Seckin D, Zara T, Cem Mat M, Demirkesen C, Vaughan DE.

Abstract

Livedoid vasculopathy (LV) is a chronic, recurrent, painful cutaneous disease with distinctive clinical features and an uncertain etiology. The skin lesions are recognizable by focal purpura, depigmentation and shallow ulcers. Thrombophilic conditions occur frequently in patients with LV. While no definitive treatment exists for LV, smoking cessation, antiplatelet therapy, immunosuppressive treatment, and anabolic steroids are often included in the therapeutic ladder. Recently, a possible link between LV and impaired fibrinolysis was established as cutaneous LV lesions responded to tissue plasminogen activator (t-PA) infusion suggesting that inhibition of the fibrinolysis through plasminogen activator inhibitor-1 (PAI-1) activity may determine the disease course in patients with LV. In this study, we investigated PAI- 1 antigen (Ag) and activity levels in 20 patients with biopsy proven LV (mean age 26 $\pm$ 11, M/F = 7/13, median disease duration 3.5 years). All patients received antiplatelet treatment with aspirin and/or dipyrimadole and 14 patients received anabolic steroids or immunosuppressive treatment. Fasting PAI-1 Ag and activity levels were measured at 9 AM in all patients. Both Ag (34 (26) ng/ml) (median (interquartile range)) and specific activity (17 (23) IU/fmole) levels of PAI-1 were moderately elevated in LV patients compared to the controls, however, PAI-1 kinetic studies demonstrated markedly enhanced stability of PAI-1 activity in plasma from patients with LV. Specific activity at 16 h was significantly higher than expected specific activity levels (7 (11) vs. 0.07 (0.09) IU/fmole, $P < 0.01$). While the exact mechanism of increased stability of PAI-1 activity is not known, it may be due to post-translational modifications or increased binding affinity for a stabilizing cofactor. In conclusion, enhanced stability of PAI-1 may contribute to the pathophysiology of LV, and systemic or local treatment with PAI-1 inhibitors may offer a potential treatment alternative in patients with LV.

J Thromb Thrombolysis. 2011 Jul;32(1):59-63.

Smoking and abdominal obesity: risk factors for venous thromboembolism among middle-aged men: "the study of men born in 1913"

Hansson PO, Eriksson H, Welin L, Svärdsudd K, Wilhelmsen L.

Abstract

Background: Risk factors for deep vein thrombosis and pulmonary embolism are mostly derived from case-control studies of hospitalized patients, and there are few long-term population-based studies.

Objective: To study the long-term risk factors for deep vein thrombosis and pulmonary embolism among middle-aged men.

Design: A prospective cohort study.

Setting: General community, "The Study of Men Born in 1913."

Subjects: A random population sample of 855 men, all aged 50 years at baseline.

Main outcome measures: Eight-hundred fifty-five men participated in a screening examination in 1963 at the age of 50 years, and 792 of these men were reexamined in 1967 at the age of 54. All the men were followed up with periodic examinations until the age of 80. **Objective** methods were used to ascertain a diagnosis of deep vein thrombosis or pulmonary embolism.

Results: Waist circumference (P=.004) and smoking (P = .02) predicted a venous thromboembolic event in multivariate survival analysis. Men in the highest decile of waist circumference (> or =100 cm) had an adjusted relative risk of 3.92 (95% confidence interval, 2.10-7.29; P<.001) compared with men with a waist circumference of less than 100 cm. For men who smoked 15 g of tobacco (15 cigarettes) a day or more, the adjusted relative risk was 2.82 (95% confidence interval, 1.30-6.13; P= .009) compared with nonsmokers.

Conclusions: Smoking and abdominal obesity were independent risk factors for venous thromboembolic events during follow-up. In addition to the prevention of smoking and obesity, a more aggressive strategy regarding the use of prophylactic agents among smokers and obese patients, in various risk situations, may be justified.

Arch Intern Med. 1999 Sep 13;159(16):1886-90

Chronic Venous Disorder Registry: A New Perspective

Yung-Wei Chi, Marlin Schul, Kathleen Gibson, Mel Rosenblatt, Lowell Kabnick, Michael Jaff

Abstract

Chronic venous disorder is one of the most prevalent medical conditions in the US that carries significant economic and health burden. The knowledge into venous pathophysiology, how it develops, and the true quality of life benefits of various treatment options are largely unknown. A truly meaningful clinical data capture system specifically for venous disorder may provide answers to the paucity of data. We describe a modern system to capture research and best practice data using the state of art information technology.

Phlebology. 2014 Aug;29(7):415-27.

Recent Methods of Evaluation of Quality of Life in Patients With Chronic Venous Disease

Andrzej Berszakiewicz, Agata Stanek, Aleksander Sieroń

Abstract

Chronic diseases permanently influence on quality of life. One of them is chronic venous disease (CVD). According to The World Health Organisation (WHO) it concerns amlost 80-83.6% of adult population of the world. As most of chronic diseases CVD is not only a medical problem but also social and financial one. This paper is an overview about impact of CVD on Qol and methods of its evaluations.

Wiad Lek. 2014;67(4):499-504.

Optimal Therapy for Advanced Chronic Venous Insufficiency

Roy L Tawes, Miguel L Barron, Abilio A Coello, Douglas H Joyce, Ralf Kolvenbach

Abstract

Introduction: While definitive therapy awaits level I evidence, controversy persists regarding the optimal operation for treatment of advanced chronic venous insufficiency (CVI). We propose a pragmatic approach to the correction or amelioration of venous hypertension resulting from hydrodynamic and hydrostatic venous reflux. We evaluated a strategy of balloon dissection, subfascial endoscopic perforating vein surgery (SEPS) with routine posterior deep compartment fasciotomy, including ligation and stripping of the superficial system, for use when reflux is documented at duplex ultrasound (US) scanning.

Methods: This is a cooperative, multicenter, retrospective review of 832 patients stratified by CEAP classification. The series consisted of 300 patients with C4 CVI, 119 patients with C5 CVI, and 413 patients with C6 CVI. A subset of 92 patients with C4 disease were prospectively randomized, and ambulatory venous pressure (AVP) was determined preoperatively and postoperatively.

All patients underwent duplex US scanning to document reflux in the deep, superficial, and perforating venous systems. Efficacy, safety, and durability were evaluated over follow-up of 1 to 9 years (mean, 31/2 years). Uniformity was attempted by adoption of the senior author's protocol and technique through on-site preceptorship in each surgeon's operative theater.

Results: This technique interrupted 3 to 14 (mean, 7) incompetent perforating veins per patient. Of the 832 patients undergoing SEPS, 460 (55%) underwent saphenous vein ligation and stripping at the same operation. In 92% ulcers healed or were significantly improved within 4 to 14 weeks. In 64 (8%) patients, ulcers failed to heal or there was no benefit from the operation. Thirty-two patients (4%) experienced recurrent ulceration or skin deterioration at 6 months-2 years (mean, 15 mo). Repeat SEPS was successful in 25 of these 96 patients, and deep valve repair was successful in 4 patients. In the 92 randomized patients with C4 disease, 41 refused postoperative AVP, leaving 51 compliant patients. The SEPS group (n = 25) had significantly reduced AVP (P <.01) compared with the control group (n = 26). Complications in 825 patients were less than 3% and consisted mostly of transient neurologic disorders (eg, paradysthesia), but deep venous thrombosis occurred in 2 patients, with pulmonary embolus in 1. No operative deaths occurred. Follow-up for 1 to 9 years (mean, 31/2 years) demonstrated durability.

Conclusion: The efficacy, safety, and durability of this operative protocol proved beneficial in our clinical experience with 832 patients during 9 years of follow-up. The SEPS subset of randomized patients with C4 disease experienced significant decrease in AVP, objectively supporting the effectiveness of reflux surgery in advanced CVI. Until definitive level I evidence is available, this operative technique is advocated as optimal therapy for CVI.

J Vasc Surg. 2003 Mar;37(3):545-51

Essential Varicose Veins and Chronic Venous Insufficiency

P *Priollet*

Abstract

Chronic venous insufficiency of the lower limbs has varied expressions: purely functional disorders, varicose veins, varicosities, oedema and trophic cutaneous disorders. For a given individual, these aspects are not necessarily increasing stages of severity of the same disease. On the other hand, many associations are possible; they are determined by the mechanism and the degree of chronic venous insufficiency, as well as by the clinical situation in which they develop. Work-up is based on careful clinical examination. Doppler examination and echography are useful for varices if radical treatment is considered. Ultrasound examination is required in case of cutaneous ulcer in order not to mistake a varicose ulcer for a trophic disorder due to incontinence of deep venous trunks, most often of thrombotic origin. Varicose veins can become complicated. Varicose haemorrhage requires immediate treatment by compression. Superficial phlebitis needs doppler examination and echography because it can be associated to deep venous thrombosis. With regard to varices and chronic venous insufficiency, treatment varies according to the concerns of the patients. Elastic compression stockings are useful whatever the clinical expression of the disease. "Phlebotropic" drugs can be used whenever venous insufficiency is associated with functional symptoms. The use of radical treatment, whether sclerosing injections or surgery, depends on anatomic lesions, the degree of venous incontinence and the severity of symptoms, but also on the desires of the patients, fully informed as to the advantages and the limitations of each technique. Personalized treatment is thus possible.

La Revue Du Praticien, (1994), 44(6)

Changes in Quality of Life for Patients With Chronic Venous Insufficiency, Present or Healed Leg Ulcers

Regina Renner, Carl Gebhardt, Jan C Simon, Kurt Seikowski

Abstract

Background: Patients with chronic leg ulcers are handicapped in daily life, both by physical complaints and social problems. The aim of our study was not only to assess a possible impairment of quality of life (QOL) of leg ulcer patients but also to evaluate if there is a real improvement of QOL after healing of the ulcer. Patients with chronic venous insufficiency served as the control group. We further analyzed if there were significant differences in the response between patients who were and were not performing compression therapy.

Patients and method: We interviewed three groups of patients (active venous leg ulcer, healed venous leg ulcer and patients with chronic venous insufficiency using the "Freiburger Life Quality Assessment für Venenerkrankungen" (FLQAv).

Results: Physical problems, daily handicaps and social problems all increased with age. Contrary to our expectations, healing of a leg ulcer did not lead to a significant increase in QOL. Instead, patients with active ulcers did not regard their QOL as lower than those in the other groups. Compression therapy also did not impair QOL in the three groups.

Conclusion: Even though ulcer healing is an admirable goal, it does not necessarily lead to an improved QOL, probably because of the numerous comorbidities in this patient group. Nonetheless, it is important to control problems associated directly with the wound to allow ulcer patients to participate actively in everyday life and minimize social problems.

J Dtsch Dermatol Ges. 2009 Nov;7(11):953-61.

Improvement of Rehabilitation Efficiency in Patients With Chronic Venous Insufficiency of the Lower Extremities

N Zhukov, S E Katorkin, Ia V Sizonenko, P F Kravtsov

Abstract

The relationship between functional incompetence, development and severity of chronic venous insufficiency of the lower extremities was investigated by the method of clinical analysis of locomotor activity. **Results** of the study may be used to choose an optimal therapeutic modality and assess dynamics of its efficiency. It was shown that the treatment of chronic venous insufficiency in the majority of the patients is inefficient unless functional activity of the lower extremities is recovered. Stimulation of the muscular-venous pump improves the outcome of postoperative rehabilitation, permits to reduce its duration, and improves quality of life of the patients.

Vopr Kurortol Fizioter Lech Fiz Kult. Jul-Aug 2009;(4):19-22.

MISCELLANEOUS

Effects of Isokinetic Calf Muscle Exercise Program on Muscle Strength and Venous Function in Patients with Chronic Venous Insufficiency

Sabriye Ercan, Cem Çetin, Turhan Yavuz, Hilmi M Demir, Yurdagül B Atalay

Abstract

Objective The aim of this study was to observe the change of the ankle joint range of motion, the muscle strength values measured with an isokinetic dynamometer, pain scores, quality of life scale, and venous return time in chronic venous insufficiency diagnosed patients by prospective follow- up after 12-week exercise program including isokinetic exercises.

Methods The patient group of this study comprised 27 patients (23 female, 4 male) who were diagnosed with chronic venous insufficiency. An exercise program including isokinetic exercise for the calf muscle was given to patients three days per week for 12 weeks. At the end of 12 weeks, five of the patients left the study due to inadequate compliance with the exercise program. As a result, control data of 22 patients were included. Ankle joint range of active motion, isokinetic muscle strength, pain, quality of life, and photoplethysmography measurements were assessed before starting and after the exercise program.

Results Evaluating changes of the starting and control data depending on time showed that all isokinetic muscle strength measurement parameters, range of motion, and overall quality of life values of patients improved. Venous return time values have also increased significantly (p < 0.05).

Conclusion In conclusion, increase in muscle strength has been provided with exercise therapy in patients with chronic venous insufficiency. It has been determined that the increase in muscle strength affected the venous pump and this ensured improvement in venous function and range of motion of the ankle. In addition, it has been detected that pain reduced and quality of life improved after the exercise program.

Phlebology. 2018 May;33(4):261-266.

Psychometric Validation of the 14 Items Chronic Venous Insufficiency Quality of Life Questionnaire (CIVIQ-14): Confirmatory Factor Analysis

J-G Le Moine, L Fiestas-Navarrete K Katumba, R Launois

Abstract

Objectives: The study aim was to confirm the factorial structure of the short (14 item) version of the Chronic Venous Insufficiency quality of life Questionnaire (CIVIQ-14) using the Vein Consult Program (VCP) results.

Methods: The international VCP study sought to evaluate the impact of chronic venous disease (CVD) on health care costs and quality of life (QoL). The factorial structure of the CIVIQ-14 was evaluated using two methods: exploratory factor analysis (EFA) to calculate the probabilities of items and dimensions remaining stable and to study the dimensionality of the scale using explained variance criteria, followed by confirmatory factor analysis (CFA) to confirm the original three dimensional structure and investigate alternative models that may have arisen from the dimensionality analysis. We also used the VCP results to evaluate the psychometric properties of the questionnaire and conducted subgroup analyses on countries with validated translations.

Results: A total of 47,149 questionnaires from 17 countries were available in the VCP. EFA revealed both items and dimensions as 100% stable. Dimensionality analysis showed that a two factor approach could be considered. CFA revealed the CIVIQ-14 three dimensional structure to be acceptable while rejecting the two dimensional model. Psychometric analysis confirmed the construct validity, internal consistency, and known groups validity of the CIVIQ-14. The results of subgroup analyses were consistent with those of the primary analysis.

Conclusions:

CFA of VCP data supported the factorial structure of the CIVIQ-14. The analysis corroborates the wide use of CIVIQ-14 as a valid instrument for reporting QoL in CVD patients.

Eur J Vasc Endovasc Surg. 2016 Feb;51(2):268-74.

Pulsatile Venous Insufficiency in Severe Tricuspid Regurgitation: Does Pulsatility Protect Against Complications of Venous Disease?

J E Naschitz, V Wolfson, I Tsikonova, D Keren, E Barmeir, D Yeshurun

Abstract

Prior observations showed that the consequences of venous hypertension depend not only on the magnitude of the venous pressure but also on the efficiency of compensatory mechanisms that protect against the effects of excessive pressures on the microcirculation. Pulsatile venous insufficiency (PVI) associated with severe tricuspid regurgitation (TR) provides the opportunity to investigate the effect of the pulsatile shear stress on the outcome of venous insufficiency. The authors conducted a study to assess the flow characteristics and clinical outcome of PVI associated with TR. Five patients were evaluated, presenting venous insufficiency associated with ectasia, varices, and visible systolic pulsations of the leg veins. Characteristics of the venous flow were assessed by duplex ultrasound. In two patients, flow in the distal calf veins was evaluated by power Doppler sonography, and the supine-to-sitting leukocyte trapping was calculated.

Results of the latter measurements were compared with measurements in five control patients who presented chronic nonpulsatile venous insufficiency. A survey of complications of PVI was conducted. On follow-up for 6 to 15 years (average 9.4 years) none of the patients developed venous thrombosis, phlebitis, or cutaneous ulcer. Flow in the distal calf vessels was increased in PVI (12-20 vessels/field) as compared with nonpulsatile venous insufficiency (0-7 vessels/field). Leukocyte trapping in the upright position was diminished in PVI (0.8-3%) as compared with nonpulsatile venous insufficiency (7-22%). In conclusion, PVI is characterized by increased flow in the distal calf veins, diminished leukocyte trapping, and a benign clinical course. These data are in agreement with experimental studies showing that pulsatile shear stress enhances secretion of cytokines by venous endothelial cells and, consequently, counteracts a predisposition to platelet aggregation, hypercoagulability, and white cell adhesion and promotes healing of leg ulcers.

Angiology. 2000 Mar;51(3):231-9.

Lower Limb Venous Angiodysplasia as a Cause of Chronic Venous Insufficiency: Specific Diagnosis and Treatment

V N Dan, S V Sapelkin, G Karmazanovskiĭ, G I Kuntsevich

Abstract

The paper presents a current understanding of chronic venous insufficiency that develops in venous forms of dysplasia. Management of venous dysplasia must be based on multidisciplinary approach including comprehensive diagnosis (predominantly noninvasive), integrative surgical and non-surgical treatment. Modern therapy must be complex and carried out in highly specialized facilities. Best functional and esthetic results can be achieved only through combined therapy. When surgical or non-surgical interventions are inappropriate or impossible, management focus must be placed on clinical control of vascular anomaly (follow-up and compression-based conservative treatment) aimed at minimization of its unfavorable impact on vital functions and at quality of life improvement.

Angiol Sosud Khir. 2007;13(2):151-5.

RESEARCH

A Study of Risk Factors of Chronic Venous Insufficiency and its Association with Features Suggestive of Preceding or Present Deep Venous Thrombosis

Ram H Malkani, Rusina Karia, and Sneh Thadani

Abstract

Background: Deep venous thrombosis (DVT), even though resolved, may damage the valves and may lead to chronic venous insufficiency (CVI). We designed the present study to examine the thrombotic markers or other ultrasound features in the absence of active thrombosis in patients presenting with features suggestive of CVI.

Materials and **Methods**: It was a cross-sectional study of 50 DVT patients. We collected a detailed history of presenting symptoms (onset, progression, and duration) and associated history of aggravating factors. After classifying the patients, color Doppler investigation for DVT and venous incompetence and blood investigations such as Factor V, D-Dimer, total cholesterol, total triglycerides, homocysteine, high- density lipoproteins, low-density lipoproteins (LDL), and very LDL were done.

Results: We found a raised Factor V significantly more in patients classified as severe under clinical classification compared with nonsevere (19% and 0%; $P = 0.05$) and in patients with a high Venous Severity Clinical Score (VSCS) compared to those with a low VSCS score (17% and 0%; $P = 0.03$). We also found that perforators were significantly more in patients with a high VSCS score (88% and 58%; P

= 0.02), in patients with a primary venous etiology compared with those without any venous etiology (97% and 1%; P < 0.0001), in patients with obstruction/reflux compared to those without any pathology (95% and 0%; P < 0.0001), and in patients with severe clinical classification compared with nonsevere patient (95% and 55%; P = 0.002).

Conclusions: Clinical or subclinical DVT, an important cause of CVI, may not always be seen on ultrasound, especially after resolution. However, they may have the presence of blood parameters (Factor V and hyperhomocysteinemia) suggestive of DVT; these can be used as proxy markers for the current or previous DVT.

Anticoagulant

An anticoagulant is a substance that prevents coagulation; that is, it stops blood from clotting. A group of pharmaceuticals called anticoagulants can be used in vivo as a medication for thrombotic disorders. Some chemical compounds are used in medical equipment, such as test tubes, blood transfusion bags, and renal dialysis equipment.

As medications

Anticoagulants are given to people to stop thrombosis (blood clotting inappropriately in the blood vessels). This is useful in primary and secondary prevention of deep vein thrombosis, pulmonary embolism, myocardial infarctions and strokes in those who are predisposed.

Coumarines (Vitamin K antagonists) Further information: Vitamin K antagonist

The oral anticoagulants are a class of pharmaceuticals that act by antagonizing the effects of vitamin K. Examples include warfarin. It is important to note that it takes at least 48 to 72 hours for the anticoagulant effect to develop fully. In cases when any immediate effect is required, heparin must be given concomitantly.

Generally, these anticoagulants are used to treat patients with deep-vein thrombosis (DVT), pulmonary embolism (PE), atrial fibrillation (AF), and mechanical prosthetic heart valves.

Adverse effects

Patients aged 80 years or more may be especially susceptible to bleeding complications with a rate of 13 bleeds per 100 person-years.[1]

These oral anticoagulants are used widely as poisons for mammalian pests, especially rodents. (For details, see rodenticide and warfarin.)

Depletion of vitamin K by coumarine therapy increases risk of arterial calcification and heart valve calcification, especially if too much vitamin D is present.[2]

Available agents

- Warfarin (Coumadin) This is the main agent used in the U.S. and UK[3]

- Acenocoumarol and phenprocoumon This is used more commonly outside the U.S. and the UK

- Brodifacoum Rat poison, not used medically

- Phenindione

Heparin and derivative substances

Heparin is a biological substance, usually made from pig intestines. It works by activating antithrombin III, which blocks thrombin from clotting blood. Heparin can be used in vivo (by injection), and also in vitro to prevent blood or plasma clotting in or on medical devices. Vacutainer brand test tubes containing heparin are usually colored green.

Low molecular weight heparin

Low molecular weight heparin is a more highly processed product that is useful as it does not require monitoring of the APTT coagulation parameter (it has more predictable plasma levels) and has fewer side effects.

Synthetic pentasaccharide inhibitors of factor Xa

Fondaparinux is a synthetic sugar composed of the five sugars (pentasaccharide) in heparin that bind to antithrombin. It is a smaller molecule than low molecular weight heparin.

Idraparinux

Major pharmaceutical Heparin recall due to contamination

In March 2008 major recalls of Heparin were announced by pharmaceuticals due to a suspected and unknown contamination of the raw Heparin stock imported from China [4]. The contaminant was later found to be a non-naturally occurring compound called oversulfated chondroitin sulfate [6 The U.S. Food and Drug Administration was quoted as stating that at least 19 deaths were believed linked to a raw Heparin ingredient imported from the People's Republic of China, and that they had also received 785 reports of serious injuries associated with the drug's use. According to the New York Times: 'Problems with heparin reported to the agency include difficulty breathing, nausea, vomiting, excessive sweating and rapidly falling blood pressure that in some cases led to life-threatening shock'.

Direct thrombin inhibitors

Another type of anticoagulant is the direct thrombin inhibitor.[Current members of this class include argatroban, lepirudin, bivalirudin, and dabigatran. An oral direct thrombin inhibitor, ximelagatran (Exanta) was denied approval by the Food and Drug Administration (FDA) in September 2004 [1]and was pulled from the market entirely in February 2006 after reports of severe liver damage and heart attacks.

Other types of anticoagulants

Many other anticoagulants exist, for use Research & Development, and more or less uses as drug candidates or diagnostics

Batroxobin, a toxin from a snake venom that clots platelet-rich plasma without affecting platelets functions (lyses fibrinogen).

General indications

Therapeutic uses of Anticoagulants include:

Atrial fibrillation, Pulmonary embolism (PE), Deep vein thrombosis (DVT), or Venous Thromboembolism (VTE), Heart failure, Stroke, Myocardial infarction, Genetic or acquired hypercoagulability

Anticoagulants outside the body

Laboratory instruments, test tubes, blood transfusion bags, and medical and surgical equipment will get clogged up and become nonoperational if blood is allowed to clot. Chemicals can be added to stop blood clotting. Apart from heparin, most of these chemicals work by binding calcium ions, preventing the coagulation proteins from using them.

EDTA is denoted by mauve or purple caps on Vacutainer brand test tubes. This chemical strongly and irreversibly binds calcium. It is in a powdered form.

Citrate is usually in blue Vacutainer tube. It is in liquid form in the tube and is used for coagulation tests, as well as in blood transfusion bags. It gets rid of the calcium, but not as strongly as EDTA. Correct proportion of this anticoagulant to blood is crucial because of the dilution. It can be in the form of sodium citrate [disambiguation needed] or ACD.

Oxalate has a mechanism similar to that of citrate. It is the anticoagulant used in fluoride (grey top) tubes.

Indian J Dermatol. 2019 Sep-Oct;64(5):366-371

Experimental models to investigate inflammatory processes in chronic venous insufficiency.

R *J Korthuis, J L Unthank*

Abstract:

Chronic venous insufficiency (CVI) is characterized by leukocyte adhesion and infiltration, venous hypertension and dilatation, and valvular dysfunction. The fact that activated white cells can direct a powerful cytotoxic arsenal at parenchymal cells following their extravasation into the tissues led to the original proposal that leukocytes may play a causative role in the pathogenesis of venous disease. A large body of subsequent work indicates that white blood cells are indeed activated in CVI. However, identification of the factors responsible for initiating leukosequestration and activation in such disorders and determinination of whether these activated cells then contribute to the progression of venous disease have been hampered by the lack of appropriate animal models that accurately mimic the human condition. Tantalizing evidence suggesting that cyclical periods of ischemia and reperfusion (I/R) may occur in diseased regions of the skin is beginning to accumulate. As is the case with CVI, leukocyte infiltration is a prominent feature in I/R and activated neutrophils play a causative role in the reperfusion component of tissue injury via the targeted release of reactive oxygen metabolites and hydrolytic enzymes. In light of these considerations, many investigators have suggested that examining the mechanisms of I/R injury in skin and skeletal muscle, where ischemia is produced by arterial occlusion, may provide a relevant model for studying the pathogenesis of CVI.

Others have suggested that venous occlusion may represent a more appropriate model, as this approach also produces the venous hypertension that is characteristic of the disease. The purpose of this review is to summarize the evidence pointing to the involvement of I/R and venous hypertension as causative factors in CVI-induced leukocyte recruitment. In addition, we will describe the evidence in favor of the view that white blood cells contribute to the pathogenesis of CVI.

Finally, we will describe several different experimental models that have been used to examine the role of I/R-induced microvascular dysfunction as it may pertain to the development of CVI, together with a discussion of the relative advantages and limitations of the various models.

Microcirculation (2000) 7, S13–S22.

Omics Profiles in Chronic Venous Ulcer Wound Fluid: Innovative Applications for Translational Medicine

Ferdinando Mannello, Daniela Ligi, Matteo Canale, Joseph D Raffetto

Abstract

Chronic venous disease represents a healthcare problem due to high prevalence and recurrence rates. Studies on chronic venous ulcer wound fluid (CVUWF) have demonstrated increased inflammation and proteolysis which can cause tissue destruction and delayed healing. This review discusses: nearly all known metabolites discovered in the past 25 years in CVUWF studies; the omics approaches characterizing the microenvironment of human venous leg ulcers; and the use of biocompounds as prognostic biomarkers and as possible targets for therapeutic approaches. A biomarker is a biological compound that can be functional or non-functional, specific or non-specific in the diagnosis/prognosis to a disease state and may be quantified to determine progression or regression of disease. Omics studies in CVUWF provide the impetus for future identification of biomarkers within the intricate network in chronic venous disease and set the basis for determining the appropriate combination of molecules that are expressed with the healing status of venous leg ulcers.

Expert Rev Mol Diagn. 2014 Jul;14(6):737-62.

About the Author

Consultant in Dermatology, in practice, from 1973.

Consultant Dermatologist in Jaslok Hospital since 1978.

Fellow of the Royal College of Physicians (Eng)

Member of the Indian association of dermatologists, Venereologists and Leprologists

Member European Society of Dermatologists and Psychiatrists Member Psychodermatology Association of India

Fellow of the American Association of Dermatology

Fellow of the European Association of Dermatology

Awards and Achievements:

Orations `

Psychological approach in Dermatology patients` at the IADVL, Cuticon, 2020.

Oration on 'Oculoctaneous Diseases' at the Maharashtra Ophthalmology Association Conference at the Amar Gian Auditorium, Mumbai 1994

Key note address : 'My tryst with Psychodermatology' Delivered at the First National Conference of the Psychodermatology Association of India, held at Kozhikode, Jan 21,2023 Life time achievement awards At the First National Conference of the Psychodermatology Association of India at Kozhikode Jan 21 2023

Life time achievement award -

IADVL, Maharashtra Branch , 2012 at Nanded.

Guide - The Premlata award - Best Research for HIV and Drug resistance, at the National IADVL, Pune 2020. A Jaslok Hospital research project.

Acievements -

President IADVL Maharashtra 1991-92.

Convenor HIV prevention programme IADVL, Maharashtra 1996-2008

Founder Member Pychodermatology Association of India, 2019

Research Gate Data -

41 Publications (Researchgate)

3,123 reads

94 citations

Immediate Goal

Passed my entrance exam for Phd of MUHS in 2020, waiting for a guide.

Training

Qualified as a Psychodermatologist by the EASDaP and by virtue of 5+ 3 years of 5 days/week Psychoanalysis.